Smile, You Sonuvabitch! A Brit's Take on Catfights, Serial Killers and Other Fun Movie Stuff

Ice Dog Movie Guide, Volume 2

Dave Franklin

Published by Baby Ice Dog Press, 2022.

SMILE, YOU SONUVABITCH! A BRIT'S TAKE ON CATFIGHTS, SERIAL KILLERS AND OTHER FUN MOVIE STUFF

First edition. July 5, 2022.

Written by Dave Franklin.

Table of Contents

Imaginative Bursts of Sadism

Do you ever do that thing, perhaps while life hasn't been treating you too brilliantly, when you start reading up on sicko Nazi and serial killer shit? You don't mean to (perhaps you've got a gap between charity commitments) but somehow you're disappearing into the bowels of the internet consuming blood-drenched pages about medieval torture instruments, Jeffrey Dahmer and Treblinka. Half an hour's slipped by and you're still trying to find the most fucked-up bit of sadism in history.

Jesus Christ, were people really draped on a wheel in the town square before the executioner broke their arms and legs, threaded their jelly-like limbs through the spokes, and put them on public display where they might take a couple of days to die? Did Ted Bundy bury his kills, dig 'em up after a few days, wash their hair, apply makeup, and then fuck 'em all over again? Were limbs lopped off and reattached to the opposite side of the body by those Jap bastards at Unit 731? Did Eichmann actually say: "I will leap into my grave laughing because the feeling that I have five million human beings on my conscience is for me a source of extraordinary satisfaction."

Man, maybe I'm not as fucked-up as I thought.

But why would anyone choose to immerse themselves in such mind-bending horror?

Well, dunno about you, but I enjoy it. Vicariously brushing up against murderous whackjobs has long been a source of titillation for yours truly. Now I guess I could be outside enjoying the fresh air, perhaps twirling atop a green hill belting out an off-key rendition of *The Sound of Music*, but that just seems like far too much effort. I prefer a dingy room's confines, a few fingers of whiskey, and the existential shivers generated by consuming the hideous misfortunes of other people. You may call a psychiatrist if you wish, but I insist there's something curiously addictive about snuffling through the likes of genocide, sexual torture, mutilation, mass graves and chemical warfare.

And, of course, once I've stopped reading there's always the movies. You remember that bit in *Pulp Fiction* where the newly freed Marsellus Wallace tells his cowed, mewling rapist: "I'm gonna get medieval on your ass."

Yes, please.

Now come join me in my enchanting world of degradation as I pick out six sickening scenes of sadism that always tickle me pink.

Tit trauma

I have no idea if being strung up by the tits is possible but that's what we get in 1970's *A Man Called Horse*. This is a handsome, influential western that spawned two sequels and arguably introduced the idea of a white man being absorbed into a 'savage' culture. Two years later *Deep River Savages* shamelessly copied its storyline, except it took its native quirks (such as grieving women immediately chopping off a finger), upped them to an eye-popping degree and chucked in rapist-cannibals as well. Still, even that energetic horror show didn't come up with anything as iconic as Richard Harris dangling by his nips.

He plays a rich Englishman in the badlands of early 19th century America. Captured by the Sioux, he's initially treated like an animal, but once he notices the chieftain's hot daughter he stops trying to run away and, ahem, opts to hang around. He kills two warriors from an enemy tribe and hands over their horses in a bid to win her hand in marriage.

Close, but no cigar.

He might've convinced them he's a hard bastard, but to get his hands on such top quality snatch he has to make his Vow to the Sun. Good grief, this is one eye-watering initiation rite (and a compelling piece of cinema). Dressed in just a leather loincloth and a thin headband, the poor bastard has to stand in front of the tribe inside the smoky gloom of a huge tepee. There's a steady drumbeat. A medicine man holds up two severed eagle's feet with their wicked black talons in front of his face.

Gulp.

Then they're agonizingly screwed into his chest before two sharpened lengths of bone are inserted lengthways into his pecs. Sweat is beading on his face, but the worst is yet to come. A rope with two nooses is lowered from a hole in the top of the tepee and looped around the makeshift fixtures on his upper torso. The drumbeat becomes feverish. With a nod from the medicine man, our somewhat anxious suitor is hauled up six feet off the ground as the braves use their spears to twirl him by the tits.

Here's hoping that piece of arse is worth it, mate.

Chilly Choking

I s'pose we're all guilty of having sucked up to the boss once in a while, but not many of us go to the extravagant lengths of a certain Nazi dominatrix.

In *Ilsa, She Wolf of the SS* our horny heroine runs Medical Camp 9. This basically means she's got carte blanche to torture prisoners to death. She takes her work seriously, though, and is keen to impress a visiting general with the progress she's made. For a start she's come up with an antidote for gangrene and a way to spread typhoid among enemy troops.

Pretty damn impressive, huh?

But Ilsa's also desperate to get her private research funded. She's convinced women are able to stand pain better than men and can therefore play a much more prominent role in the war by taking frontline positions.

The general, however, is not impressed. "You must not waste Germany's time on your own personal projects," he sternly tells her.

But for someone as resourceful as Ilsa this objection is a mere bump in the road. And where there's a will, there's likely to be a suffering prisoner. "Tonight we have a very special surprise for you," she replies.

And so what is this surprise?

A candlelit dinner held in the general's honour. Very nice. But wait, there's more. A naked woman is standing *on* the end of the table. The general walks up to her and has a good look at her bush. "Remarkable," he comments as Ilsa stands alongside. "Remarkable!" Something's a bit strange, though. He reaches out to stroke one of her trembling legs. "But her legs... They are so cold. Like marble." The general reaches down and pushes away the numerous vases of flowers surrounding and obscuring her feet. She's standing on a block of ice!

Ilsa is beaming. "Look further, general."

Her boss does just that, his vision travelling up her goosebump-afflicted body to the poor woman's neck. There's a noose around it. "While we eat..." He snaps his fingers to illustrate the moment of her impending death.

"Exactly," Ilsa says, unable to keep the giggly pride out of her voice. "I thought it would amuse you."

The general loves it. "*Wunderbar*!" he cries. "*Wunderbar*!"

And so the general proceeds to heartily eat, sing patriotic songs and get drunk as the ice slowly melts, a lengthy process that ensures we get plentiful close-ups of the victim's terrified face.

Wunderbar indeed!

Sucked brains

Ever seen a human milkshake?

No?

Then *Blood Sucking Freaks* AKA *The Incredible Torture Show* is the one for you. It's an ultra-camp, enjoyably amateurish piece of exploitation-splatter that has gained a cult following, partly because its two lead actors met grisly ends not too long after filming wrapped. Then again, their deaths are strangely fitting in that *Freaks* does have meta aspects.

Listen to Sardu (Seamus O'Brien), our *Master of the Theatre of the Macabre*, as he addresses the audience during his latest off-Broadway show: "This is just a theatrical presentation. A show, which offers no reality, not a fraction of reality, and just allows us to delve into our grossest fantasies far beyond erotica. Tonight we begin with torture. I warn you if you find what you see is a little upsetting to your stomachs, then just pretend we're playacting. Or if you're sceptical or bored, then just pretend what you see is real."

As it happens, it *is* real. A naked woman has her hand amputated with a hacksaw before dying on stage, although a watching critic dismisses the performance as a 'third-rate magic show'. Can you see what director Joel M. Reed is doing here? Having fun, as far as I can tell, while naughtily prodding the line between illusion and actuality. It reminded me of that bit in *Henry: Portrait of a Serial Killer* in which we see a terrified family being assaulted in their living room, only for the camera to pull back and reveal Henry in an armchair watching a recording he made of the event. Yes, we're repulsed by real-life sadism, yet many of us are drawn to watching it on screen.

Why?

It's not a comfortable question to try to answer because 1) it means we're voyeurs and 2) it starts gingerly moving us toward the same page as the likes of Sardu and Henry.

Much easier and safer to condemn screen violence instead, a reaction that *Blood Sucking Freaks* certainly prompted back in the mid-70s with its plentiful violence, full frontal nudity and sexual torture, even though it's obviously all tongue in cheek. For example, take the human milkshake bit. Sardu calls in a doctor to attend to an abducted girl, who hasn't responded well to her change in circumstances. For a good ten seconds the doc appears sane, but that mask dissolves when Sardu offers him the chance to perform an operation rather than pay a fee.

"What kind?" he asks.

"Oh," Sardu replies with a twinkle in his eye, "you make it up."

And so the doc does. After removing a woman's teeth one by one without anaesthetic (a bout of dramatic dental surgery accompanied by a snatch of opera singing and a confession he still lives with his mother) he shaves the top of her head. Next he picks up a power drill, unable to contain his boyish enthusiasm as he bores downward. Then he inserts a transparent straw into the six-inch deep hole and starts merrily sucking away, although like all kids it's not long before he starts blowing down the straw and making bubbles.

Brain bubbles.

A horrifying point

I hate it when I get an eyelash in my eye. Irritating as hell. Still, I guess it's preferable to a six-inch-long wooden splinter.

Once seen, Paola Menard's gruesome death in *Zombie* AKA *Zombi 2* AKA *Zombie Flesh-Eaters* is not easily forgotten. You keep expecting the director to pull away, to have some goddamned discretion. The power of suggestion and all that. But no, he just keeps going and takes the inspired scene all the way through to its bloody, inexorable end.

Paola plays a scared doctor's wife stationed on a Caribbean island. The dead have recently started coming back to life, the radio's stopped working, and she's drinking too much.

"I don't want to stay on this island one hour longer," she tells her possibly mad hubby. "You won't be happy until I meet one of your zombies."

Prophetic words.

After Paola treats us to a full frontal in the shower, we know trouble's afoot when a decaying hand is pressed up against a windowpane. Paola dries herself off and slips on a loose-fitting dress, but gets spooked when she hears something moving around outside. She tries to take refuge by jamming a chest of drawers up against a door, but the zombie smashes through the louvers, grabs hold of her long hair and starts pulling her head toward a nasty-looking sliver. Fair play, this is a well-directed scene as we get alternating close-ups of her widened eye and the tip of the splinter. Paola's screaming and thrashing, but she's just not strong enough to break free. In goes the shard, like a needle into custard. It even breaks off, leaving a jagged stump poking out of her ruined peeper.

Aspirin, please!

Violently abducted? Check.

Beaten for two days and two nights? Check.

Ice pick stuck in balls? Check.

And still no dice? Check.

Sometimes it's a breeze being a gangster and sometimes you gotta work for your dough. Look at Nicky Santoro in Scorsese's *Casino*. He's been given a job by the bosses, but getting info from Tony Dogs about a fatal bar shoot-up is proving a lot trickier than anticipated.

"To be truthful with you, I had to admire this fucking guy," Nicky tells us in a voiceover. "He was one of the toughest Irishmen I ever met."

Nicky's an enterprising hoodlum, though, and it's not long before he's thought of a possible solution to this unfortunate impasse.

Put the motherfucker's head in a vice.

And so the bloodied and bruised Dogs, who already has one eye swollen shut from the relentless abuse, is laid on a workbench on his back with his head nestling in the device's wooden jaws.

Nicky leans over, looking down at the guy's face.

"Dogs," he says. "Can you hear me, Dogs? Listen to me, Anthony. I got your head in a fucking vice. I'm gonna squash your fucking head like a grapefruit if you don't give me a name. Don't make me have to do this. Please. Come on. Don't make me be a bad guy. Come on."

Dogs manages a gasping reply.

Unfortunately, it's not the required one. Worse, it's impolite. Nicky, never the most patient of men, is sent into a handle-turning frenzy. Meanwhile his criminal associates, who've probably seen an eye-opening thing or two in their time when it comes to trauma, grimace and turn away. Nicky, however, gets the name he's been after.

Not that it calms him down.

"You make me pop your eye out of your fucking head to protect that piece of shit?" he bellows.

I dunno. You just can't please some people.

Bathroom of brutality

There's a saying: *You are what you eat.* Can't say I've ever bought into it, although I occasionally grasp its relevance whenever I happen to spot some flabby, wheezing cunt in trackypants waddling out of McDonald's.

No, I prefer to believe *You are what you think.*

And so if your thoughts keep returning to a subject, that's what you are. It's your identity, even if you don't tell a soul. If you dwell on sailing, of cruising across the open sea, you're a sailor. If you dream of winning the world chess championship and spend every other moment visualizing killer opening strategies, you're a chess player.

Of course, being consumed by something doesn't mean this is what you will externally become. Life usually gets in the way. Most people have to compromise. Lots of wannabe actors wait tables, you know. That doesn't mean the thoughts go away. It doesn't dampen the dream. Oddly enough, the inner frustration might even strengthen such tormenting fantasies.

Just listen to that Radiohead song about aliens observing us, the one in which they conclude humans are 'weird creatures who lock up their spirits, drill holes in themselves and live for their secrets.'

To paraphrase, you are what you think.

Serial killers nicely fit such an adage. Ninety-nine and a half percent of the time they wear a mask. They mimic emotions, copy how others behave and do their best to blend in.

And so John Wayne Gacy wasn't a shoe store manager, Harold Shipman wasn't a doctor, Dennis Rader wasn't a security alarm installer, Peter Sutcliffe wasn't a truck driver and Dennis Nilsen sure as shit wasn't a copper.

First and foremost they were serial killers. All the rest was bullshit. Beneath the mask they obsessed, fantasized and seethed. All day long and deep into the night. It's the same with every compulsive murderer. Usually they fixate on sex stuff, but that's a smokescreen. Sex, or more accurately rape, is merely one of the methods they employ to achieve what they crave most: control over another human being.

Now as we all know the movies have long loved serial killers, an affection that mushroomed after the enormous Oscar-winning success of *The Silence of the Lambs*. Australia was slow on the uptake but got in the on the act with the likes of 2005's *Wolf Creek* and the socio-realist horror of 2011's *Snowtown* AKA *The Snowtown Murders*. Here we meet John Bunting (an electrifying Daniel Henshall). He's a man who likes to pose as a helpful neighbour, a father figure, and a moral crusader in a rundown part of Adelaide.

And like all those other serial killers, he's wearing a bullshit-caked mask.

Bunting just wants to make up for his inadequacy, his failures, his general invisibility in the state of things. At least in his own head. If he can exert control over one of his fellow creatures, then at least he'll be important in that person's life. No one can argue otherwise. After all, a serial killer is the most significant person a victim will ever meet.

Nothing illustrates Bunting's love of control better than the prolonged suffering he gloatingly inflicts upon a rapist. Beaten and chained to a bathroom pipe, the poor fuck even has his big toenail removed with pliers.

This is just the entrée, though. Time for the main course.

An accomplice has already looped a cord around the rapist's throat. Bunting crouches at face level and orders the cord to be tightened, all the while staring into his victim's eyes.

Not that Bunting wants him dead just yet.

After fifteen or seconds of severe suffering, he tells his partner in crime to *release* the tension. And then to ramp it up again, only slackening off whenever death gets near. At this point Bunting retains human form, but everything else is unrecognizable and off the scale. In his world other people exist for his benefit, his gratification. His life is ashes, but at least the fire can be rekindled when someone's under his power. "Head up," he tells the rapist before the choking cycle restarts yet again. Bunting doesn't want to miss a thing, feeding off his victim's acute distress while perhaps trying to locate the possibility of a soul, the life spark, in the man's banging, fading vision. Whatever the case, he's genuinely fascinated, witnessing what so few others have ever seen in this intimate, maskless ritual.

This is power, this is control, this is life and death in *Snowtown*.

Annoying Fuckers

Most people are annoying.

It doesn't matter whether they're a droning colleague, that snarky online twat who just won't see sense, some random queue jumper, a younger sibling, yet another vacuous, overpaid celeb, the halitosis-afflicted taxi driver taking the long way round, a right wing foreign president, a neighbour loudly playing music or that hotty in the supermarket who just looked straight through you.

At least, this has been my experience. Perhaps that's why I rarely venture out and instead pretend a life of watching movies is not only an acceptable, hassle-free alternative to dealing with the hoi polloi but also a rich and rewarding one.

Whatever the case, the cinematic worlds I spend so much time within strongly suggest I'm not the only one having to grin and bear it. I guess that's part of the attraction of movies. They make you feel less alone.

Anyhow, here are three characters who take the biscuit when it comes to winding others up.

The sexist pig truck driver in *Thelma and Louise* (1991)

What is it that happens to some guys when they slip behind the wheel? Why does a combination of locomotion and being encased within metal and glass so routinely turn them into aggressive, mouthy nobs?

Even harmless little me has been on the receiving end of this phenomenon. More than once I've been strolling down the street minding my own business only for a couple of guys to zoom past yelling "Wanker!" It's baffling conduct, but it's often worse for women who have to put up with such stuff as "Show us yer tits!" and "How much for a fuck?"

Boy, am I glad I've grown out of that behaviour.

In one of Ridley Scott's best efforts he gives us the personification of sexist vulgarity in the marvellous, knuckle-dragging form of Marco St. John. He plays an unnamed truck driver, initially appearing courteous as our heroines cruise up behind his massive tanker. He indicates for them to pass on the straight stretch of highway, prompting Thelma (Geena Davis) to say: "Oh, isn't that nice? Truck drivers are always so nice."

But Marco's civility is what is known as lulling someone into a false sense of security. The first clue he's not the most progressive chap is his mud flaps being adorned with the mirrored silhouettes of a busty, reclining woman. As Thelma and Louise pull up alongside, Marco's still on his best behaviour, grinning down from his cab and waving.

Man, he's good at this false sense of security thing.

The oblivious Thelma says thanks and waves back which, of course, prompt him to reveal his true colours. Out pops his waggling tongue like a sexed-up electric eel. Christ, is this how he performs cunnilingus? He must get lockjaw in forty-five seconds flat.

The women nip ahead, expressing their disgust as Marco keeps honking in the background. Thelma shakes her head. "That's gross! What's he gotta do that for, anyway?" Louise (Susan Sarandon), whom we've come to rely on as the sassier and smarter of the two, offers her interpretation. "They think we like it," she says. "They think it turns us on."

Nope.

Men don't engage in such crassness to 'turn women on.' Even a shithead like our unenlightened truck driver knows that. They do it to *intimidate*.

But by the time the girls bump into Marco again it's a different ball game, their calamitous road trip having been indelibly soured by contact with one male shitkicker after another.

And Marco ain't gonna do anything to change any of that. Now he's wolf whistling and treating them to his gift of the gab. "Hey, baby!" he cries. "You ready for a big dick?" (Well, to be fair, such a blunt verbal approach has gotta expend a good deal less energy than all that manic pseudo-cunnilingus stuff).

Now it's Thelma and Louise's turn to have a go at the false sense of security thing. They all stop at a dusty outpost, which leads to the pitiful shots of Marco squirting freshener into his mouth and removing his wedding ring, as if he doesn't want his imminent conquests to think badly of him for cheating on his wife. Clearly energized, he jumps out of his cab, dances on the spot and blows his waiting belles a kiss.

Things don't quite go as planned, though.

"We think you have really bad manners," Thelma tells him.

Marco can only laugh.

"Where do you get off behaving like that with women you don't even know?" Louise adds. "How'd you feel if somebody did that to your mother? Or your sister? Or your wife?"

"Huh?" is his only response, giving us a sense not of evil or even hardcore misogyny but lamentable ignorance. This is a man with an inability to read body language, pick up on the women's tone of voice, hold a conversation or even muster a retort. By now an apology for his ungentlemanly antics is being demanded, but Marco's not the sort to say sorry to the gentler sex. Within seconds, his rig's tires are being shot out before his beloved truck is blown to kingdom come. The girls can only look on in open-mouthed wonder as poor Marco sinks to his knees against a backdrop of burning ruins. "You bitches!" he yells while waving both fists in the air. "You bitches from hell!"

This is a magnificently satisfying piece of cinema, so memorable that I have little doubt it provides the perfect fodder for female revenge fantasies. In other words, fellahs, watch your mouths the next time you're cruising around and happen to spot a female or two coz one day you might just bump into a pair 'ready to get serious' all over your arse.

The weaselly parole officer in *Straight Time* (1978)

None of us like having a boss. Even as children we chafed against mum and dad making us eat our veggies or go to bed at a certain time. Let's face it, other people telling us what to do *sucks*.

Well, in the lesser known crime drama *Straight Time*, newly released prisoner Max Dembo (Dustin Hoffman) is in the glum position of being back on the street but barely having control over *anything*. He still has to meet his rigid parole conditions, a requirement made a hundred times worse by his supervisor Earl Frank (M. Emmet Walsh) being a controlling pain in the arse.

Now Walsh is not a household name, but you probably know him from supporting performances in such quality fare as *Serpico*, *Slap Shot*, *Blade Runner* and especially *Blood Simple*. This guy's been around. In *Straight Time* he's great, really, really great, and spends every onscreen moment unwisely annoying the shit out of the desperately-trying-to-comply, seemingly reformed Dembo.

Upon their first meeting at the Department of Corrections, we see Frank's a paunchy, balding, mildly dishevelled man. He neither wears a tie nor sits up straight in his chair. Dembo actually looks the more together of the two, but there's no doubt about who's in charge. At first Frank's polite and courteous, but this is the thinnest of masks, and his contempt for Dembo's criminal past soon starts radiating off him. Things threaten to turn ugly when Frank is dissatisfied with Dembo's explanation for spending the previous night at a motel instead of a halfway house.

"I just spent six years in prison," Dembo tells him. "I just wanted to look at the lights, wanted to feel free, wanted to walk around, not have somebody tell me I gotta get in bed at ten o'clock."

Frank jumps in with both feet, telling Dembo he has a 'serious attitude problem.' In that one line, we know he's got it in for the ex-con. "My friend," he says, flashing his practised fake smile, "I see that you're gonna force me to deal with you."

And deal with him he does, later resorting to snooping around his room and slapping handcuffs on him after finding a book of matches that one of Dembo's mates had used to cook heroin. Sincere protests about his innocence are not only a waste of time but music to Frank's ears. Suddenly Dembo's back inside for a suspected parole violation, losing his newly acquired job and home as a result.

And, of course, when his drug test proves clean, that insincere bastard Frank is there to belatedly pick him up and return him to the halfway house while lording it over his charge every minute of the way.

Fucking hell, Frank's a pathetic son of a bitch. Even when he's not reminding Dembo who's boss, his attempts at chitchat reveal him to be a vaguely bigoted bore. He's insincere, condescending and in possession of a misplaced superiority complex. Most of all, he loves the power he wields over Dembo, obviously seeing himself as a cat playing with a mouse. But just like our sexist pig truck driver, he badly misjudges the situation, leading to a fantastic, richly deserved denouement that's on a par with Marco's fate.

Walsh is brilliant throughout and I love the way he instantly switches between apparent helpfulness and vindictiveness. His jagged interplay with the quietly seething Hoffman, which puts the viewer in the curious position of rooting for the imminent menace to society, is a joy to behold.

The world's worst house guest in *Sexy Beast* (2000)

"People say: Don't you miss it, Gal? I say, what? England? Nah. Fucking place. It's a dump. Don't make me laugh. Grey, grimy, sooty. What a shithole. What a toilet. Every cunt with a long face shuffling about moaning, all worried. No thanks, not for me."

It's fair to say that the cashed-up, ex-crim Gal (Ray Winstone) has no regrets about moving to sunny Spain. He spends pretty much every day lounging by the pool working on his tan, eating calamari at his favourite restaurant, hanging out with friends, and dancing in the balmy night-time air with his beloved wife.

Everything's great.

Well, apart from a rolling, bouncing hillside boulder missing his head by inches, the barbecue flames leaping out in an apparent bid to incinerate him, and weird dreams about man-sized rabbits hunting *him*.

It's almost as if such ominous signs suggest trouble's afoot in paradise.

Then Gal gets news of a London phone call through his friends. The very much non-retired Don Logan (Ben Kingsley) wants him for a bank heist and is on his way over from England. Gal's wife gives a simple response: "Oh, Christ."

Gal might as well have been told that a human combination of the Prince of Darkness, Ebola and nuclear war is coming to visit. Gal can't think of an excuse to decline, any kind of sop that will lessen the force of the approaching tornado. Suddenly a funereal pall is hanging over his luxurious villa with every character drained of colour and looking like they're about to gnaw off their fingernails.

Gal's wife suggests an impromptu holiday, prompting him to sigh. "That would be like a red rag to a bull," he says.

And with this foreboding brilliantly established, we finally get to meet the bald, goateed Don as he confidently strides through the airport like *The Long Good Friday's* Harold Shand. Accompanied by thumping, energetic music that suggests unchecked momentum, Don doesn't smile. Neither does he sweetly pinch the cheeks of any children. He's a model of concentration, moving forward with fixed vision like a shark zeroing in on a hapless target.

Gal does his best to politely say no. He really does. "I'd do anything not to offend ya, but I can't take part," he tells him. "I'm not really up to it."

Don half-smiles. "Is this a fuck off, Gal?"

From this point on Don turns into a relentlessly cajoling, haranguing, capricious force of nature who uses words to slash like a shit-smeared knife. There's no intimidating trick he won't try whether it's a prolonged, unnerving stare, childishly repeating words like a schoolyard bully, rhapsodizing about your wife's porno past or kicking you in the face while you're sleeping.

Then, of course, there's his exceptional talent in channelling his inner drill instructor Hartman and letting fly with an amazing array of creative insults.

"You're revolting," he spits at Gal. "Look at your fucking suntan. Like leather. Like a leather man, your skin. You could make a fucking suitcase out of you. A holdall. You look like a crocodile. A fat crocodile. Fat bastard. You look like Idi Amin."

Now suggesting the paunchy Gal resembles the black, grotesquely obese Ugandan dictator is taking things a bit too far, but that's Don Logan in a nutshell. He *does* take things too far.

Not that a way over the top slur results in him finishing trying to grind Gal down. There's just no letup in the verbal barrage whether they're in a bar, at the beach, sitting by the pool or in the car.

"What do you think this is? The *Wheel of Fortune*? Make your dough and fuck off? Leave the table? Thanks, Don. See ya, Don. Off to sunny Spain now. Lie in your pool like a fat blob laughing at me. You think I'm gonna have that?"

Perhaps my favourite bit, though, is the moment we glimpse a different side of this piss-poor conversationalist after Gal reveals he's happy living a retired life in Spain.

"I won't let you be happy," Don shrilly counters, laying bare his essential pitifulness. "Why should I?"

The Oscar-nominated Kingsley shines during his nightmare cocktail of motor-mouthed aggression, instantaneous violence, chilling paranoia and plain old stubbornness. He puts in a shift that has to be one of cinema's greatest examples of casting an actor against type.

Fucked-Up Films #1: The Exterminator (1980)

Synopsis

Life is war whether you're in Nam or the Big Apple

Director

James Glickenhaus

Cast

Robert Ginty, Christopher George, Steve James, Samantha Eggar

I have a clear recollection of standing in a video shop aged twelve with *On Golden Pond* on one side and *The Exterminator* on the other. I can't remember too much about the cover of the first, except it featured smiley old farts and had the word *pond* in the title. Even at that tender age I knew there was no way a good movie could be made about *ponds*.

And then there was *The Exterminator*, some ripped guy in a black motorcycle helmet wielding a flamethrower with the tagline: *If you're lying... I'll be back.*

Well, which one do you think I pestered dad to rent?

Turned out this urban thriller's heady mix of Vietcong war crimes, gangster-shredding violence and the odd canine fatality was far from healthy viewing but just the ticket for me and my hooting mates.

What are these sick bastards doing? John Eastland (Ginty) is one of those unlucky bastards that exploitation flicks couldn't function without. He's a decent guy but can't catch a break to save his blue-collar life. Firstly we see him getting blown up and captured in Vietnam, eventually escaping after his best buddy Michael (James) saves his life. Things don't improve back in New York when Michael has his spine rearranged by the rampaging members of a street gang called the Ghetto Ghouls.

What's a man to do? Write a hand-on-heart letter to the local TV news station, that's what!

'The people of New York have been terrorized by criminals for too long,' the letter-reading newscaster subsequently tells viewers. 'Politicians have stood idly by as thugs and killers have taken over our streets, our parks, our lives. As of today, this will no longer be true.'

And, of course, the missive is signed *Chuck Bronson*.

No, hang on, I mean *The Exterminator*.

Is the villain any good? One of the interesting, vaguely surprising things here is we don't get a chief bad guy for Eastland to face off against. Just when you think he's settled on eliminating one piece of scum, up pops another target.

How skuzzy are the other men? Pretty skuzzy. You can take your pick between racist, badly dressed, beer-stealing street punks whose *raison d'être* is to piss off honest, hardworking citizens or the hooker-torturing, paedophilic inhabitants of a horribly painted, none-too-legal brothel. There's a definite lack of male role models throughout.

How do the lovely ladies fare? Not great, but I've seen a lot worse. Hookers get the brunt of the abuse, although an old dear is smacked across the face and kicked on the ground by three members of those fun-loving Ghetto Ghouls. Mind you, given she was out at night, taking a shortcut through a park and carrying groceries she was clearly asking for it. There's also a kindly doc looking after Eastland's crippled buddy but as she doesn't get raped, set on fire or thrown off a building I fail to see the point of her role.

Would the violence make a vicar faint? Back in the day *The Exterminator* generated a lot of negative press, perhaps fuelling its surprisingly decent box office performance. Plenty of moral crusaders were convinced cinematic brutality had hit a graphic new low, their handwringing objections centring on the Vietcong's machete-wielding, head-removing shenanigans in the opening minutes.

And fair play, it's a cool scene.

Even so, times have moved on. To give you an example, I caught *Rambo: Last Blood* the other day in which Sly also gets saucy with a machete by chopping off a baddie's foot rather than a head. It's such a convincing act of extreme violence I not only gasped '*Ooh!*' but suspect an extra was genuinely mutilated, having agreed to the amputation after the producers offered a crate of beer and the post-hospital chance to hang out with Sly for a day or two.

Not a bad deal, I guess.

Anyhow, despite a decent body count, *The Exterminator* never made me go '*Ooh!*' Many of its sadistic episodes, such as a screaming Mafia boss being fed into a meat grinder, are implied rather than shown (probably because the budget was running out). In short, if you could keep a vicar away from this movie's groovy start, I reckon he *might* get through this one (although he'd still be in serious danger of awkward silences, multiple blushes and the occasional stammering objection).

How fucked-up is this film? The ex-Vietnam Vet running amok was probably first introduced with 1974's pretty good cult horror flick, *Deathdream* AKA *Dead of Night*, reaching its commercial peak eleven years later with Rambo returning to the South East Asian country to refight the war ("Do we get to win this time?")

In *The Exterminator* Eastland is not presented as a nut or misfit, never once coming across as anywhere near as deranged as *Taxi Driver's* Travis Bickle or *Rolling Thunder's* Charles Rane. The only suggestion of post-traumatic stress is a sporadic Nam flashback. Eastland's just tired of being surrounded by scummy bastards in his hometown. He doesn't go in for Bond or Arnie-style quips (*I'll be back* is said quite straight). Neither does he see himself as some sort of saviour. Hell, he doesn't even appear to get off on the violence. Ginty gives a buttoned-down performance, almost managing to convince us that the burnings, shootings and explosions are *necessary*. Indeed, some of the flick's quieter moments, such as a silent Eastland dripping mercury into dumdum bullets before meticulously filing them down, are among the most effective.

Saying that, things are still all over the place. It starts superbly with a spectacular explosion that sees Eastland thrown about thirty feet into the air, his tumbling body silhouetted against a wall of flame. I also like the way the (disappointingly brief) war segment segues into a night-time swoop around New York harbour as a heartfelt ballad kicks in. Indeed, there's a lot of outdoor filming, an approach that brings the city's markets, streets, parks and grimier locations to vivid life.

However, it's baffling why director Glickenhaus fast forwards through some pretty damn important events. In four scenes flat (that all take place on the *same day*) we get the life-ruining assault on Michael, Eastland informing his wife he'll never walk again, a pinioned gang member being threatened with a flamethrower, and Eastland bursting into the Ghouls' graffiti-daubed HQ for his first spot of murder.

Chuck in the CIA, a pervert senator, the Mob, an irrelevant bit of romance, a ludicrous scene in a steakhouse toilet which involves defecation and a ninja-like abduction, and I'd have to say *The Exterminator* doesn't go the way you'd expect.

However, it has a little more intelligence and ambition than it's generally given credit for and remains far better than the simplistic nihilism of something like *Death Wish II*. Dare I say it, but *The Exterminator* might be due a bit of reassessment. It's not top-notch or anything, but it's a key vigilante flick and has its strengths. Most of all, it's gotta be better than watching those Oscar-winning fogies Henry Fonda and Katharine Hepburn catch tadpoles at their stupid pond.

Starring Debuts Part Two

Jeffrey Combs in *Re-Animator* (1985)

It's apt that Herbert West (Combs) resembles both Harry Potter and Scottish necrophile Dennis Nilsen.

His small stature and precocious schoolboy looks suggest he's harmless, enabling him to obscure a deep-rooted fascination with corpses while committing murder if necessary.

It's a plum role and Combs seizes it with such memorable relish that he now enjoys a well-deserved place in horror's long, blood-spattered tradition of mad scientists.

West arrives at a Massachusetts medical school to further his neurological studies under the tutelage of Dr. Carl Hill (the wonderfully off-centre David Gale). Straightaway it's plain that the new student has limited social finesse.

"How can you teach such drivel?" he asks during his first class before accusing the respected surgeon of plagiarism and outdated research on brain death. Hill tries to take the arrogant outburst on the chin. "I'm going to enjoy failing you," he mutters.

Like so many of his Frankenstein ilk, West has a sweaty intensity that makes people uncomfortable. He might be a student but you're never going to find him partying on campus and drunkenly egging the dean's windows. Girls don't interest him. He's capable of a smile but there's never any warmth behind it, as if the exercise is merely a required social nicety done under mild duress. On the whole he will suck the fun out of any room.

What matters are his career and the acknowledgement of his outrageous genius. To this end, he's secretive, free of doubt, and indifferent to distress. Every waking thought is directed toward pushing the boundaries of medical science. Convinced his limited, vaguely stupid colleagues are blundering in the dark, it doesn't matter how much chaos he wreaks in the obsessive pursuit of his goals. Indeed, when it comes to bringing his dream to its sacred fruition he literally has a never say die attitude.

West's roommate Dan Cain (Bruce Abbott) is soon sucked into his twisted orbit via a recently deceased pet cat. "Don't expect it to tango," West tells him before injecting it with his glowing serum. "It has a broken back."

Cain's eyes are opened at the death-defeating results, even if his former pet no longer shows him the same degree of affection.

"We can defeat death," West seductively whispers in his ear. "We can achieve every doctor's dream. We'll be famous... and live lifetimes."

Now you might disagree, but I believe the 80s was the last decade in which good horror movies were consistently produced. *Re-Animator* popped up slap bang in its middle, securing my vote as the second greatest horror comedy of all time after *American Werewolf*. It's a brisk movie, aided by good production values, excellent special effects, some splendid nudity, and nicely judged support.

However, what makes it stand out is the way it truly commits to its premise, never once shying away from pushing its pronounced streak of black comedy as far as possible, even if that means depicting a reanimated severed head slobbering over pinioned female flesh.

Combs' unhinged, justly celebrated performance stands at its centre, encapsulating the way in which egomaniacs often validate their bloody deeds by insisting they're on the side of right.

Dustin Hoffman in *The Graduate* (1967)

There's a scene in *The Graduate* where Benjamin Braddock (Hoffman) is lying supine on a hotel bed while Mrs. Robinson (Anne Bancroft), the sophisticated older woman who's introduced him to the mysteries of sex, sits alongside clad in a black bra slowly unbuttoning his white shirt and running her hands over his smooth chest. Accompanied by *The Sound of Silence*, Benjamin's got this amazing expression. He's gazing dumbstruck up at her and everything's shiny and new, the world's been reinvented and he's as alive as he'll ever be. It's so simple and beautiful and yet terribly sad because it must crumble.

After all, such wondrous moments can never endure. Life doesn't work like that.

Great actors can do this, they can make you fall into their world without saying a word, and Hoffman achieves it here in much the same way the repressed Anthony Hopkins does when he's cornered in his private room and transfixed by the feminine playfulness of Emma Thompson in *The Remains of the Day*.

Still, there's an awful lot more to Hoffman's performance than the occasional glimpse of mute reverie. Indeed, he spends most of this coming of age classic in an acute state of bewildered discomfort. Having recently graduated from an East Coast college, he's at a loss as to why such a high point isn't providing the easy, logical stepping stone to the next part of life. As a student he was an award-winning track star but now...

There are just so many *questions*, the existential ones he's asking himself and the suffocating ones continually being lobbed at him by parents and their ilk about what he's going to do. The turmoil is written over his face from the second we first encounter him sitting on a plane, prompting his concerned father to immediately ask upon his return to their swish Californian home: "What's the matter?"

From here Benjamin starts feeling like a fish in an aquarium. He's choking under the relentless curiosity, smothering expectations and constant suggestions, not to mention his bristling dislike at the assumption of dutiful conformity. His 21st birthday present of scuba equipment proves especially apt, enabling amused onlookers to peer down at him after he's forced to jump into the backyard swimming pool and breathe underwater.

All Benjamin knows is what he *doesn't* want, having no doubt that an offer of a soul-crimping career in plastics would do little more than turn him into a plastic man. The best he can do is yearn for a 'different' future.

"I've had this feeling ever since I've graduated, this kind of compulsion to be rude all the time," he says. "It's like I'm playing some kind of game, but the rules don't make any sense to me and they're being made up by all the wrong people."

Then Mrs. Robinson makes her fateful move, complicating matters even further. The virginal Benjamin gives us a vivid portrait of simultaneous dread and desire, his mouth full of objections yet his panicky eyes telling a different story. He's a boy stumbling into an adult's world, the terror so plain on his face that sometimes it's like he's attending his own execution. When he isn't bumping into things, he's failing miserably at playing it cool, inanely repeating stuff in a thick voice that's always threatening to break, and even driving on the sidewalk. He goes into such a deep tizzy at the thought of Mrs. Robinson fishing around in his underpants that he can't help sweating in her cool, classy and deeply unsettling company. Even when they finally end up in a hotel room he's still a cack-handed klutz desperate to wangle his way out of it.

"Maybe we can do something else together," he suggests, trying to throw everything into reverse. "Mrs. Robinson, would you like to go to a movie?" He wants out but his elegant seductress knows how to push his buttons and it's not long before the deed is done.

The intense confusion dissipates and she becomes his world.

At least for a little while.

Christ, how good is Hoffman in this flick? Has anyone ever given such a convincing performance of sustained, consistently amusing discomfort? *The Graduate* is a riveting triumph, immeasurably bolstered by one of the great starring debuts, and remains as fresh today as it was at the tail end of the sixties.

Benjamin's newfound joy of fucking means he no longer gives a fuck about all those other big questions. Plastics...? Graduate School...? Who wants to think about such mundane shite when he's got access to a hot cougar, good weather, a swimming pool, a chunk of change in his pocket, a red

Alfa Romeo, and the many privileges of youth. His eyes are open and that troublesome smoke's cleared. Now he's spending his days lying on an inflatable pool lounger, drifting literally and figuratively, before spending his nights in carnal bliss. It's a situation his nearest and dearest can hardly fail to notice. "Would you mind telling me what those four years of college were for?" his father asks. "What was the point of all that hard work?"

Benjamin shrugs. "You got me."

But this state of contented indifference can never last. After the giddying high comes the sour crash, prompted by his desire to have an actual conversation with his clothes-shedding temptress. Perhaps he's also chafing against being in the traditionally female role. After all, he was the one who was pursued and conquered. In his subsequent attempt at a discussion he discovers Mrs. Robinson's extreme sensitivity about her daughter Elaine (Katharine Ross), a sensitivity doubtless rooted in sexual jealousy and the fear of aging, as well as the belittling verdict that he's not good enough to date her. Beforehand Benjamin was always sweet and polite, but this putdown is a real slap in the face.

"I'm not proud of myself spending time with a broken-down alcoholic," he cruelly tells her while hunting around both for his clothes in their hotel room and some leverage. "And if you think I come here for any reason besides pure boredom then you're all wrong. This is the sickest, most perverted thing that ever happened to me."

Aah, the corrupting nature of sexual contact.

But after a horrible circular argument all he can do is take his trousers off again, get back into bed and say: "Let's not talk at all."

And there's another life lesson, buddy: Men fuck, women *talk*.

Everything's falling apart, Mrs. Robinson isn't the answer anymore than plastics, and he's right back at square one. Before long he's mumbling: "My whole life is such a waste. It's just... nothing."

Hello darkness, my old friend.

All that's left is to break the 'rules' by taking Mrs. Robinson's gorgeous daughter out. However, Benjamin's so confused by his lack of direction and all this head-spinning female contact that he has to pretend to be another person during the disastrous date. He drives like a fuckwit, gives one-word answers, walks too fast, wears dark sunnies that mask his eyes, smokes, and takes her to a strip joint. Is there a funnier, sadder moment in sixties cinema than a busty stripper spinning her tassels in opposing directions while he asks the lovely, refined Elaine: "How'd you like that? Could you do it?"

Christ, where has Benjamin gone? Who is this dislikeable schmuck?

But his confused blundering isn't over yet. He still has to upset a landlord, break into a house, try his hand at stalking, swing a giant crucifix, thump a cuckold, and ruin a wedding. He's on a perilous, question-filled journey, all right, one that strangely takes him all the way from a plane seat to a bus seat. By the time he sinks into it, having decisively, *finally* seized a direction in life the exhilaration drains and cold reality begins to set in.

There's only one question left: Is this the answer?

Dolph Lundgren in *Rocky IV* (1985)

Look, I'm not gay.

Yes, I love *The Wizard of Oz* and did once find myself in a gay nightclub via a drunken youthful mistake, but don't go trying to give me all that *lady doth protest too much* shit.

I'm not gay.

All right?

Saying that, I must confess to a sneaking admiration for the physical attributes of Mr. Lundgren in this particular sports drama. It's nothing sexual, no wish to touch his 'front bottom' as Don Logan says in *Sexy Beast*, but just a simple aesthetic appreciation. And by that I mean the way the guy's been put together. Blonde, eight feet tall, and looking like he's capable of dismantling all of America's institutions and traditions with one gargantuan punch.

This admiration of his strapping physique is no different to the way I feel when I see other well-designed structures, such as Sydney's Opera House, the Taj Mahal or St. Paul's Cathedral. They're handsome entities, aren't they? But I don't wanna shag them anymore than I do Dolph. Or even run my hand over his smooth, finely chiselled chest when he's not looking. That would be daft.

Right, on with the review.

Now Mr. T was a good, memorable villain in the second sequel but Lundgren takes things to a whole new level here. He's superb and surely the main reason *Rocky IV* became the franchise's biggest hit with a $300million box office take. Pity Tommy Morrison (the poor schmuck who had to try to follow in Dolph's footsteps) in the dismal *Rocky V*.

Anyhow, early on in *Rocky IV* we're told the average heavyweight boxer punches with the force of 700 pounds of pressure per square inch. Via some computer wizardry Captain Ivan Drago is shown achieving 1850 psi, an enormous thump that we later see has increased to a phenomenal 2150.

"The results are quite obvious," his manager tells a bunch of awestruck onlookers. "Whatever he hits, he destroys."

Out of curiosity I Googled the bite pressure of the most fearsome predator of Earth (and no, I don't mean Harvey Weinstein) and found that a 21 ft Great White can sink its choppers into you at 4000 psi.

Now this isn't exactly an irrefutable scientific conclusion, but I believe this means Drago punches with the equivalent force of a bite from a 10ft long hungry shark. Is it me or does this conjure up the wonderful picture of Drago dancing around the ring armed with a pair of razor-toothed sharks on the end of his wrists?

Bloody hell, no wonder Apollo ended up dead. Perhaps the only surprise was that Drago didn't slowly circle him as he lay face down twitching on the canvas, soaking up the boos while taking the occasional chomp.

Then again, everything about Drago is impressive. Introduced before the glare of America's media, he looks dashing in his army uniform with his impossibly broad shoulders. He's a 261-pound 'mountain of muscle' and 'the most perfectly trained athlete ever.' He's the undefeated world amateur boxing champion. There's no need for any showboating or trash talk. Indeed, he barely utters a word but what he does say is priceless ("You will lose", "I cannot be defeated", "I defeat all men", "I must break you" and that classic, chilling statement of indifference: "If he dies, he dies.") Even his nickname The Siberian Express is the coolest in the history of the sport.

Then there's his unsmiling demeanour. Boy, does this guy know how to intimidate. Look how many shots we get of his sweat-beaded face in profile before his head slowly swivels to unleash that knee-quivering stare. And on top of everything else, he appears emotionless, as if he's some sort of pugilistic Terminator. Certainly there are moments when he gives a machine-like impression of Skynet disdain for the puny mortals clamouring around him. This explains his faint bemusement with James Brown belting out *Living in America* alongside showgirls in the minutes before the fatal exhibition match. Not that such a load of Western razzle-dazzle could possibly make any difference to Drago's concentration. No one has their eye on the ball like him. He can neither be distracted nor goaded, especially by some dancing, has-been ninny in an Uncle Sam getup who pays the ultimate price for underestimation.

Frankly, I would've ended the flick right there with Rocky wishing he'd thrown in the towel to save his best mate from the threat of decapitation. Drago's the best. Hell, even his towering *missus* looks like she can kick Rocky's arse.

But I guess movies don't work that way. After all, Rocky's always been the underdog, hasn't he? Even so, it's still hard to believe he's gonna get in the ring with this shark-man.

In Russia.

On Christmas Day.

After giving up his belt.

For *free*.

No wonder a distraught Adrian (Talia Shire) bleats: "You've seen him. You've seen how strong he is. You can't win!" Or as that understandably smug Slav manager pronounces at the subsequent press conference: "It's physically impossible for this little man to win. Drago is a look at the future."

Now we all know Rocky's got a huge heart, an indomitable spirit and the simmering need to avenge Apollo, but duking it out toe to toe with this cyborg?

It's simply inconceivable.

Whatever next? The Soviet Union falling apart virtually overnight?

I have to say *Rocky IV*, written and directed by Sly, is brilliant at building Drago up. By the time our slightly shorter hero has made the decision to take on the steroid-fuelled 'death from above' and singlehandedly heal East-West relations, the ultra-confident Drago's already become a near-mythical figure. In a way his eventual defeat after fifteen bruising, bloodied rounds is the only mistake the movie makes, especially as he then has to gallingly listen to his victor's simplistic guff about how 'everybody can change.'

Well, Drago doesn't need to change. He's fucking perfect.

Or am I being blinded by love?

Emily Lloyd in *Wish You Were Here* (1987)

That arch wit Morrissey obviously knows a thing or two about holidaying in dismal seaside towns. Just listen to the brilliant *Everyday is Like Sunday* in which he dreamily yearns for such places to be bombed: *This is the coastal town that they forgot to close down. Armageddon, come Armageddon! Come, Armageddon, come! Everyday is like Sunday. Everyday is silent and grey.*

Well, at least Morrissey could leave. It's much worse for sixteen-year-old Lynda Mansell (Lloyd). She has to *live* in one. The opening shots of this coming of age classic tell you all you need to know. Threatening skies, horrible muck-like sand, a cold, uninviting ocean, and crying, swooping seagulls. Swimmers and sunbathers are as rare as Lynda's grasp of decorum.

Witness her soon-to-be-fired antics in front of her straitlaced father in a packed tearoom. "We all piss in the teapot," she gleefully tells the appalled customers while standing on a chair. "I'm pregnant. In the club. A man's willy has entered my person. Am I the only one who does it? What do you lot do, eh? Hands up all those who like willies." By now her fists are pumping the air as a manager runs around frantically apologising. "I like willies! Sex!"

It's no real surprise Lynda's got to this point. *Wish You Were* Here introduces her in a black and white photograph as a gasmask-clad child, as if the stuffy air around her is not quite fit for her inhalations. Soon afterward she's racing along the wet promenade on a bike flashing her legs at the startled boys, mooning neighbours, out-psyching psychiatrists, and doing rude things in a garden shed.

"You're in such a rush," her exasperated father (Geoffrey Hutchings) tells her. "Why be in such a rush about it all?"

But rush she does, a whirlwind-like need for attention that's no doubt been generated by the early death of her beloved mother. Despite the conservative moral climate of 1950s Britain, she has no qualms about pre-marital sex. Employers (and adults in general) are viewed with disdain as they try to clip her wings. Then again, boys her age also disappoint. Jobs come and go, invariably ending in funny public spectacles.

Her poor dad can't quite give up trying to rein in his bored, unapologetic offspring, even though the reward for showing paternal concern is to bounce between embarrassment, shame and mortification.

"There's something wrong with you, my girl," he concludes.

Things aren't helped when his bookie friend Eric (Tom Bell) takes a creepy interest in her. This is a snake-like man who looks at Lynda as if she's a nice, warm mouse. "Think you're it, don't you?" he tells her, reaching under her dress while they stand in her living room. "I think you're all the same. Don't know what you've got it for. All you young girls, you're scared. All talk, scared of a real man, ain't yer?"

Her response? "Hope yer finger stinks."

Still, it's in this relationship that we start to grasp Lynda's glaring contradictions. She knows Eric's a wrong 'un but still lets him have his way. She's tough but vulnerable, defiant but desperate to be accepted, intelligent yet occasionally quite dumb.

A typical teenager, really, just a bit more of an exhibitionist than most.

Throughout it all, Lloyd (and her very expressive face) vibrantly portray the myriad sides of this brilliantly fleshed-out wild child, especially the way she spits out the choice dialogue.

Up yer bum!

Ralph Macchio in *The Karate Kid* (1984)

There are wish fulfilment movies and then there's the fucking *Karate Kid*.

Macchio plays Daniel LaRusso, a wholesome, 17-year-old kid who's arrived in LA with his upbeat mom. A five-strong gang of bullies, who've been taught 'no mercy' by their evil karate teacher, zero in.

Well, big deal.

Daniel still gets the buxom, high-class girl (a blonde cheerleader, no less) before whipping his chief tormentor's arse fair and square in public. It doesn't matter he's so ill-prepared for the climactic tournament that he's spent two months painting fences, waxing cars and kicking ocean waves rather than going anywhere near an actual sparring partner or even learning the rules of engagement.

Not only that but the beaten bad guy (whose girlfriend has already been stolen by Daniel) then happily tells him he's 'all right' and *gives* him the trophy, the equivalent of rolling over and showing his belly.

It's pie in the sky stuff. Christ, the last shot should have been Daniel humping the cheerleader doggy style while smugly winking into the camera.

So why don't I hate Daniel, this clean-cut kid who doesn't drink, smoke or swear? Especially as the little fucker shows so much character, discipline and bravery to overcome his problems, traits I routinely eschew in favour of cynicism and a dive into the nearest bottle of Jack Daniels.

I guess because Macchio puts in such a winning performance. He's 22 here, five years older than his character, but looking two years younger. It's a perfect piece of casting and he displays engaging range whether talking to himself, trimming bonsai or coming over the cheerleader's tits. Sorry, I made that last bit up, and shall promise not to make any more sexual references to Ali (Elisabeth Shue) and her curiously erotic fondness for sweaters and tank tops.

Still, Macchio does prove himself a good actor. I like how he gets beaten up on the beach and splutters "Just leave me alone!" as Ali offers comfort while he lays face down in the sand trying not to cry. Better still is the way his face does all the acting as he slowly realizes Mr. Miyagi (Noriyuki 'Pat' Morita) has been slyly training him through a series of back-breaking menial tasks ('wax on, wax off') rather than exploiting his youthful labour.

Daniel barely gets any good lines, though, and isn't the movie's most interesting character. That honour goes to his elderly mentor, a war hero who can slice the necks off four standing beer bottles with one karate chop. Miyagi is terrific, but it's the way the wide-eyed Daniel meshes with him that produces one of the decade's greatest double acts.

Nevertheless, it remains surprising how often *Karate Kid* slips into fantasy. Witness Mr. Miyagi sparking out *five* teenage aggressors despite being four feet tall and in possession of a bus pass. This should be a Graham Chapman moment but the movie has banked so much goodwill by this point that I'm happy to let it slide. Then there's the way he fixes Daniel's shattered leg by briskly rubbing his hands together to produce some sort of Oriental equivalent of a Deep Heat bath.

Not that such nonsense matters a jot. *Karate Kid* works. It's a memorable, feel-good classic that oozes charm like those other 80s winners *Splash*, *Back to the Future* and *Crocodile Dundee*.

Still, I would have preferred Mr. Miyagi's unorthodox training regime to have been nothing more than an elaborate grooming exercise, resulting in a disillusioned, embittered Daniel joining his tormentors' gang through some gruesome initiation ceremony before putting Ali on the game. Movies rarely go the way I want, though.

Then again, perhaps I need to ditch the tedious cynicism and take greater note of Mr. Miyagi's enduring wisdom: A man who can catch a fly with chopsticks can accomplish anything.

Aaron Eckhart in *In the Company of Men* (1997)

Perhaps the key scene in Neil LaBute's caustic directorial debut is the one in which business exec Chad (Eckhart) gets a junior colleague to expose himself.

It's during this brief humiliation that we grasp *Company's* true interest: the increasingly unpleasant methods Chad will use to clamber over other men in the workplace.

A fair chunk of viewers, however, struggle to get past the movie's nasty premise (the deliberate emotional and psychological destruction of a vulnerable young woman) and therefore mark it down as a misogynist's twisted dream.

Company's far too smart to fall into such a trap. Chad simply uses misogyny as a *tool* to climb the corporate ladder and get what he wants: power and control over his defeated brethren. However, even before he hatches his memorably evil plan, it's clear he's obsessed with work's competitive nature. Listen to him talk about the younger guys: "Bunch of vultures waiting for me to tire out. I get low numbers two months in a row, they're gonna feed on my insides." He *hates* his male colleagues. They're all threats, obstacles and 'a special strain of fucker.' No wonder we get periodic bursts of tribal music. *Welcome to the jungle, we've got fun and games...*

And then there's his alma mater buddy Howard (Matt Malloy), who's just forged ahead in the pecking order. They've been sent out on a temporary job to a chaotic branch office with Howard hesitantly in charge. Although Chad expresses no resentment, it appears odd. After all, Chad's the confident, handsome, smooth-talking extrovert whereas Howard has got the glasses, slightly nerdy haircut and dull personality. How come he gets to give the orders, especially when he has difficulty standing up to his own mum? Perhaps Chad senses a glitch in the matrix...

Whatever the case, they do share one thing in common: a growing intolerance of the way women have treated them. Chad's misogyny is evident straightaway. He tells hateful jokes and imagines Howard's rebellious fiancée ending up on a pyre in the village square if they lived in India. Worse is to come. Chad wants to find a 'wallflower type' during their six-week assignment, 'some corn-fed bitch who'd practically mess her pants if you so much as sharpened a pencil for her' that they can both woo before simultaneously dumping.

"We will laugh about this," he tells Howard, "till we are very old men."

It's queasy stuff, all right, and can be difficult to watch, especially as Chad chooses Christine (Stacy Edwards), a self-conscious *deaf* typist who's got a voice like 'Flipper the dolphin'. From this point on, the male chauvinism flies thick and fast. "Women," Chad says. "Inside, they're all the same. Just meat and gristle and hatred."

But everything comes down to this arch-manipulator's overall game plan, best illustrated when he shuts his office blinds and asks an intern to drop his pants, a compliance that *might* persuade him to recommend the guy for a management trainee program.

"I just wanna make sure you've got what it takes," Chad says in a reasonable tone of voice. "Show. Me. Your. Balls." Still the stammering intern hesitates before Chad reveals business is all about who's 'sporting the nastiest sac of venom.' Once the intern submits, Chad knows he's got the better of him and visibly relaxes. "Get me a cup of coffee," he adds, just to underline his dominance.

It's not hard to see Chad's a human rattlesnake. It wouldn't be difficult to imagine him working for Aktion T4, the Nazis' program of forced euthanasia that happily said bye-bye to the less Chad-like members of society. And you could be sure he'd look damned good strolling around the office adorned with a pair of lightning bolts. As it is, he works in *marketing* which, as we all know, is even fucking worse.

Eckhart gives a memorable portrait of a chain-smoking corporate sociopath, boyish and charming one moment, bone-chillingly cruel the next. Sure, this baby Gekko is not helped by LaBute's static direction, the relentlessly mundane locations and the failure to disguise the movie's stage origins, but he still revels in the role. Few flicks deliver such piercing dialogue or so resolutely refuse to sell out its despicable main character. Or as Chad tells his decade-long, increasingly bewildered mate: "Never lose control. That's the key, Howard. That is the total key to the universe."

Gene Wilder in *The Producers* (1967)

Comedians often suck when they try their luck on the big screen.

They might be established stand-ups able to sell out 3,000-seater venues or a much-loved part of *Saturday Night Live*, but something invariably starts to stink during their feature-length stuff. To be fair, it's very difficult for any performer to make consistently funny flicks. There are anomalies, such as Woody Allen's 70s work, but most of the time we get a string of unfunny flops or mediocre time killers from the likes of Ricky Gervais, Dan Akroyd, Bill Murray, Russell Brand, Chris Farley, Adam Sandler, Tom Green et al before they retreat to a banal sitcom. For every *Arthur* there's a *Best Defense*, *Blame it on the Bellboy* and *Wholly Moses!* Eddie Murphy initially looked to be a wonderful exception before going on to typify the unfunny comedian adrift in a sea of cinematic dross. Paul Hogan, anyone? Even John Cleese only managed three outstanding comedies in half a century.

I don't know why so many comedians flounder. Perhaps it's a straightforward inability to get their hands on a top-notch script packed with quotable one-liners, but I suspect it also has something to do with being an *actor* first and foremost, someone who instinctively grasps the importance of timing. My sole reason for that (pretty weak) suggestion is Gene Wilder. His background wasn't comedy but that doesn't prevent him from getting my vote as the funniest guy in 70s cinema, especially his sheep-loving turn in *Everything You Always Wanted to Know About Sex*. His collapse into dudsville during the 80s (the awful *Haunted Honeymoon*, the strained *See No Evil*, the fitfully amusing *Woman in Red*) still makes me a bit sad, but nothing could besmirch the reputation he forged during Mel Brooks' holy trifecta of *The Producers*, *Blazing Saddles* and *Young Frankenstein*. Some people are pretty damn fond of *Willy Wonka*, too. In terms of significance, pop culture, sustained humour, quotability and legendary performances, these movies cannot be criticized.

Or rather they can, but if you take the trouble to look up the dictionary definition of *twat* it will inform you that's someone who doesn't rate Mel Brooks' holy trifecta of comedies.

Anyway, after a minor role in *Bonnie and Clyde*, Wilder got his big chance as a colluding accountant in *The Producers*. Filmed less than twenty-five years after the end of World War Two, it was arguably the first time anyone had taken the piss out of the genocidal Third Reich at length, an approach that brought strong condemnation from some quarters.

Fucking numpties.

With its dancing Hitlers, naughty stable boys, unreconstructed Nazis and dips into 'little old lady land', it remains a sublime viewing experience, as well as testament to the power of ridicule and a sly, affection-laced commentary on the pretensions and excesses of theatre. Wilder plays Leo Bloom, a nervous, over-sensitive man prone to hysterics. He's sent by his firm to audit the books of the rapidly fading, cardboard belt-wearing Broadway producer Max Bialystock (Zero Mostel) and quickly comes under the older man's corrupt influence.

"I'm a nothing," Leo realizes. "I spend my life counting other people's money, people I'm smarter than, *better* than. Where's my share?"

Together they cook up a scheme to rip off a multitude of investors by putting on a deliberately dreadful show called *Springtime for Hitler*. It's in such monumental bad taste that they can't envisage it doing anything other than folding after one tumultuous night, thus enabling them to keep all their backers' money.

Like the vast majority of Wilder's comic creations, Leo is sweet-natured, a characteristic typified by the way he's still carrying a comfort blanket. Even when things turn to shit and prison beckons, the best insult he can muster is to call his corrupter a 'fat fatty'. Throughout *Producers* he provides a perfect foil to Max's seedy, much coarser nature as shown by their contrasting approach to sex. Apart from wooing rich old dears all day long, Max is happy to use the investors' money to treat himself to a mindless, gyrating, sexpot secretary who barely speaks a word of English. Leo, however, can only stare open-mouthed at her, obviously helpless before her voluptuous femininity. It's not much different when he meets the play's flamboyantly gay director, Roger De Bris (Christopher Hewett). The timid Leo is mortified, prompting him to deliver one of the movie's best lines. "Max..." he says in a neutral voice while blankly staring into space, "he's wearing a dress." The poor guy. Leo even gets flustered when inadvertently putting a hand on the bare arse of a marble statue.

In his only Oscar-nominated acting turn, Wilder might be overshadowed by the grotesque Mostel but he still manages to deliver laugh out loud moments, as well as put in place all the comic mannerisms that I came to love over the years. Here we get the manic bursts of enthusiasm and panic; the drawn-out pauses in which half a dozen emotions cross his face; his eyes sliding to the side as if he can't believe what he's just heard; and a sober, professional demeanour that frequently disintegrates into childish tantrums.

The Producers might have spelled 'winter for Poland and France', but it was also springtime for one of cinema's greatest comedians.

Wilder was in bloom.

Mark Hamill & Harrison Ford in *Star Wars* (1977)

Star Wars remains the dog's bollocks, a bona fide pop culture phenomenon, and an astonishing exercise in world-building with its fucking cool lightsabres, eye-melting jumps through hyperspace, hokey Jedi mind tricks, planet annihilation, and lovable stormtroopers, none of whom are capable of hitting a cow's arse with a banjo. Only a retard can fail to enjoy such a glorious intergalactic spectacle or acknowledge its gargantuan impact on cinema.

It was also Hamill's film debut, which must surely rank among the most successful and iconic of all time. Ford, however, had already appeared in eight flicks, including quality stuff like *The Conversation*, but this was the first time a studio gave him a proper go. Fuck knows why. It's obvious he's a Proper Movie Star, underlined here when (among the good guys) the handsome bastard walks away with the pic.

You do feel a bit sorry for Hamill because even though he's just landed on his feet in one of the biggest franchises ever, he can't compete with Ford's overpowering charisma. Is that because he's bland? A bit insipid? Or would anyone come off that way next to a prime Ford and his scene-stealing charm? At any rate, *Star Wars* proved to be the launch pad for Ford, who over the next eight years turned in one artistic triumph after another whereas the fresh-faced, much shorter Hamill never escaped his Jedi identity.

Hamill plays Luke Skywalker, a dutiful, vaguely resentful farm boy with daddy issues who yearns to leave his home planet for a bit of action. He wears a judo outfit, repairs droids, plays with a toy plane and doesn't appear to possess a snowball's chance in hell of snaring any pussy. He's an all-round nice guy, loyal, respectful and sincere, but also pretty anaemic. When he bumps into Obi-Wan Kenobi (Alec Guinness) and is given the chance to save a princess, he turns into a whiney teenager. "I can't get involved," he bleats. "I've got work to do. It's not that I like the Empire, I hate it, but there's nothing I can do about it right now." Luckily, the two remaining members of his immediate family are turned into burnt skeletons by the bad guys, helping him ditch the weedy persona. He's not quite Bronson yet but at least this farm boy has just had a super-itchy bug shoved up his arse. "There's nothing here for me now," he tells Obi-Wan. "I wanna learn the ways of the Force and become a Jedi like my father."

As you can probably tell, he doesn't get any killer lines (perhaps one of the few weaknesses of Lucas' script), delivering the clunkiest one when he bursts into Leia's execution cell disguised as a stormtrooper: "I'm Luke Skywalker and I'm here to rescue you."

Luke does complete a fine character arc, though, initially pansying the place up by getting knocked out by one of the not-too-scary Sand People before letting an old man save his skin in a bar fight. However, it's not long before he becomes a doubting disciple of the Force, turns in a credible impersonation of Tarzan swinging on a vine, and kicks major butt as an all-action fighter pilot hero.

Ford, meanwhile, has a much cushier time as Han Solo, so relaxed that he doesn't even bother putting in an appearance for the first forty-five minutes. He's a cocksure, self-centred smuggler, flitting around the galaxy with a seven-foot tall 'walking carpet' who behaves like an aggressive, unshaven drag queen off her meds. Solo's main concern is not overthrowing the evil Empire, but evading the gangster Jabba the Hutt to whom he owes a shit load of money. About the only things he cares about are his own skin and his super-fast ship, the Millennium Falcon. He treats Luke like an annoying younger sibling, frequently calling him 'kid' while lecturing him that

"Travelling through hyperspace ain't like dustin' crops, boy." Obi-Wan fares little better, getting dismissed as an 'old fossil'. And the Force? "Hokey religions and ancient weapons are no match for a good blaster at your side. No mystical energy field controls *my* destiny."

In other words, Han is sneering, condescending, argumentative, money-obsessed and combative. Shit, what's not to like?

In fact, he bickers with whomever he meets, especially Leia (Carrie Fisher). Han's definitely an old school kind of guy when it comes to the ladies, wary of 'female advice' and happy to resort to frequent sarcasm ('your highness', 'your worship') to deal with the growing sexual tension. Disappointingly, he never makes fun of her ludicrous hairdo while it's probably the tiny whiff of her pussy that makes him risk life and limb on what should have been a suicide mission against the Death Star.

And another good guy bites the dust.

Still, Han and Luke do make a memorably squabbling team, providing a solid foundation for 1980's even better *Empire Strikes Back*.

Bring on those AT-ATs.

Joe Spinell in *Maniac* (1980)

Joe Spinell was a haemophiliac who bled to death in 1989 at the age of 52. Throughout his 17-year film career, he overwhelmingly played bit parts, but had an extraordinary knack for picking the right projects. We're talking the first two *Godfather* and *Rocky* movies, as well as *Taxi Driver*, *Sorcerer* and *Cruising*. Pretty good, huh? The reason he rarely got a starring chance was probably down to his lack of a leading man's looks: he was a heavyset, mean-looking bastard born to play loan sharks, enforcers, and bent cops.

However, once the post-*Halloween* slasher boom got underway, there was a market for the less photogenic type, resulting in Spinell finally taking front and centre in the controversial *Maniac*. Here he plays a mother-obsessed, scalp-harvesting serial killer roaming the Big Apple. Not the sort of role you could see Robert Redford going for, you know?

Maniac, cheaply put together by a former porno director, immediately ran into difficulty with its violent content, but has since become a cult favourite that was remade in 2012. It's essentially plotless, preferring to offer a portrait of a man whose traumatic, scar-inflicting childhood has pushed him over the edge into insanity.

Frank Zito (Spinell) doesn't have much of a life. No job, no friends, no hobbies, and a pudgy body that's fast slipping into heart attack country. At least he has a roof over his head, even if it's a shabby, one-bedroom apartment. Somehow, though, he's getting plenty of female attention.

Wait a minute, there's something up with those ladies draped around his place. They're not exactly the life and soul of the party. Oh, I see. They're *mannequins*, dummies with badly fitting, nailed on wigs and blood-streaked faces. Well, who needs bingo, TV or the pub when you can instead play dress up with the clothes and scalps of butchered hookers and talk to them all through the night?

Maniac is the antithesis of glamour, one of those late seventies/early eighties flicks determined to present a decaying, graffiti-daubed New York as the preferred hangout for the most fucked-up criminal scumbags on Earth. The whimpering, beanie-clad Frank is not some highly intelligent, publicity-loving outsider who gets off on baiting the cops. With his sweaty, doughy face, rambling impersonations of his mother, and compulsion to punch holes in flesh, he's little more than a sorry, woman-hating loser. "Fancy girls in their fancy dresses and their lipstick, laughing and dancing..." he moans and half-sighs to no one in particular before handcuffing himself to a bedded mannequin for the night. "But you stop them, don't you? I can't stop them, but you do, don't you? Then they can't laugh and they can't dance anymore." Murder doesn't even improve his mood, often reducing him to a state of victim-blaming, babbling incoherence. Frank, however, is comforted by possession. His 'ladies' can't leave, and warding off loneliness appears to be his one true driving force.

This is not a perfect movie. It's weakly written and has much implausibility, especially when Frank strikes up an instantaneous, respectful friendship with a gorgeous fashion photographer. It's meant to show a different side to the character, but takes the flick straight to la-la land. I also dislike his occasional displays of Herculean strength, lifting one garrotted victim off his feet, and the nonsensical shock ending.

However, I do enjoy him morphing into a camp hairdresser, mock-chiding a mannequin for the state of her hair as he enthusiastically brushes it. "It's just a little blood," he tells her. "It'll wash out."

Maniac has plenty of gruesome violence, especially its notorious shotgun decapitation in a car. There are also some suspenseful sequences (such as the stalking of a nurse) and an extremely seedy atmosphere, boosted by Spinell's full-blooded, whacked-out performance. Zito is a creepy, pathetic killer, carrying on like a chubby, sex-obsessed Apache who's become a wee bit confused after wearily wandering into the wrong century.

Lorraine Stanley in *London to Brighton* (2006)

"Nice, isn't it? To see a bit of colour."

So says Kelly (Stanley) as she looks at the green fields through a train window on the way from London to the seaside.

It's a banal observation and yet so telling. There is no colour in Kelly's life. No joy, no hope, no normality. Every day is an animalistic struggle for survival. For Kelly is a terrified hooker with a pasty, smashed-up face on the run from her less than saintly pimp.

And who is she talking to?

An eleven-year-old runaway that she was forced to procure for a rich nonce, an arrangement, shall we say, that could have gone better.

As you can tell, *London to Brighton* is no Merchant-Ivory film. It's a grimy, foul-mouthed wallow in the underbelly of British big city life. It features unprotected street sex, cowardly, manipulative pimps, a pock-faced gangster, an uncomfortable interrogation about the state of a child's hymen, a straight razor being put to surreptitious use, and a constant sense of desperation and menace.

Kelly is like a rusty pinball, careening between shit-stained bumpers and potholed ramps, any one of which may lead to her doom. It's easy to take the high ground and condemn her for initially sinking her streetwise hooks into the runaway Joanne (Georgia Groome), but a two-hundred quid finding fee buys a lot of fags. Plus, there's the fact she's got no choice. That's one of the things poverty does: it eliminates options.

London to Brighton is Paul Andrew Williams' stellar directorial debut, clocking in at less than eighty minutes. It gets the grubby details of every scene right and should be lapped up by *Mona Lisa* fans. Stanley is excellent throughout, fully embracing the character's shabbily-dressed, stringy-haired, chain-smoking mannerisms. She's rough as guts (her first words are a bellowed *fuck off* in a graffiti-daubed toilet), an authenticity that's never undermined by any trite speeches or bursts of working class wisdom. Crucially, however, she hasn't lost her humanity and it's her burgeoning relationship with an equally terrified surrogate daughter that offers the chance to show she's a bit more than a bottom feeder.

Just for a cheery change of pace, Stanley next appeared in the hoodie-horror, *Eden Lake*.

Commando (1985)

Director

Mark L. Lester

Synopsis

Meet Arnie. He eats Green Berets for breakfast.

Cast

Arnold Schwarzenegger, Rae Dawn Chong, Alyssa Milano, Vernon Wells

If you're the sort of guy who dresses his semi-automatic rifle in a see-through negligee just before beddy-byes and snuggles up tight while dreaming about his erect penis turning into the aforementioned weapon and walking butt-naked down the street spraying cock bullets at all those other puny men, then *Commando* is the one for you.

This flick is so tough it will slap your face and make you clean the latrines with a toothbrush if you don't salute it every fifteen minutes. It cannot be criticized in any way, shape or form, and anyone who suggests a better title would be *Penile Gun Armageddon* had better dive for the nearest foxhole pronto.

Just like it's impossible to say how many grains of sand are on the average beach, it's impossible to keep count of how many men Arnie kills during this awesome 85-minute bout of murderous mayhem. He's a retired Special Forces colonel living in a secluded mountain retreat with his young daughter. He's got a name and you can be damned sure it's not anything lightweight or vaguely silly like Arthur Looney-Warde. Still, I forget what it is because I'm too busy salivating at the sight of him emerging from the forest carrying a fucking *tree* on one shoulder. My god, this is a man. The movie's only four minutes old and I'm already on my knees in a state of worship. I'll try again with his name. It might be Super Army Soldier. No, that's not good enough. In this testosterone-fuelled universe it would be an insult to call him anything other than *Death*.

Anyhow, a bunch of aggressive fuckwits are in town, one of whom is a deposed South American dictator. He wants Death to eliminate his successor because, as we all know, his countrymen are incapable of violence. All day long they do little but sew, bake yummy pastries and braid each other's hair. There's no way of finding even one killer for hire in that 400-million-strong bunch of pansies. No, when you need an irritating, job-stealing bloke killed, it's best to fly to the next continent to coerce Death into doing the job by abducting his nearest and dearest. And you know Death loves his child because he acts so out of character around her, doing weird shit like smiling, hugging and not breaking her arms for shoving an ice-cream in his face. He even allows her to feed a friendly deer when (if alone) he surely would've pulled apart with his bare hands and eaten raw.

Some army bloke arrives who's not Colonel Samuel Trautman. No matter. He warns Death that things are looking screwy and leaves behind two of his best men as security. This is stupid. Why does he think Death needs protecting? After all, this is a man who's so tough he can not only hear an approaching chopper before it's even fired up its blades but *smell* a hidden would-be assassin at a distance of two hundred yards. And apart from that, he's confident enough to make jokes about Boy George's perceived lack of masculinity. Sure enough, the two 'protectors' prove to have ridiculously small cojones and immediately get killed by the ex-dictator's non-baking contingent. The daughter is whisked away and Death (after leaping from a departing aircraft) has eleven hours to save her life.

Hang on, some frizzy-haired black chick at the airport is getting involved. What the hell? We don't need ladies in this red-blooded world of gun-toting alpha males. All she's doing is screaming and putting her hands over her face. Not once does she punch anyone, let alone dangle a dwarf one-handed over a cliff. Hindrance personified. For Christ's sake, she's so inept she doesn't even know how to use a rocket launcher. She makes the rockets go *backward*. C'mon, Death, just give this Silly Girly a slap and move on. Her role, as far as I can see, is to show men are vastly superior while providing a running commentary on the constant display of virility. Hence, in between painting her nails and whining about wanting a baby, she says stuff like "These guys eat too much red meat", "Did anyone ever tell you that you have a lot of hostility?" and, worst of all, "I can't believe this macho bullshit."

Heresy! Burn her! Burn the witch!

After a lot of car chases, phone booth destruction and security guard disrespect, they eventually get to the island where Death's daughter is being held hostage. Stupidly, the redundant South American dictator has only protected himself with two hundred heavily armed paramilitaries. Oh, he's also hooked up with a slightly tubby Aussie guy that I'm certain appeared gyrating in some of Madonna's early videos. However, despite his soft, boyish skin, meticulously groomed tash, chunky necklace, chainmesh vest, fingerless gloves and leather pants, I don't think he's going to be man enough to stop Death.

Talk about gnats whining around the master's ankles.

Meanwhile, Death's disguising himself with camouflage paint. Initially, I can't get a handle on this as he's not engaging in jungle warfare but launching a full-frontal assault on a handful of buildings in broad daylight. But, of course, I've made a dumb mistake. It's not a case of camouflage or trying to look tough. Those temporary, superficial stripes are actually *bullet deflectors*. That's the only way to explain how a man can get cornered in a shed and survive having three-hundred bullets pumped into it. At this point Death doesn't even have a gun. Not that he needs one. He's got a garden fork which (when given the correct military training) will always outperform an automatic weapon.

As for Death's daughter, are you surprised she's rescued unharmed? Sure, there's a threat of throat-slitting at a couple of points, but frankly I suspect such a fate would've been kinder than the one she's destined to meet. For no one, *no mortal man*, can live up to the impossible standards of heroic manliness set by that demigod she calls daddy. She'll try, of course, she'll go through the motions with the dating thing, but every man will fail with their paltry thirteen-inch biceps and disinterest in slaughter, leaving her to become a broken-down, alcoholic man-hater.

Right, enough talk.

I'm off to join the army. I don't care I'm in my fifties, chronically unfit, have a long criminal record for sexual deviance, and weigh less than Arnie's right leg. So fucking what? I've seen *Commando* more than ten times. What's more, I know I won't even have to pass on such pertinent information to the recruiting officer. I'll just hold up the DVD, puff out my chest and give him *that* look, the look that gun-loving, battle-hardened beefcakes across the globe all recognise.

And then, finally, I'll be able to launch my own penile gun Armageddon.

A Handful of 80s British Faves

"Don't threaten me with a dead fish!"

Full marks if you recognize an indignant Withnail trying to be tough with a gruff poacher in a pub. As far as British movies go, *Withnail and I* gets my vote as the decade's best along with the bewildered Harold Shand in *The Long Good Friday*. Nothing else comes close to those two gems when Maggie ruled the roost, although there are plenty of other goodies to enjoy. Here are five I can happily re-watch.

Gregory's Girl (1980)

There are times on your cinematic journey when you no longer have a yen for watching an eyeball being skewered by a long wooden splinter.

You get tired of terrorists running amok. Gangsters have become passé. The decapitations, explosions, alien invasions and the prospect of seeing Jennifer Jason Leigh's tits yet again no longer float your boat.

Instead you want your night's entertainment to be a little... different. Maybe something less full on. You know, *gentler*.

You can do it, right?

Well, let me suggest *Gregory's Girl*.

Now I love a high corpse count as much as the next guy so it's always one hell of a surprise that I enjoy this malevolence-free picture of high school life as much as I do. There are no bullies loitering in the corridors, no arguments with siblings, no teacher clashes, and zero bitchiness. Yes, we get a bit of perving on an undressing woman ("That's a brassiere. She's got a brassiere!") but it sure as fuck ain't *Porky's*. It's devoid of conflict so I have no idea how this movie works.

But work it does.

Gregory (a marvellous John Gordon Sinclair) is a gangly, gormless idiot. He's not only awkward, self-conscious and possibly a little touched in the head, but unable to locate a single muscle on his beanpole frame. He's the sort of teenager who spends his time dancing horizontally or doing nocturnal cat impressions. If a waitress happens to ask if he wants black or white coffee, he'll frown and reply *brown*.

He's also the malfunctioning striker in his school soccer team, having not scored in eight consecutive defeats. "It's a tricky time for me," he tells his despondent, long-suffering coach before offering the excuse that he's 'growing'.

But the coach wants fresh blood, his subsequent trial for new players unexpectedly attracting a *girl* (Dee Hepburn). The thing is, Dorothy's not only much more skilful than the other boys but knows how to score a goal, a skill that quickly sees her replace Gregory in the team.

Gregory's best mate is unimpressed ("If women were meant to play football, they'd have their tits somewhere else") but Gregory doesn't care. He's smitten, even if he does have to jealousy watch the cool and confident Dorothy getting kissed whenever she scores. "That's disgusting," he objects. "Perverse. On a football field. With kids watching. That's the sort of thing that gives football a bad name."

There's a fair bit of role-reversal in this beguiling Scottish pic, such as one boy being an ace pastry cook while Gregory has to take advice about fashion, the opposite sex and even bathing from his ten-year-old sister. It's all intensely sweet-natured and full of quirky, offbeat moments but never cloying. The youngsters are often given intentionally grownup attitudes and dialogue, my favourite example being a reporter from the school magazine keen to do an article on the fifteen-year-old Dorothy. "I want to interview you and that girl in 2A who had the triplets," he tells her in the dressing room. "You're an interesting girl, but I want to find the real Dorothy, the one underneath the football strip. Dorothy... the *woman*."

Eye of the Needle (1981)

Donald Sutherland had a lot of luck with World War Two. *The Dirty Dozen*, *Kelly's Heroes* and *The Eagle Has Landed* are bona fide classics and he managed to make it four in a row with this terrific spy thriller. Unlike the others, though, this one's no jolly adventure that might lead to a gold-stuffed bank or, better still, a romp on the beach with a nubile Jenny Agutter.

Oh, no. This one's *mean*.

And that's all down to Sutherland's character, Henry Faber, a Nazi spy operating in England who gets wind of the Allies' invasion plans to land in Normandy. Codenamed The Needle, he's an experienced killer, a man who will stick his switchblade in you whether you're male or female, young or old, a stranger or friend, in uniform or not, able-bodied or in a wheelchair, on your own or in a crowded place. He'll chuck you off a cliff and then bang your wife five minutes later. He's the personification of steely, blue-eyed nastiness.

We don't get too many clues why he's turned into such a badass, though. He was rebellious at his military academy and flogged, met Hitler before he came to power, and appears resentful toward his pushy, well-connected parents. At one point he pretends to be a writer while worming his way into the affections of a deeply lonely woman (an appealing Kate Nelligan). When she asks what he writes about, he replies: "The war. Not battles and killing, but isolation, the feeling some men have of suddenly being separated from other men."

Well, Faber's a loner, and that's probably why he's so good at his job. He's an intelligent and highly capable blend of spy, serial killer, Nazi, expert liar and chameleon.

Needle is a movie that flies under the radar of great WW2 flicks. It has excellent production values that manage to conjure up a convincing depiction of wartime Britain. It's old-fashioned with its dash of romance and bursts of swirling orchestral music, but thoroughly modern in its lack of sentimentality and the cold way Faber dispatches his numerous victims.

Welsh director Richard Marquand does an excellent job, his evident talents helping secure the reins of the slightly better known *Return of the Jedi* two years later. In that movie Darth Vader is the biggest baddie in the galaxy but ends up losing his nerve.

Faber never does.

Educating Rita (1983)

I can remember a question on my English Literature exam at university in which I was supposed to write an essay on the black page in Sterne's *Tristram Shandy*. If you're not familiar with that particular 18th Century 'comic' novel, the black page is just that: a black page. You know, an oblong splash of ink.

Sigh.

My discontent with academia had been building for a while, but I guess it was only then I truly grasped the need to get the hell away from such pretentious absurdity and do something proper. I mean, I had mates who were sparks and mechanics and there I was at the age of twenty-one having to spend forty-five minutes or so gushing about a *colour*.

As Steve Coogan's student-hating alter ego Paul Calf might observe: "Bag o' shite!"

Anyhow, *Educating Rita* does little to make me rethink my rather low opinion of academia. Arts students and their educators still seem like they're divorced from reality and living in a pseudo-important bubble.

English Lit ones for sure.

In *Educating Rita* Julie Walters plays the titular character, a chirpy, working class hairdresser in her mid-20s who's desperate to avoid a destiny of nappy changing supplemented by weekend pub sing-a-longs with her family. She signs up for the Open University, a degree course that involves studying through TV programs and a weekly tutorial at a real university. It's here she nervously meets Dr. Frank Bryant (Michael Caine) on her journey to becoming an insufferable, up-her-own-arse monster.

Frank has long worked out academia is a bag o'shite. That's why he can't be bothered to wear a tie, trim his hair and beard, or even stay sober. Soon we see him in class slouched in a chair staring out the window. Asked by one of those irritating student dweebs if he's drunk, he replies: "Of course I'm drunk! You don't really expect me to teach this when I'm sober?" To him William Blake is nothing more than a 'dead poet'.

Not long afterwards he tries giving Rita the brush-off in his private room, but she insists he tutors her because he's a 'crazy mad piss artist.' Now Rita might be appallingly dressed in just about every scene, but at least she's initially likable. She gives Frank the occasional Nazi salute, writes one-sentence essays, and calls Macbeth's wife a 'cow'.

It can't last, though. Before long she's bristling when Frank calls her funny, charming and delightful.

"I don't wanna be funny," she says. "I wanna talk serious with the rest of ya." You see what earnestly studying boring old literature can do? Her husband of five years is also suffering, bewildered by her tedious transformation. Eventually, he's forced to throw her books on the fire, an understandable move that's still not enough to stop the rot. Rita's down to earth persona has been replaced by affectation. She's swapped hairdressing for working in a poncy *bistro* and has the constant need to 'talk about things that matter.' What's more, she's surrounded herself with fawning, lightweight student friends, the sort of people that need machine-gunning en masse.

Like her husband, Frank is appalled at the monster he's helped create. "I've done a fine job on you, haven't I?" he says, his voice breaking. "Why don't you just go away? I don't think I can bear it any longer."

Hear, hear.

As you can probably tell, I'm on Frank's side. You're better off listening to his jaded wisdom ("All I know is that I know absolutely nothing") otherwise you run the risk of spending year after year pointlessly studying American poets, *Peer Gynt* and Chekhov before turning into someone as intolerable as Rita.

Still, my intense dislike of Julie Walters' character doesn't stop me from loving *Educating Rita*, especially Caine's drunken dancing and all-round performance. Usually, I don't care much for movies based on plays as they're too talky, have limited action and small casts. Something like the lauded *Who's Afraid of Virginia Woolf?* strikes me as little more than four angry drunks shouting at each other for two hours-plus. It looks like a filmed play, you know? *Educating Rita's* an exception, a terrifically likable flick that manages to disguise its stage origins.

I think I'll pop up to the attic now, fish out that long-neglected copy of *Tristram Shandy*, and burn it.

Mona Lisa (1986)

Like any director who's been around a long time, Neil Jordan's had a hit and miss career. He's done big-budget boring misfires (*Interview with the Vampire*) and pretentious drivel (*The Brave One*) but also good stuff like *The Crying Game* and *The Butcher Boy*. However, *Mona Lisa* is the one that makes me want to shake his hand. It's a pearl, the sort of movie that unfurls so confidently during its opening minutes you *know* you're in for a treat.

George (Bob Hoskins) is a gangster who's just been released after a lengthy stretch. We meet him wandering around London enjoying his newfound freedom while dreamily accompanied by Nat King Cole's *Mona Lisa*.

Well, this is going to be a nice little tale, yes?

However, George soon finds himself adrift on a scum-tinged tide of filth in a man's world where females are relentlessly exploited, abused and attacked. After looking up his old boss Denny Mortwell (Michael Caine), he lands a job driving a 'tall thin black tart' called Simone (Cathy Tyson) around the West End's poshest hotels to service wealthy clients. At one place a suspicious manager latches onto what she's up to. "Pretend you know me," she urges George while grabbing his arm in the lobby and trying to shake the manager off.

"I don't fucking know ya, do I?" he replies.

It's an ominous bit of dialogue that taps into the deceptive relationships and illusory appearances on display throughout. *Mona Lisa* likes to blend reality with art as shown through the movie's title, the appearance of a white rabbit, a mention of *The Frog Prince*, and the way George happily discusses detective stories with his friend Thomas (Robbie Coltrane). Don't go thinking there's anything poncy or artsy-fartsy about this flick, though. Even our goodhearted, curiously naïve, tea-drinking hero George is racist, violent and not averse to having sex with a bruised, underage hooker.

And then there's Mortwell, the parasitical blackmailing boss whom George took a seven-year fall for. Now Caine's no stranger to playing mean bastards as he showed in the classic *Get Carter*, but he's exceptionally unpleasant here and gives the immediate impression of having been marinated in sleaze. "Don't be sorry," he tells George. "It's bad to be sorry."

Mortwell's far more sophisticated than George and moves in upper class circles with ease, but even in a tux he looks suspicious. This is an ugly, ugly character that radiates disdain, contempt and menace. Before long he's pestering George to gather dirt on one of Simone's wealthy clients but after he's brought an innocuous photo he explodes into rage.

"Get something better!" he cries, prompting George to ask *what*. "I mean, dirty, slimy, nasty, *kinky*!" Honestly, the way the snarling Mortwell jumps to his feet and forces George back with the intensity of his outburst provides one of my all-time favourite Michael Caine moments. Now Hoskins is consistently great in this movie (giving a performance that almost matches his IRA-misjudging turn in *Long Good Friday*) but Caine threatens to steal every scene out from under him.

Tyson also deserves praise as the sad, feisty but never self-pitying high-class hooker. "Everyone should have someone to rush home to," she tells George in between bouts of Mace-spraying and telling blokes to fuck off. "I'm different... I'm the girl they rush home from."

Despite its grim subject matter and carefully orchestrated bursts of knife and gun violence, *Mona Lisa* doesn't make the mistake of being unrelentingly dark and depressing. It's far too smart, nuanced and well-rounded for that. George's burgeoning relationship with his estranged daughter, as well as the wonderful humour generated by his nourishing friendship with Thomas, provide the perfect counterpoint to the sleaze.

Rita, Sue and Bob, Too (1987)

Is it possible to bite off more pussy than you can chew?

Well, our married hero Bob (George Costigan) does his best to find out when he starts shagging two sixteen-year-old schoolgirls in his car.

"Jesus," Rita (Siobhan Finneran) says upon getting a glimpse of his condom-encased penis, "it looks like a frozen sausage."

As you can probably tell, this bawdy, foul-mouthed comedy is full of dirty chuckles, knickers being whipped off and demands for a 'jump.' There's finger inserting but thankfully no finger wagging. Lively performances abound and it's got a lovely, ultimately life-affirming flavour, marking it out as a welcome alternative to all those dour depictions of British working class misery in borefests like *Ratcatcher* (1999) and *Red Road* (2006).

Bob's a middle-class businessman who's getting on a bit but still fancies himself as a Jack the Lad. He's married to the uptight Michelle (Lesley Sharpe) who only wants sex once a week after popping out two kids. "The trouble with you, Bob," she tells him, "is you're sex mad."

Now this might be true but the randy bastard doesn't exactly show his diplomatic side by retorting: "When we have sex it's like shagging a bag of spuds."

Luckily the babysitters are to hand and they barely need seducing. All it takes is a night-time trip to the moors and he's banging one after the other, his frozen sausage never showing the slightest sign of thawing. All three are up for the raunchy, guilt-free arrangement to continue with Bob occasionally trying to lure them away from school for a bit of lunchtime nookie. Of course these days he'd be labelled a predatory pedo and hauled off to clink, even though the girls are of age and 100 per cent willing.

It's true both Rita and Sue (Michelle Holmes) look too old to play teenagers, but otherwise they convincingly portray a pair of good-hearted slappers with their mullet hairdos, plastic jewellery, fondness for pastel colours and awkward dancing to Bananarama. Neither has much going on upstairs, nor any interest in trying to develop it through education, but they are determined to have a good time. Indeed, Bob is the highlight of their week. Well, that's not much of a surprise given they live on a crappy council estate that's dotted with boarded-up ground floor windows, fighting dogs, and a kooky, balcony-inhabiting neighbour shouting whacked-out stuff.

There's a lot to like here with gritty issues such as class, race, miscarriage, adultery, alcoholism, domestic abuse and sexual jealousy all touched upon. However, director Alan Clarke (*Scum*) maintains a good-natured overall stance, typified by the decision to make Sue's permanently sozzled dad a harmless, brilliantly funny idiot while also including an apt appearance by the legendarily bad, novelty pop band Black Lace singing *Gang Bang*.

Controversial in its day for its candid depiction of teenage female sexuality and a non-judgmental attitude toward a middle-aged philanderer, its critics tend to ignore the fact it was written by a woman based on her own experiences and filmed on the same council estate she grew up on. However, *Rita, Sue and Bob Too* is a good example of The Kind of Movie That Wouldn't Get Made Today. If it were put out in the 21st Century, it would have to focus on 'abuse of power', 'economic exploitation' and 'victimization'. It certainly couldn't straightforwardly depict a pair of cock-happy bubbleheads looking forward to having Bob's bobbing butt between their legs. I mean, what sort of message is that to send?

Aah, modern movies. Don't get me started.

Anyhow, *Rita, Sue, and Bob Too* might have the slimmest of stories, but it's still a satisfying slice of earthy working class life.

Superb final freeze frame, too.

Dishonourable Mentions

Chariots of Dire (1981), *The Boys in Poo* (1982), *Pink Void: The Pall* (1982), *Howling II: Your Sister is in a Bad Movie* (1985)

Fucked-Up Films #2: Romper Stomper (1992)

Synopsis

Heil Crowe!

Director

Geoffrey Wright

Cast

Russell Crowe, Daniel Pollock, Jacqueline McKenzie, Alex Scott

What are these sick bastards doing? Worshipping the Third Reich, threatening to chop off people's legs with an axe, mourning a decapitated mother, and terrorising the Vietnamese in a Melbournian suburb.

Is the villain any good? The heavily tattooed, permanently unshaven Hando (Crowe) is a neo-Nazi so committed to white supremacy that he attacks a Jap-made car and refuses to eat pasta because it's 'bloody wog crap.' Never seen without his skinhead clobber, he probably sleeps in his Doc Martens. As expected, his bedroom is adorned with far right memorabilia. Terrified of becoming a 'white coolie' in his own country, he objects to 'boatloads of human trash' arriving on his Footscray doorstep. "I want people to know I'm proud of my white history and white blood," he says. "One day that might be all I have. I don't wanna go the same way as the fucking Abo."

Hando is not all talk, though. He will beat up stray Vietnamese, especially if his gang outnumbers them. Oh, he might kill the odd Asian shop attendant, too.

He continually looks down on others, apparently oblivious to the fact he's standing on nothing. The man's a violent, parasitical Dole-bludger, attacking workers who are actually contributing to Australia and trying to build a life. It's fair to say self-awareness is not Hando's strongpoint. There's also a lingering suspicion he's gay, given the homoerotic charge underpinning his dealings with his right-hand man and second-in-command, Davey (Pollock). I probably wouldn't mention this to him, though.

People often confuse a villain's charisma with the glorification of whatever shit they're into. *Romper Stomper* certainly copped such flak back in the early nineties. *Nope*. Hando's undeniably magnetic here, but nothing can disguise he's a loser of the first order. There's a straight line between his beliefs, actions and demise.

Hollywood beckoned for Crowe on the basis of this tremendous performance.

How do the lovely ladies fare? As expected, neo-Nazi skinhead society is not an egalitarian paradise. The gang's terribly-dressed two girlfriends are more hangers-on than anything else, constantly ordered around and treated with contempt. They are fucked and verbally abused at whim. On a good day they merely cook, cry over their fallen men, and get slapped. For the most part they don't seem to grasp they're neck-deep in a misogynistic world, only opting to flee when Hando vows firearm-backed violence after being driven out of his HQ by some seriously pissed-off immigrants.

Still, this pair of Aryan ladies fares better than others. Vietnamese women simply get punched in the face without hesitation.

Things get more complicated with the arrival of the seriously messed-up, epileptic rich girl, Gabrielle (McKenzie). She's a hippy-like free spirit who spouts bollocks about reincarnation, but can still be vengeful, turned on by aggro and more than capable of putting the boot in. She doesn't get an easy ride, though. There's one excellent scene where Hando's reading aloud a treasured excerpt from *Mein Kampf* and she's got this dreamy, childlike look, as if being seduced by Hitler's poison. Gabrielle's power slowly grows, eventually becoming pivotal.

How skuzzy are the men? I think this is another case of toxic masculinity. Hando's gang is a snarling bunch of super-aggressive, overgrown adolescents heavily into binge drinking, partying, crime, property destruction, misogyny and pranks. They can't even dance nicely. When a neo-Nazi Canberra contingent comes to visit, it's to sell Hitler Youth memorabilia rather than discuss the opera or ballet.

There's a telling moment when a former skinhead returns to the gang's HQ after joining the navy. Hando ridicules the sight of his non-shaven head and asks: "You enjoy being cannon fodder for the system?" The ex-skinhead can only shrug. "It's a job," he replies before half-heartedly mirroring a Hitler salute. Here we can see he's rejected the dead-end existence of neo-Nazi life and is starting to grow up. After all, you can only be a racist, aggro-fuelled tool for so long. Sooner or later you've gotta get on with the mundane (but ultimately more constructive) stuff like becoming a working stiff. Otherwise you end up dead or in prison.

Outside of the gang, things don't improve much as Gabrielle's father is an incestuous predator. Perhaps the only decent bloke in the whole shebang is a pub landlord who chucks out underage kids and is happy to serve 'gooks'.

Would the violence make a vicar faint? *Romper Stomper* has long had a reputation for nastiness, but it's probably undeserved. Despite a large amount of fights, there's no real graphic stuff. However, street violence is introduced in the opening scene, helping ensure the threat of imminent head-splitting hangs over the pic's entirety. We get a lengthy pitched battle, the realism of which is amped up by the tremendous use of a handheld camera. There's simmering hatred on all sides that's certainly not dissipated when the cops turn up. Racist punk songs litter the soundtrack with lyrics like: 'Smack him if he's yellow/Smack him if he's black/Smack him till he fucks off and doesn't come back'. The whole vibe of the movie is caught early on when a member of Hando's gang gives the camera the finger and bellows 'fuck off!' straight at the viewer.

Vicars probably don't like that sort of thing.

How fucked-up is this film? With its energy, verve, convincing sense of place and unpredictable turns, *Romper Stomper* is among the best Aussie movies. It's an uncompromising, well written and smartly directed ninety-five minutes that avoids finger-wagging and easy moralizing. The three central performances are dynamite, although it's especially sad to know the depressed, 23-year-old Pollock committed suicide before getting to see the completed film. With lines like "We came to wreck everything and ruin your life. God sent us" it's the best skinhead flick I've seen. It's far, far better than *American History X*.

The Natives are Getting Restless

Man has long excelled at picking on animals and fucking up the environment, a dismal trait I'm fine with as long as it generates good eco-horror movies. This sub-genre is staggeringly rich and diverse, tackling everything from sentient frogs and mutant sea creatures to walking plants and extraterrestrial viruses that powderise your blood. It has undoubtedly produced classics, such as *King Kong* and *Jaws*, while also providing the foundation for many other quality flicks, like Summer Isle's pagan inhabitants deciding the best way to counteract a catastrophic crop failure is to enjoy a virgin pig barbie.

Of course, part of eco-horror's charm is that it's also responsible for some of the all-time daftest films in which the most innocuous entities are turned into man-eaters. And by that I mean the escapades of carnivorous tomatoes, giant bunnies, and oversized slugs and worms. These days the trend is to not only embrace such absurdity but to up the ante to fantastic extremes. Don't be surprised to stumble across enormous, lava-breathing tarantulas (*Lavalantula*) or shark-spewing tornadoes (*Sharknado*). Whatever the case, eco-horror has fascinated filmmakers pretty much from day one and remains an astonishingly popular way to explore climate change, pollution and disease.

Island of Lost Souls (1932)

I'm no film historian and have little idea if eco-horror originated in 1932 but that seems like an impressively early enough point to begin. Don't be put off by *Souls* being the best part of a century old for this pre-Code cult flick has plenty of bite and a great central performance.

Charles Laughton plays Dr. Moreau, a man so bonkers he wears a three-piece white suit and tie all day long in the *tropics*. Having begun his career by speeding up plant evolution, like any mad scientist worth his salt he's gone on to develop that worrying tic called ambition.

Grandiose ambition.

Or as he tells a shipwreck survivor on his lush, volcanically enriched South Seas island: "Why not experiment with the more complex organisms?" Soon he's fanatically dedicated to transforming animals into people via blood transfusions, plastic surgery and a whole gamut of agonizing procedures.

Pretty sick, huh? With his terror-inspiring House of Pain and indifference to suffering, this guy is a Mengele forerunner. I love the way there's no conceivable point for turning animals into people (other than to see if it can be done) just like it was senseless for the Nazi doctor to sew children together or inject chemicals into their eyes.

Not that Moreau sees it that way. He's actually pretty chuffed with his pioneering scientific genius, the latest example being Lota, the Panther Woman. She's his pride and joy, as well as the only woman on the island. Now I'm against this kind of appalling animal experimentation, but I have to admit I am intrigued by the sexual possibilities of turning a panther into a slinky, feline she-creature with limited intelligence and speech. Just imagine: after you've done the bizzo you could tether her to a post outside your home and have a pretty nifty guard. Hmm, did I go too far there?

Anyway, this is an eerie, seventy-minute movie built on sadism. Vivisection, madness, death and screams of pain abound. With his neatly trimmed facial hair, clipped tones, obvious intellect and penchant for cracking a bullwhip, Moreau is a fantastic character. He's the supreme puppet master, drunk on power and control, although he does take time off to sip tea. Watch out for his classic line as he stands in the half-shadows, an observation that helped the hugely controversial *Lost Souls* cop a decades-long ban in some countries: "Do you know what it means to feel like God?"

The Beast from 20,000 Fathoms (1953)

In the early years of the atomic age, it was little surprise that filmmakers couldn't get enough of cautionary tales about the bomb.

"Every time one of these things goes off I feel as if we're helping to write the first chapter of a new *Genesis*," a scientist says moments before detonating an explosion in the Arctic Circle.

"Let's hope we don't find ourselves writing the last chapter of the old one," another egghead replies.

This time round such an Earth-quaking event unleashes a newly thawed Rhedosaurus that's been blissfully dozing in the ice for one hundred million years. Yes, I know that's beyond the wildest dreams of the most dementedly optimistic cryonicist, but it'll have to do as the premise for this stodgy outing. However, the cop-eating, rollercoaster-wrecking amphibious beastie is early testament to Ray Harryhausen's astonishing talent, especially when it rises out of the ocean, clambers onto a rocky outcrop and wrecks a lighthouse.

Beast's main claim to fame, though, is being the first bomb-annoyed giant monster flick, a frontrunner directly responsible for inspiring 1954's iconic *Godzilla*. A year after that Harryhausen was busy pissing around with a giant radioactive octopus in *It Came from Beneath the Sea*.

Them! (1954)

"Ants are the only creatures on Earth, other than man, who wage war," an expert tells a top-secret taskforce that's been set up to battle some bothersome giant ants. "They campaign, they are chronic aggressors and they make slave labourers of the captives they don't kill." Fair enough, but that doesn't mean a good flick can be made about them.

Them! was the first big bug creature feature, but it's a pompous, meandering dud full of ham-fisted dialogue. Typical of its failings is a machine gun-wielding cop who blows fifty holes in the first monstrous ant to turn up, only to lower his smoking weapon and ask: "What is it?" Huh? Presumably he can identify a normal-sized ant, so why's he struggling when the fucker's right in front of him and eight feet long?

Anyhow, radiation's the culprit again, but whereas the Rhedosaurus holds up thanks to Harryhausen's magic, the stiff, mechanical ant models are devoid of dexterity and speed. It's telling that the best part of *Them!* is the mildly suspenseful opening half-hour in which the sugar-stealing darlings *don't* appear. As soon as one shows up everything goes to shit.

Twenty years later another attempt was made to make ants frightening with *Phase IV*. They remain the same size in this one, but super-clever. Are you scared? No, me neither. A burst of solar activity or something has changed their behaviour so that all the different species unite and decide to attack. Two po-faced scientists set up a hi-tech dome in the middle of the Arizonian desert to investigate, but soon those brainy insects are scaring horses, blowing up generators, causing cars to crash and short-circuiting computers. *Phase IV* features some nicely composed shots while its sense of isolation gives it a similar feel to that outback classic *Walkabout*, but it stretches absurdly all the way. Some of the ants' acting is very good, though.

Then came 1977's *Empire of the Ants* in which a bunch of superimposed ants snack on leaking barrels of toxic waste, surround pre-*Dynasty* rich bitch Joan Collins and attempt to come up with a solution for typecasting.

Conclusion? Just like violent vegetation movies are rubbish (1962's *Day of the Triffids*, *The Vines*, *The Happening*), don't go making ant stuff, either.

The Birds (1963)

The Birds is regarded as classic Hitchcock, although I feel without a Shadow of a Doubt that it's nowhere near his best. The titular creatures inexplicably start attacking the inhabitants of a small Californian seaside town, perhaps driven mad by a diet of discarded burgers and having to witness Tippi Hedren's acting. Nothing convinces here. There's a ridiculously contrived pet shop opening, terrible special effects, a po-faced ornithologist spouting off in a diner, and the characters doing nonsensical stuff like leaving their indoors haven to wander outside. Most of all, apart from one great bird's eye view of a fire-engulfed petrol station, it's boring right through to its non-ending.

Vicious sparrows...? Oh, fuck off, Alfred.

Planet of the Apes (1968)

There seems to be a fair chunk of people that insist the book is always better than the movie. As a level-headed chap, whose bouts of homicidal egomania are definitely on the wane, I take things on a case by case basis. However,

I will say Pierre Boulle's *Monkey Planet* is inferior to Franklin J. Schaffner's remarkable flick. *Monkey Planet* is a short, unsatisfactory read with cutesy bookending, but please don't think I'm having a go at Mr. Boulle. I'll always be grateful to the guy for coming up with such a brilliant premise. If he hadn't put pen to paper, we would never have got the newly crash-landed Charlton Heston musing two thousand years from now: "I can't help thinking that somewhere in the universe there has to be something better than man."

So why is the iconic movie a hundred times better? Four reasons: racism, vividness, nastiness and its extraordinary ending. At their core both works are about racism, but *Apes* produces one of the greatest-ever leaps of imagination. There's simply no better movie out there dealing with prejudice in such an ingenious and memorable way (and that includes *Blazing Saddles*).

Apes is able to explore racism so well because it adds layer after layer to its satirical source material, thereby creating a much more convincing simian society. Every aspect is superbly thought through. Chuck in the excellent sets and costumes, as well as the groundbreaking makeup, and you get a wonderfully realized upside-down world.

Thirdly, the book lacks brutality. This has always surprised me in that Boulle suffered two years of bloody grim, life-threatening custody during WW2. His personal experience of degradation is only touched upon in his novel whereas *Apes* is seriously brutal. The savagery begins as soon as the rifle-wielding apes arrive on horseback, beating the cornfield's tall plants in a bid to round up as many of their human prey as possible. From here on it's all halters, bullwhips, clubs, grinning hunters posing next to piles of corpses, jails, strung-up captives, lobotomies, experimental surgery, racism and talk of extermination.

Christ, it's so *human*.

Schaffner directs with real flair, occasionally finding disorientating camera angles to reflect Heston's acute bewilderment. Dwarfed by the forbidding landscape, the passage of time and his gradual understanding of the mindboggling events, he gives his most famous performance. Then there's his classic dialogue, such as "It's a madhouse! A madhouse!" and "You cut up his brain, you bloody baboon!" and most famously of all: "Get your stinking paws off me, you damned, dirty ape!" (a line I like to spit out whenever I'm arrested).

Co-written by *Twilight Zone* genius Rod Serling, it's no surprise *Apes* provides plenty of food for thought in depicting its clash between faith and science. It retells the story of Darwin and the virulent objections to his revolutionary theory of evolution. I love the pompous, infuriating religious authorities spouting 'self-evident' sacred truths when it's clear they've got nothing but backward bullshit and threats of execution in their determined bid to smother genuine knowledge and progress.

One of the marvels of 60s cinema, *Apes* is a bold, energetic collision of imagination, intellect, verve and action, as well as being another warning about Man's radiation-infused yen for self-destruction. God, I haven't even touched upon Jerry Goldsmith's menacing score and my fondness for that mute Amazonian hottie, Nova. Plus, no matter how many times you see it, that ending never fails to ignite a tingly sense of awe.

No Blade of Grass (1970)

Set in Britain, this is an inept, poorly acted mess masquerading as an end of the world story. A grass-killing disease has led to famine, cannibalism and chaos. "Do you know what I think caused the virus?" one pontificating pub-goer says. "It's coz them Chinese fertilize everything with human shit." Unfortunately, we don't get any shots of our Sino neighbours defecating on crops so we'll have to put that particular observation down to racism for, as we all know, the Chinese are actually ruining everything by eating bats.

There's nothing subtle about *Grass*, a movie that opens with a lengthy montage of dying Earth images, replete with a boring song gently telling us things have gone to shit before a voiceover hammers home that things have gone to shit.

Still, if you want to see *horned* bikers on the rampage, real-life footage of a birth, and a mum and her sixteen-year-old virginal daughter gang-raped to groovy sixties music, then this is the one for you.

Soylent Green (1973)

It's time for some more square-jawed heroics from Chuck Heston.

He's popped off to the future again and unsurprisingly things ain't too rosy. Instead of lobotomy-performing apes, he's gotta deal with overpopulation, pollution, scarcity of basic resources, an energy crisis, a year-round heat wave and his best mate Edward G. Robinson wearing an effete beret. Things are so shite that the mere sight of a stick of celery or a bar of soap can induce rapture.

There's nothing futuristic about this 2022 vision of New York City. Progress has stalled somewhere in the 70s so that we get crappy computer games, awful interior décor and the massed poor having nothing to do except sleep. Interestingly, female emancipation has hurtled backwards. Women are now known as 'furniture' in that they're owned by men and expected to endure a bit of wear and tear. This subtext doesn't lead anywhere, but back in 1973 it must've irked the average feminist.

As for Chuck, he's a gruff cop who looks like he got blindly dressed in a charity shop. His morals seem a bit dodgy, too, in that he's happy to ransack a murdered rich man's apartment while swigging a bottle of all too rare bourbon. However, he's a dogged investigator, discovering the victim is a key man in the food production industry with political connections. Suddenly doors start closing and Chuck's being followed. Or as he concludes: "Something stinks here."

Soylent might be a little unfocused, but I'm fond of it. It's got two memorable scenes: a food riot that sees protestors literally treated as garbage and Robinson's send-off (an assisted journey into death replete with vivid images of Earth's former bio-diverse richness) made all the more poignant by the distinctive *Double Indemnity* actor knowing he was terminally ill in real life.

And, of course, while *Apes* has the famous ending, *Soylent* boasts that much-loved last line.

Jaws (1975)

It's always amazed me that it took until the mid-seventies for filmmakers to get round to doing a proper shark story. After all, real-life attacks had long mesmerized the public (*Jaws* mentions the 1916 Jersey Shore fatalities while the 1945 sinking of the USS *Indianapolis* prompts one of cinema's great monologues). Given that a shipwreck victim gets munched as far back as 1932's groovy *The Most Dangerous Game*, why the delay in putting a great white or tiger front and centre?

Well, I don't have the answer, but the enormous success of Peter Benchley's very readable novel ensured an, ahem, sea change.

And thank fuck for that.

Blessed with the most memorable opening in cinema, *Jaws* is packed full of superb moments. You know the ones. Fingernails being dragged down a blackboard, an impromptu jetty tow, a severed leg sinking to the ocean bottom, an underwater head popping out of a holed hull, and a grieving mother delivering a public slap. Its tautly directed two hours remain a magical watch.

Former New York cop Martin Brody (Roy Scheider) has moved to New England's Amity Island for a quieter life, although he still has to deal with rampaging pre-adolescents karate-chopping picket fences. Things don't improve when a missing skinny dipper turns up in less than pristine condition on the beach. I love the way the water-hating Brody looks down at the remains of her crab-covered corpse, takes off his glasses and glances out to sea, as if he already knows there's a reckoning to be had.

The lethal attacks continue, mainly because the shit-kicking mayor puts the mighty dollar above human life. Indeed, *Jaws* is excellent at illustrating people's stupidity when faced with a frightening threat, its first half offering numerous examples of knee-jerk reactions, half-assed solutions, irrationality, incompetence, hoaxers and exploitation.

It's not long before Brody's hooked up with a youthful marine biologist Matt Hooper (Richard Dreyfuss) and a crusty, charismatic, possibly deranged seadog Quint (Robert Shaw) to hunt the 25ft, three-ton shark. "What we're dealing with here is a perfect engine," Hooper says. "An eating machine. It's really a miracle of evolution. All this machine does is swim and eat and make little sharks."

The interplay between the three seafaring misfits is the stuff of legend, especially when they drunkenly compare scars. This light-hearted bonding leads into Quint's mesmerizing recollection of a top-secret maritime mission that ended in disaster with hundreds of men in the water able to do little against an army of marauding sharks. Not sure if I believe him, though, when he says he once saw a shark eat a rocking chair.

Director Steven Spielberg conjures up a marvel on a $9million budget. Some things are simple, like the departing *Orca* being viewed through the gaping skeletal jaws of one of Quint's earlier conquests. At other times Spielberg repeatedly generates compelling drama through nothing more than the antics of a few floating yellow barrels.

Then there's the more tricky stuff. Good grief, the tense sequence with a panicking Hooper in an anti-shark cage is as attention-grabbing as anything I've ever seen. But that's *Jaws* for you. It's simply brilliant at mastering so many elements, such as riveting action, sly comedy and perfect characterization. Throw in *that* score and you not only have Spielberg's best movie but the greatest eco-horror movie of all time.

In the wake of *Jaws'* unparalleled success, the whole eco-horror thing received a massive boost as filmmakers scrabbled to come up with their own take or cash in. One of the first was *Orca: The Killer Whale*, a fascinating fishy fuckup that features a gorgeous pre-stardom Bo Derek and the slightly less sexy Indian giant Will Sampson. You might remember him humanely smothering a lobotomized Jack Nicholson in the days when he could recognize a decent script. Frankly, after watching this turkey, he should've stayed inside the nuthouse or at least smothered his agent.

Nothing works in this strangely watchable dud, especially its preposterous dialogue. Listen to this early snatch from whale expert Charlotte Rampling (!) illuminating a typical killer whale trait: "Like human beings, they have a profound instinct for vengeance." Hmm, don't think so, love, but I'll go along with it for the movie's sake.

Richard Harris stars, apparently unbothered that his Ahab-style character is a confused cunt. He wants to capture a whale to sell to an 'aquarium', but thinks an explosive harpoon is the way to go. Five minutes later he's slaughtered a pregnant beast as her anguished mate vows Bronson-style revenge. Next it's killed one of his crew and sunk a couple of boats in the harbour. How long before it's slithering down the high street packing heat?

Understandably shaken, Harris seeks answers from that bastion of common sense, the Church. "Can you commit a sin against an animal?" he asks a reverend, who doesn't even need to check the bible's killer whale section. "You can commit a sin against a blade of grass," comes the sage reply.

Bloody hell, the magnitude of this one's ineptness is off the scale. Mind you, it deserves credit for refusing to blink during its ninety minutes of face-slapping lunacy. I'm just disappointed it isn't called *Orca: The Face of Death* or *Orca: The Evil That Whales Do*. At least we know where that third *Jaws* sequel dredged up its farcical storyline.

Next off the conveyor belt was 1978's *Piranha*. There's a glimmer of an idea here as the wee beasties in question are the result of Operation Razor Teeth, a top-secret Vietnam-era governmental attempt to breed a super-weapon to use against the VC. Its opening fifteen minutes promise some tongue-in-cheek fun, but its bursts of piscine savagery soon wear out their welcome.

Right, I'm done with bad fishy flicks and can't be bothered to sit through the unappealing giant octopus spectacular, *Tentacles*. Let's try a couple of flicks from Down Under.

Long Weekend (1978)

Australia had a go at eco-horror with 1977's Aborigine-flavoured *The Last Wave*. Its main merit is showing Aborigines are just as dumb as Christians and all those other pious nitwits when it comes to banging on about that elusive (but apparently ever-present) looming apocalypse. And so we get freakish weather and bad dreams and... Oh, I don't care. Wouldn't it be nice if one of these religious or quasi-religious bunch of numpties came up with a prediction in which God was chuffed with mankind's progress and wanted to hold a lovely big barbecue to celebrate? Instead, *Last Wave* goes the traditional, catastrophe-just-round-the-corner route. Sure, it offers the odd creepy shot, but gets sunk by ropey acting and a plodding pace.

Much, much better is *Long Weekend*. Written by Everett De Roche, who went on to pen the bacon-and-tusks-flavoured *Razorback*, this is one eerie motherfucker. A squabbling Aussie couple goes on an isolated camping trip. Peter's an arrogant, careless bastard, the sort of trigger-happy bloke who flicks lit ciggies out the car window and chucks beer bottles into the surf to shoot at. His wife Marcia is hard work, too, in that she's a brittle, resentful, tantrum-throwing adulterer.

The thing that sets *Long Weekend* apart is its abortion underpinning. Peter and Marcia's three-day break is designed to bring them back together as they've spent the last couple of months subconsciously trying to deal with the deliberate destruction of their unborn child. Sex has died, arguments have increased, and they're heading for the rocks.

During their holiday Marcia becomes fascinated with an eagle egg while Peter finds a doll on the beach and an abandoned child's tea set in the bush. They hear animal cries that sound just like a baby. Best of all, is when Peter investigates a submerged vehicle and glimpses a child-like entity on its back seat.

Long Weekend has the potential for *Jaws*-style attacks, but prefers a much subtler, nuanced approach that worms its way under your skin. It's steadily

paced with excellent photography and good performances. It also manages
to find a satisfying ending.

Humanoids from the Deep (1980)

I'm afraid my objective journalistic analysis of moviedom is about to slip
with this one. You see, I have a personal reason for *Humanoids'* inclusion that
has nothing to do with its suitability or quality. I just enjoy watching one of
its cast get killed.

Over and over.

The dude's name is David Strassman and he's an enormously successful
ventriloquist/comedian. You might have heard of him. I briefly met him in
1996 and I can still remember his disdainful handshake that transmitted a
flashing neon message to my brain: *You're no one so I'm not gonna bother with
you.*

Then he was off to spend time with more worthwhile people.

The fact his withering verdict was true did not soothe my hurt. I just watched
his sold-out show instead, determined not to be entertained while the
painful memories of that fateful handshake began to turn septic. The years
passed and my desire for revenge only intensified.

Then I happened to catch *Humanoids* and was taken by surprise to see a
youthful Strassman pop up in his only movie to date.

In a tent on an isolated beach with a gorgeous chick.

Bastard.

Then she peels off her top to reveal some bloody impressive norks.

Double bastard.

Now she's fully nude.

*Life's so unfair! Do I have to watch my transgressor doing the sort of stuff with a
hot babe that only exists in my tortured dreams?*

But then, lo and behold, things get miraculously better.

A monster rips its way into the tent, the terrified girl screams, and Strassman is sporting a hideous shoulder wound.

Justice for Davey!

Unfortunately, the monster loses interest in mutilating Strassman any further and instead lumbers after the naked fleeing girl. I guess I can understand its priorities.

Humanoids is a prime example of schlock. Short, filled with boobies, explosions and continuity lapses, it's the sort of flick any teenage boy appreciates. If you want the plot, big business has inadvertently released genetically enhanced salmon into the surrounding waters, resulting in coelacanths feeding on them and abruptly turning into rape-loving dog-haters in thick rubbery suits.

Well, count me in.

This is not a good movie, but it is gory fun. The world needs more tiara-wearing, bare-breasted beauty queens battling ravenous mutant fish-men. Plus, there's half-decent direction, an effective score, appealing scenery, racial undercurrents, a reasonably convincing depiction of life in a Californian coastal town, an upright female scientist who specializes in stating the bleeding obvious, and a brazen *Alien* rip-off moment.

Not to mention Strassman's demise. And even though his onscreen death happened sixteen years before belittling me with his disapproving press of the fingers, I'm still gonna put it down to a particularly deserving case of karma.

Cujo (1983)

As we know, those never-ending Stephen King adaptations have been doing their best to smother cinema for a while now. Back in the early days there were classics like *Carrie*, *The Shining*, *The Dead Zone* and *Misery*, as well as half-decent, non-horror stuff like *Stand by Me* and *Shawshank*. These days we get junk (*It* and *Doctor Sleep*), mediocrity (*1922*), and bum-numbing epics in which Tom Hanks can't piss properly (*The Green Mile*). How long before a studio gets hold of the great man's shopping list and runs with that? Couldn't be any worse than 2019's *Pet Sematary*.

Cujo, on the other paw, is neither great nor crap. It has a professional gloss in the directing and acting departments, but misses the mark partly because its disparate elements (such as adultery and dodgy cereal) don't gel.

Dee Wallace is married to a nice, good-looking guy who's not only kept himself in shape but is a brilliant father to their little boy. Her response? To drop her panties for the local bearded stud. Meanwhile, the nearby white trash mechanic's St. Bernard is bitten on the schnozzle by a rabid bat. Dee gets car trouble and so pops out to get it fixed, resulting in the nutzo mutt keeping her pinned in the vehicle.

Story and music-wise, *Cujo* doesn't feel like a horror movie for its entire first half. However, once the pooch becomes a postman's nightmare, the animal trainers do their job well. It's a convincingly skuzzy, mad and miserable beast, especially when it begins headbutting the sweltering car and chewing off door handles. Still, there's only so much mileage in such a flimsy setup, even if I did appreciate Dee barking: "Fuck you, dog!" It would be nice if her lengthy confinement could in some way be interpreted as 'punishment' for her shitty decision to enjoy extra-marital cock, but the screenplay's far too standard for anything so daring. Instead, it's a simple, small story.

Too simple, too small.

Razorback (1984)

"Razorbacks. Vicious, shit-eating, godless vermin. God and the devil couldn't have created a more despicable species."

Razorback didn't do great business on release, but has deservedly picked up a fair few fans since. It boasts superb cinematography and many attention-grabbing shots. Just look at its opening frames of a kangaroo grubbing around by a barbed wire fence silhouetted against an apocalyptic setting sun. Images of savage beauty abound, a feature that sometimes gives the outback landscape an extraterrestrial feel.

In a telling echo of Australia's infamous dingo baby case, nice old guy Jake Cullen (Bill Kerr) is looking after his grandkid when a massive wild boar smashes through the wall of the house and carries off the tender treat to devour. Barely anyone believes his account of events until two years later when a no-shit female investigative reporter, who specializes in exposing animal abuse, also vanishes...

Razorback packs a terrific amount of incident into its opening twenty-five minutes. It's strong on thrills, mood and atmosphere so we get everything from a night-time car chase and the threat of rape to a shaggy camel sticking its head through a pub window to grab a can of Coke. *Texas Chainsaw* fans should enjoy the dodgy meat packing plant, the sense of isolation, the heat and dust, the scattered animal bones, and some of the uncultured, possibly insane locals.

Director Russell Mulcahy, who at this point already had an enormously impressive CV helming innovative pop music videos, knows what he's doing and gets mostly good performances from an entertaining cast. I also enjoyed the dialogue such as "What's up your hole?", "Haven't seen a taxi round here since about 1953 and he was lost", "One fart and you're a hamburger" and "Wakey! Wakey! Hands off, snakey!"

The outback has provided the setting for some very good flicks, such as *The Proposition*, *Mad Max 2* and especially *Wake in Fright*. Likewise *Razorback* capitalizes on its location. It's a distinctive slice of eco-horror with an uncompromising edge and very strong visuals. Keep your eyes peeled for an outstanding piece of comedy involving a fast disappearing TV set.

Safe (1995)

I guess unleashing genocide on gypsies or Jews is frowned upon these days, but I can't see much wrong in wiping out rich suburbanites like Carol White and her pathetic, whiny ilk.

You see, there's no point to Carol's exceptionally comfortable life. She calls herself a *homemaker* in a fancy bid to cover up the fact she doesn't work, knowing full well *housewife* doesn't sound too impressive when other women with a bit of get up and go are running businesses, piloting jumbo jets or winning Olympic medals. Carol spends her blank days having manicures at the hairdresser or getting upset when the wrong-coloured couch is delivered to her fastidiously neat and tidy home. She doesn't enjoy sex.

Or anything else for that matter.

She's stiff, brittle and self-obsessed. Even though she's in her early thirties, the most energetic thing she can muster is a gentle burst of Madonna-accompanied aerobics. Otherwise she's a pale human tortoise, convinced she's under 'a lot of stress.' Her circle of cookie cutter friends amplifies her vacuous, pampered shortcomings. They talk about fruit diets and self-help books while dithering over decaf or herbal tea. At a baby shower Carol asks one bestie if she wrapped the present herself.

"Oh God, are you kidding?" the friend replies with an embarrassed laugh. "I wish I were that creative."

Armageddon, come Armageddon! as Morrissey might muse.

But at least Carol's buried self-loathing is subconsciously allowing her to grasp she's a non-entity. Her body wants out and is starting to shut down. First it's a nosebleed, then bouts of puking. Panic attacks follow. Her doctor can't find anything wrong and suggests a shrink, but feeble-minded attention-seekers like Carol are never likely to truly grasp their irrelevance.

No, she prefers to blame her symptoms on the environment. Toxins, pesticides, exhaust fumes, even her mystified husband's cologne... You name it, they're the root cause. And, of course, there's a growing army of pseudo-scientific rip-off merchants standing by with their hippy self-love bullshit to convince her she's got an 'environmental illness' and needs to establish 'toxic-free zones'. Or as one tells her: "There are 60,000 chemicals in our environment, but only ten percent tested for human toxicity."

As you can tell, *Safe* is not an action-packed thriller, but an overlong, quietly intriguing peek into neurosis and paranoia. Director Todd Haynes draws a terrific, anxiety-ridden performance from Julianne Moore, who shows how a seemingly intelligent, rational type can get sucked into such a mind-fucking vortex. Sure, there's a *possibility* Carol's body is reacting to pollutants, but I'd rather believe such a psychosomatic waste of space needs shooting.

Great, I've turned into a Nazi.

Waterworld (1995)

The first shot we get is Kevin Costner having a slash, although if *Waterworld* wanted to open with a more representative act of its quality he'd be shitting.

Well, maybe that's a bit harsh. *Waterworld* is a big-budget mess that often feels like a sodden *Mad Max 2*, but its campiness and energetic direction just about keep it afloat. However, its 130 minutes contain far more chuckles than thrills.

For a start there's Costner himself. Presumably he has his uses (though I'd be hard-pressed to name one), but he's a bad fit as a surly, eyeball-eating action hero. I mean, he does his best swinging through the air like Tarzan and, er, rescuing tomatoes, but he's continually undermined by the costume department having decked him out in striped trousers, a topknot and a barnacle earring. Oh yeah, then there are the gills and webbed feet which enable him to swim so fast underwater he can leap dolphin-like out of the drink. It's a tricky movie to take seriously, you know?

And after factoring in its $175 million budget, you start to think the western world's priorities are a little out of whack and maybe such an obscene amount of cash should be used to feed the poor or at least given to me.

Anyhow, it's five hundred years into the future and all that important ice stuff has melted. Dry land is as rare as a good Dire Straits album cover. Kev's become a nameless drifter, although at one point he's amusingly labelled a 'Gentleman Guppy'. He's a hard-bitten loner on a fancy boat who trades dirt. And no, I don't mean porno mags, butt plugs and incriminating info. I mean actual dirt. After inadvertently getting caught up in Dennis Hopper's attack on a trading post, he escapes with a brat who's got a map tattooed on her back. Hopper badly wants that map, although fuck knows how he learned of its existence in the first place. He's convinced it will lead him and his followers to the long-desired dry land, so the chase is on.

Hopper doesn't come out of this one too well, either. Clad in a codpiece and shoulder pads, he looks like a down-market, one-eyed Gary Glitter. Whereas Gary was backed by the Glitter Band, Our Den leads The Smokers. Can you guess how they get their name? Mind you, given that the average corner shop is thousands of feet underwater, I have no idea how he's obtained a constant supply of Benson and Hedges Superslims. In fact, he's got so many ciggies he even offers one to the map-adorned kid. "Never too young to start," he says with a gleam in his eye.

My God, everyone's lost at sea in this increasingly tongue-in-cheek, way over the top piece of flotsam. It's gibberish yet somehow perfectly predictable, featuring a shit load of explosions, an over talkative child badly in need of drowning, a pinch of semaphore, and Hopper describing Kev as a 'turd that won't flush'.

Amen to that.

Open Water (2003)

We're told Mother Nature nurtures us but you try telling that to the hapless heroes of this deeply unnerving existential flick. There's no 'villain' here, no man-made threat, no example of the radioactive chickens coming home to roost. Instead it's a case of two stranded ordinary Joes trying to deal with the environment's ego-squashing indifference to their horrifying plight.

Daniel and Susan (Blanchard Ryan and Daniel Travis) are two hard workers who take a much-needed diving trip. Unfortunately, the dive master screws up the headcount of the returning divers, leaving the poor lambs to resurface and find their boat gone.

Land cannot be seen. They're caught in a current. The sun keeps beating down. There's no food. And the local wildlife is growing unfriendly...

Open Water has the simplest setup of any movie I've seen yet it's devastatingly effective. It really is a nightmare scenario, its creeping horror generated by little more than two decent human beings bobbing on the warm ocean waves.

"We're gonna get through this," Daniel reassures his girl at one point.

But you sense they're not.

Tormented by the possibility of rescue from distant boats on the horizon, it's not long before cramp, vomiting and jellyfish stings start to snuff out hope. Neither can believe the situation.

"The best part is we *paid* to be out here," Daniel shouts amid the arguments, recriminations, rage, terror, and the inevitable *I love yous*. "We paid those incompetent fuckers to drop us out in the middle of the ocean."

Susan's bleakly funny response? "I wanted to go skiing."

Unbearably tense at points, this is survival horror of the highest calibre. It's fascinating how Daniel is aware of his puniness in the face of such a vast, aeon-spanning wilderness but still bellows into the void, apparently determined to assert the weight of his existence even as Mother Nature obliviously destroys him.

Not Taking The Michael

Some talented actors appear to have a bitch of a time choosing a worthwhile script. It's almost as if a load is dumped in front of them, they close their eyes and pick one. Travolta's a prime example, having appeared in nine thousand flicks but only a handful of classics since he first got going in the mid-seventies. Now I suspect there's an awful lot of luck involved in ending up in a half-decent movie, let alone a top-notch one, but I assume doing your utmost to select a promising screenplay is the first step.

Actors are always walking a tightrope when it comes to signing on the dotted line, desperate to be in the next *Pulp Fiction* and nowhere near an *Ishtar*. Of course, there are a few mercenaries like the legendary madman Klaus Klinski, who's on record as wanting the most money for the least work, but I'm sure the vast majority of thesps do their damndest to choose something *good*.

At his peak few could match Michael Douglas' knack for getting his hands on quality, button-pushing fare. This was a man obviously attracted to thorny issues, the sort of stuff that prompted prime water cooler discussions. Sexual harassment, vigilantism, insider trading... Oh boy, he knew how to turn it into box office gold, not to mention get tongues wagging.

Now Kirk Douglas was a bloody tough act to follow, given the quality of *Paths of Glory*, *Spartacus* and *Ace in the Hole*, but I reckon Michael's ability to fish out meaty, provocative scripts enabled him to surpass the old man's achievements.

Coma (1978) *& The China Syndrome* (1979)

Douglas' fifteen-odd year run of plum cinematic roles got underway with the medical thriller *Coma*, playing the boyfriend of Genevieve Bujold. In truth, he's second fiddle not only to our plucky heroine but the incredibly creepy central concept of turning the various internal bits of healthy patients into a lucrative black-market business. Douglas doesn't do anything special, but he's still part of a memorable flick with a couple of standout scenes.

Coma was a deserved hit, quickly followed by a project about a nuclear accident released less than two weeks before a real-life fuckup at a Pennsylvanian power plant. Now while I prefer flicks that depict full-on disasters to *near* disasters (coz, you know, lots of mangled corpses), this is still a worthwhile and admirably tense affair.

Douglas is a hot-headed TV cameraman, whose unappealing beard is matched by a wardrobe that includes everything from a flat cap to a tweed jacket with elbow patches. Dreadful. Anyhow, he happens to be doing a puff piece at a nuclear plant with lightweight reporter Jane Fonda when its core is almost exposed, a sphincter-loosening event that could have resulted in southern California being wiped off the map. He naughtily keeps filming the panic-stricken staff as they struggle to regain control, even though he's been told any form of photography of the control room is a security breach.

Back at the TV studio the big boss won't run his incriminating footage, prompting the memorable insult 'chicken shit asshole' before he starts lobbing around words like *conspiracy*. This still isn't prime Douglas, but he does get to label Fonda (who's more concerned with hanging onto her good job than rocking the boat) 'a piece of talking furniture'.

Fair play to the writers of *Syndrome*, they enable the viewer to follow the incredible complexities of a nuclear accident without boring us silly. It's well-acted and has ongoing merit, especially as we've since had further radiation boo-boos at Chernobyl and Fukushima. *Syndrome's* main worth is to remind us we do occasionally need to think about Important Stuff, such as clean, green energy sources, before gleefully plunging back into cinematic worlds that are awash with bare boobies and bullet-ridden bodies.

The Star Chamber (1983)

"I got bodies piling up all around me and I'm passing out the ammunition."

It's fair to say Judge Steven Hardin (Douglas) is getting frustrated with the legal system. When he's not being forced to let go baddies that shoot little old ladies in the head for their welfare checks, he has to release murderous child pornographers whose lovely handiwork makes seasoned cops throw up.

Both cases fail because of ridiculous technicalities, leaving one of the alleged kiddie rapists to mutter: "God bless fucking America."

All Hardin can do is bitch to his wife ("I feel like I'm on the wrong side") and take his frustrations out on the prosecutors who aren't properly preparing their cases ("You've hinged everything on a shaky search and dropped it in my lap. Terrific!") Things continue to spiral downwards when he's confronted by the outraged father of an adorable murdered munchkin and only able to proffer platitudes about the bind he's in when it comes to the law's rigid nature.

"What about justice?" the father counters. "You ever deal with that? Is that ever fed into this little crossword puzzle you call the law?"

The Star Chamber ensures it presents Hardin as a Bastion of Decency. He's honest, good at his job, and supported by a loving family in his up-market home. We're clearly supposed to view him as a right-thinking man, especially when he starts saying the system has been turned into a 'giant Rubik's cube that can be twisted into any pattern that fits'.

So what's he gonna do?

Luckily, his older mentor Judge Benjamin Caulfield (Hal Holbrook) has a neat solution to this Dickensian the-law-is-an-arse problem. Hardin just needs to join the nine-strong 'Court of Last Resort', thereby helping arrange to have holes blown in any slimy criminal bastard who slips between the cracks.

As you can tell, *The Star Chamber* is a rightwing wet dream, the natural successor to pro-vigilante flicks like *Death Wish* in which glib, smirking scumbags finally get what's coming to them. This is one bunch of fascist judges that even Dirty Harry would be happy to sit down with and shoot the breeze (or any passing perps). For the most part it's simplistic, button-pushing stuff where the viewer is led by the nose into understanding, if not sympathizing with Hardin's decision.

Or as the doubt-free Caulfield tells him: "Time to get your fingernails dirty, kiddo."

Saying all that, *The Star Chamber's* not a bad watch. It's never dull and provides food for thought amid the killings. Douglas puts in a restrained performance, much more so than Pacino's pissed-off, super-charged lawyer four years earlier in the similarly themed *...And Justice For All*. He does a lot of smoking and staring into space while wrestling with his tortured conscience, although he still gets to do some signature Douglas moves, such as pacing and banging things as his initially calm voice rises to a short, frustrated shout.

The Star Chamber runs with a fascinating idea and is given a professional sheen by director Peter Hyams. Shame it badly loses its nerve. Douglas would go on to make better stuff, but any pic in which our refined and supposed betters hand out extrajudicial verdicts via an emotionless, silencer-equipped assassin is probably worth a look.

Romancing the Stone (1984)

This magnificent adventure-comedy was the start of Douglas' golden age and the one in which his previous onscreen personas coalesced into a recognizable whole.

He plays the gruff Jack T. Colton, a rugged, self-reliant bird poacher in the Colombian jungle who only thinks about number one. He's bumbling along quite nicely until the successful romantic novelist Joan Wilder (Kathleen Turner) inadvertently causes her bus driver to crash into Colton's stationary jeep, resulting in fifteen grand's worth of exotic birds flying away.

"Lady, you are bad news," he tells her. "What'd you do? Wake up this morning and say: Today, I'm gonna ruin a man's life."

It's telling, though, that the only object he rescues from his ruined jeep is a photo of a sailboat, a yacht he plans to buy and travel around the world in. Just like his newfound acquaintance, he's a romantic, although he doesn't know it yet.

In the meantime he needs to get rid of Joan, a hapless ninny who keeps doing stupid things like trying to recover a lost button in the dense undergrowth. Indeed, she's the embodiment of a Silly Girly, a cat-owning, dowdily-dressed dreamer in dire need of a damn good root to straighten her out.

Colton, however, is indifferent to this damsel in distress and does his best to abandon her, only changing his mind when a price is agreed for his help. I like the way she looks at her suitcase, obviously expecting him to act the gentleman and carry it, only for him to pick it up and drop it at her feet while passing her.

With its hair-raising escapades, such as a muddy waterslide down a hill and a *drive* over a waterfall, this is an imaginative, fast-paced and well-executed movie. It's got a good Lee Van Cleef-lookalike villain, excellent comedic support from Danny DeVito as an incompetent criminal, and a great romantic ending on a par with *An Officer and a Gentleman's* Richard Gere sweeping Debra Winger off her feet. The unseen way Colton retrieves the titular stone from its reptilian guardian is beyond fucking pie in the sky, though.

Surprisingly, *Stone* also has a fair bit of edge. We get the odd rape joke, Colombia described as a 'Third World toilet', a stabbing, and blood spurting from the stump of a bitten-off hand.

Good-o.

Douglas makes a brash action hero, convincingly wielding a pump-action shotgun while also demonstrating a previously untapped flair for comedy. Best of all is the way he brilliantly meshes with Kathleen Turner, their joyous chemistry resulting in a further two outings together.

The Jewel of the Nile was the first, a mechanical flick I wish had started with a paunchy, balding Colton slumped in an armchair nursing a beer and watching baseball while his shrew-like missus bangs around the kitchen trying to calm their bawling baby. You know, a telling snapshot of how romance and sexual love inevitably disintegrate into drudgery and the possibility of murder.

Instead we get a charmless, contrived adventure built on the flimsiest of foundations. Poor Colton is pussy-whipped throughout, continually doing things he doesn't want to do and obviously dreading the day he gets to meet the prospective mother-in-law.

I think there's some sort of lesson to be learned here, guys.

Wall Street (1987)

Even though *Jewel of the Nile* sucked, it did decent business. With four hits under his belt Douglas was sitting pretty, but 1985 landed him with the equivalent of *Cats*. Now I haven't seen *A Chorus Line* coz a Real Man has nothing to do with mincing musicals. Indeed, the last one I endured was the Oscar-winning *Chicago*, an unfortunate occurrence that can be explained by being in a state of extreme disorientation following several savage blows to the head in a street fight with at least four pensioners.

Anyway, Douglas' Midas touch swiftly returned in 1987 when he starred in *two* blockbusters. *Fatal Attraction* was the first, a slick, plausible and intensely memorable thriller that'll make any married guy think twice when offered frizzy-haired sex on a plate. Unfortunately, its melodramatic bathroom finale is so rotten I think I would have preferred Glenn Close getting stuffed down the bog or boiled on the stove. At least that would've been funny.

Then there was *Wall Street*.

Now I don't believe anyone understands the stock market's myriad financial complexities. I know I don't. Shares, commodities, publicly owned companies, blue chips, the Dow Jones... And, of course, given my near-total level of ignorance, I guess it was inevitable I invested a couple of grand in an Aussie telco back in the early 2000s. After six weeks I was a thousand bucks up, convinced I was the new Gordon Gekko. I even started wearing braces, a tie clip, avoiding lunch and contemptuously telling bemused passersby that if they wanted a friend to get a dog.

Then the share price of my beloved telco, my ticket out of the rat race, began falling. Not rapidly but steadily, an unspectacular decline that resulted in many pep talks with my reflection that usually went along the lines of *Just hold your nerve, Davey boy, things'll recover.*

And did they?

Did they fuck.

Two years later my display of monetary verve had resulted in depression, a minor alcohol problem, the meek sale of the cursed stock for less than half my outlay, and the ongoing vandalisation of any public telephone I happen to spot. To this day *Wall Street* remains a faintly traumatic watch as it's a reminder of my own lack of stock market nous. I'll never be a financial whizz-kid, just like I'll never make a woman meow in bed. Saying that, Gekko is still one of the all-time great villains.

"Please allow me to introduce myself, I'm a man of wealth and taste..." So sang a deceptively languid Jagger in *Sympathy for the Devil* and that sinister tune often pops into my head whenever Gekko's on screen. He's a potent mix of God, Mephistopheles, Dracula and Scarface so it's no wonder Bud Fox (an excellent Charlie Sheen) looks shit scared before his long-anticipated meeting with the ruthless kingpin.

Wall Street does a great job of building Gekko up. We first learn he's a money-making machine who had an 'ethical bypass' at birth. Next there's a glimpse of his beaming face on the front cover of *Fortune* magazine before a snatch of his authoritative voice is heard as subordinates troop into his office.

Our first meeting doesn't disappoint. Sporting top-notch threads and slicked back hair, Gekko paces his humongous office barking orders down the phone at his minions. This is a man who radiates power, a perpetually hungry wolf in an impeccable suit whose steely gaze is always weighing everything up and seeing what's in it for him. His single-minded commitment to the greenback is nothing short of fanatical.

The ambitious but wet-behind-the-ears Bud can do little but sweat and blunder in front of him, offering one dud financial tip after another. He knows his chance of gaining a foothold in Gekko's seemingly unattainable world is growing slimmer by the moment until Gekko delivers the key line, the one that sets everything in motion.

"Tell me something I don't know," he says, which not only underlines the man's insatiable lust for information, but happens to be code for *sell your soul, pipsqueak.*

Poor Bud can't resist, offering up inside info on his father's airline company. Soon Gekko has taken Bud under his leathery wing and is schooling him in the dark arts of fiscal manoeuvring. He doesn't value hard work or persistence; it's all about pertinent info. "If you're not inside, you are outside," he tells his new protégé. "I bet on sure things. Read Sun Tzu's *The Art of War*. Every battle is won *before* it's ever fought." Gekko's language is full of violence, littered with references to war, fighting and slaughter.

He's also a two-faced liar, a relentless man who will pose as your friend in public and private while all the time sharpening his fangs to sink into your jugular. With his devilish grin, he loves stripping a company's assets in the same way he enjoys pulling the clothes off a piece of top quality arse on his private jet. It's all about *conquest*, you see, planting his flag on top of whatever's wreckable.

Not that he can't defend his corner.

"I am not a destroyer of companies," he publicly tells the shareholders of a company he's about to destroy. "I am a liberator of them. Greed, for lack of a better word, is good. Greed is right. Greed works. Greed clarifies, cuts through, and captures the essence of evolutionary spirit. Greed, in all of its forms, greed for life, for money, for love, for knowledge has marked the upward surge of mankind."

Bud is bewitched, hopelessly corrupted by his shiny new baubles and unable to see that a driven, obsessive man like Gekko is actually *ill*. Maybe he might understand if he were privy to some of Gekko's more nefarious remarks. How about this doozy to Bud's high-class new girlfriend, a woman he's long had under his duplicitous control: "You and I are the same. We're smart enough not to buy into the longest myth running: Love. A fiction created by people to stop them jumping out of windows."

Oh God, isn't Gekko great? He's got all the answers, except to the one question at the root of it all: How much is enough?

On the face of it, the superb *Wall Street* is the story of Bud's rise and fall in a frantic, dog-eat-dog world. Sheen is very good, especially the way he blubs at work after unleashing the Kraken on his principled, blue-collar father, literally breaking the man's heart. However, this is Douglas' best-known role and for good reason. He's an absolute powerhouse, dominating the avarice-fuelled proceedings like Anthony Hopkins in *Silence of the Lambs* and Orson Welles in *The Third Man*.

And remember, kids: "It's all about the bucks. The rest is conversation."

Black Rain (1989)

Some flicks fall into the category of what I call Airplane Movies. They're watchable at 35,000 feet, but have pretty much left your head by the time you're standing at the baggage carousel vaguely disappointed that you once again never got a sniff of joining the Mile High Club. *Black Rain*, much like Ridley Scott's later *American Gangster*, is a classic Airplane Movie.

After the dizzying highs of *Fatal Attraction* and *Wall Street* this one has to go down as a disappointment, especially as Douglas was at the zenith of his powers. Surprisingly, it's the first time he played a cop since his *Streets of San Francisco* days on TV back in the 70s. However, although I don't care for *Black Rain*, perhaps its main merit was providing Douglas with the blueprint for *Basic Instinct's* turbo-charged Nick Curran three years later. Practice makes perfect and all that because the similarities between the two characters are remarkable. Both are gruff, macho loose cannons, in trouble with Internal Affairs, hate rules and procedures, have an ex-wife, smoke like shit, and get involved with a blonde hottie who knows how to fill a dress. They even share the same first name. The chief difference is *Basic Instinct's* Nick Curran sports a less embarrassing haircut while hunting his AC/DC quarry with a permanent hard-on.

So why is Paul Verhoeven's controversial, balls to the floor thriller ten times better? Well, *Black Rain* has an irrelevant beginning, weak foundations, by the numbers plotting, some groan-inducing implausibilities, and a so-so cast. It's not dull, but there's no verve, no razzle-dazzle, no *oomph*. Douglas plays the dick-swinging Nick Conklin, who happens to be in a restaurant with his eminently reasonable partner Charlie Vincent (Andy Garcia) when a Jap gangster Sato (Yusaku Matsuda) kills two other baddies in front of fifty horrified witnesses. Despite catching him after a chase and a bit of fisticuffs, the US authorities bafflingly decide to return Sato to Osaka. On the trip over there those butterfingers Nick and Charlie allow Sato to be whisked off the plane by his own gang members posing as cops.

I have to say it's a rushed, if not plain daft setup.

Nick gets the odd decent line ("Sometimes you gotta forget your head and grab your balls") but the lightweight Charlie provides bland support, especially when compared to the excellent George Dzundza in *Basic Instinct*. "Ladies of the eighties are going for shoes," Charlie chirps at one point, a fair indication of his lack of decent lines. Please cut this man's head off. Similarly, the spiky-haired, shades-wearing Sato is no match for Sharon Stone, particularly in the tit department.

Not much is made of the culture clash, either. In one brilliantly original scene, we discover Nick's not very good with chopsticks. Given how impulsive ('Fuck patience!') and unreconstructed he is, there's a disappointing lack of racial aggravation and non-pc slurs thrown around. Nick says 'nip' once and even then he thinks the guy he's disparaging won't understand. Likewise, the straight arrow Jap cop (Ken Takakura) he chafes against is similarly unimaginative in his insults. "Perhaps you should think less of yourself and more of the group," he tells Nick while trying to remove the rod from up his arse. "Try to work like a Japanese."

Yes, very level-headed, clap clap, but hardly memorable stuff.

Tellingly, *Black Rain*'s best bit has nothing to do with the routine action and uninspired dialogue. It arrives at an outdoor eatery when the straight arrow cop asks Nick if he's guilty of taking dirty money back in New York. Nick, having earlier raged at Internal Affairs that he's clean, simply stops eating his noodles and looks down. "I'm not proud of it," he says with unexpected candour and contrition. "I had a divorce, kids, bills..."

It's the only moment in this Airplane Movie that emotionally connects.

The War of the Roses (1989)

I'm a loner and have been all my life, although I did once live with a woman. Well, I say 'live with' but the truth was more to do with tolerating her company under the same roof as she paid the rent. It was an uncertain period in my life so the functional arrangement and occasional fuck suited me fine, but when she bafflingly started dropping hints about marriage and babies I was gone before the accusation 'user' could be spat out.

To this day I have no idea why people get hitched and/or reproduce. Seeing the same person pretty much every day of your life? Being tied to an ungrateful kid or two for a couple of decades? Christ, why would anyone go in for such irritating, restrictive and damaging nonsense? Please provide some proof that people are meant to be together for a long period of time.

That's why I have a sly fondness for *War of the Roses*, a bitter, savage depiction of a collapsing marriage. *Look what I avoided*, I always think when the credits roll. *Doesn't Davey know best*?

Then I have a smug wank to celebrate my profound loneliness.

Oliver Rose (Douglas) has been married for eighteen years to Barbara (Kathleen Turner) and they live in a mansion. To the outside world they're a hugely successful couple, but it's not hard to see their relationship is filled with mind games, sarcasm, passive-aggressive bullshit, deeply irritating mannerisms and habits, the exhausting need for diplomacy in the face of the ever-present threat of conflict and the continual headbutting involved in trying to establish once and for all WHO'S IN FUCKING CHARGE.

You know, like most other couples.

Everything comes to a head when Oliver painfully experiences what he thinks is a life-threatening wobble only to find his wife doubling down on not coming to the hospital by asking for a divorce.

Why? he asks.

"Because when I watch you eat, when I see you asleep, when I look at you lately, I just wanna smash your face in," she replies before punching him.

Fair enough.

They say all wars are fought about territory and *Roses* brilliantly encapsulates this in a microcosm as the pair rapidly descends into an unholy battle over who gets the house. Before long they're trading insults on the stairs, throwing crockery and destroying property. Cats and genitals don't fare too well, either.

"You have sunk below the deepest layer of prehistoric frog shit at the bottom of a New Jersey skunk swamp," Oliver tells Barbara in a divorce lawyer's office. He's actually the sympathetic character here, although he's happy to land the odd low blow. Take his standout scene when he drunkenly arrives home as Barbara hosts a black tie dinner party for her business clients.

"I would never humiliate you like this," she says while he stands on a chair in the kitchen pissing on the fish.

"You're not equipped to, honey," is his priceless retort.

Douglas and Turner rekindle their chemistry in *Roses*, a deranged, take-no-prisoners black comedy which memorably illustrates the dangers of digging your heels in.

Or at least sawing them off your wife's shoes.

Basic Instinct (1992)

In a Hollywood first, Nick Curran is a cop on the edge.

Not that you can immediately tell. On his way to a murder scene, he's well-groomed, asks questions in a measured tone, and looks like he's got it together. Yes, he has a penchant for inappropriate remarks, but we'll forgive him as he no longer drinks, smokes, snorts coke or shoots dead hapless tourists.

Then he gets dazzled by a flash of Catherine Tramell's (Stone) vulva and goes off the deep end.

Now I know she's got a degree in psychology, but it's still amusing how fast she messes with the inside of his head ("Have you ever fucked on cocaine, Nick?") In two meetings flat he turns into the equivalent of a horny werewolf with a badge. Suddenly he's swigging Jack Daniels again, chain-smoking, publicly threatening to 'kick the fucking teeth in' of a goading member of Internal Affairs, and virtually foaming at the mouth.

Not to mention slamming the psychologist assessing his wellbeing (in the wake of the aforementioned tourist shootings) up against a wall, tearing her blouse open and bending her over a couch during an arse-baring display of rape.

"You've never been like that before," she says while numbly gathering up her ripped clothes. "Why?"

"You tell me," he replies with a shrug. "You're the shrink."

Jesus Christ, what's he gonna do if he gets to spend any more brain-scrambling time with Catherine? Have a go at bestiality? Walk into McDonald's with an AK47? Try to get New Kids on the Block to reform?

Whatever the case, *Basic Instinct's* first forty minutes provide the perfect evidence for Douglas' willingness to take on less than saintly roles. I mean, could you see a fellow A-lister like Tom Hanks doing something as fantastically in your face as this?

But hang on, Nick's not finished yet. My god, his pussy-pickled brain is now telling him it's OK to wear a V-neck green sweater sans shirt in a nightclub. Somehow Catherine thinks this is acceptable foreplay and they finally get it on. During sex, Nick looks like he's losing his mind, trying to be the boss with some manly thrusts but ending up tied to the bed. Is she going to whip out her favourite murder weapon and treat him like a giant human ice cube?

Nope.

Instead she rides him to ecstasy before releasing him from his silky bonds, his evident relief resulting in him embracing her like she's his mum. Honestly, this is fucked-up stuff.

However, it gets even better.

After padding nude to the luxurious bathroom, he delivers a fantastic line to Catherine's lesbo lover, Roxy, who's been secretly watching their nuclear-powered humping. Without attempting to cover himself up, he just looks at her. "Let me ask you something, Rocky, man to man," he says, deliberately getting her name wrong as his voice drips with smugness and contempt. "I think she's the fuck of the century. What do you think?"

He then gets back into bed with the game-playing Catherine. When she wraps his arm around her and meekly kisses his hand, he obviously thinks he's tamed the tigress.

Douglas would never be this brave again. Sure, he's overshadowed by Stone's feral, star-making turn, but he's still fucking great in *Basic Instinct*, one of the most astonishing, full-on movies Tinsel Town ever pumped out.

Falling Down (1993)

Fuck knows how you follow something as jaw-droppingly provocative as *Basic Instinct* but Douglas managed it with this bloody fantastic urban dystopia. This is the one where he's got the military-style haircut, the glasses, a perfectly understandable penchant for pointing a pump-action shotgun at garishly dressed golfers, and a simple, but overwhelming desire to get home.

Except, of course, in this case *home* means death.

I must say I do love this flick's beginning, a near-wordless five minutes which demonstrates how simplicity can sometimes be gold. We meet a sweaty, fly-bothered Bill Foster (Douglas) marooned in a ghastly traffic jam during the rising heat of the morning rush hour. His tie is rammed up to his throat. There's not enough air and what he can get into his constricted lungs is tainted by exhaust fumes. There's nothing to do except listen to shrieking school kids, look at dumb bumper stickers and hate people. You can almost hear the needle-like thoughts jabbing his feverish brain: *Is this what it's all about? And I fucking do this five days a week?*

Questions, no doubt, that many of us have asked at one time or another. We're fully on his side at this point. He's mad as hell and he's not gonna take it anymore. Having reached boiling point, Foster pushes open his car door and steps out. He might be carrying a briefcase but that accessory soon proves little more than the most superficial of attempts to present a civilized front. In essence, from this moment on he's walking in ever decreasing circles toward a landmine.

But what an incident-packed journey across a God-awful inner-city landscape packed full of hustlers, beggars, placard-waving protestors, yet more road works, overcrowded buses, giant advertising billboards, the homeless, uncooperative fast food managers, knife-wielding would-be muggers, abusive drivers, and homophobic, nigger-hating white supremacists. Basic civility is at a premium. Graffiti and gaudy street art are everywhere. Sure, there's some clumsy exaggeration of LA's inhabitants to the point of cartoonish excess, but I still love director Joel Schumacher's dysfunctional vision of stifling heat, stressed individuals at breaking point and a prevailing lack of courtesy.

What's also clear is the significance of territory. Time and time again Foster encounters people trying to eject him from their turf. Gang members, shopkeepers, construction workers and golfers all instruct him to leave. Hell, even the mother of his little girl doesn't want him anywhere near his former home. This is a guy who might be in motion but in reality has nowhere to go. He's a middle-aged man wearing worn-out shoes and sleeping in a single bed, silently sharing strained meals with his scared mother. He has no job, no family, no *function*. A man out of time. No wonder he compares himself to a stranded astronaut on the dark side of the moon.

"I'm past the point of no return, Beth," he tells his ex-wife on the phone. "Do you know when that is? That's the point in your journey when it's longer to go back to the beginning than it is to continue to the end."

You'll never hear the rationale for murder-suicide put better.

Still, there are some brilliantly funny scenes along the way that capture modern life's intensely annoying facets, especially the fake chumminess of retail staff and their rigid adherence to pointless policies and schedules. Who doesn't want to pull out a semi-automatic weapon when faced with such pinheads? And aren't we naughtily on Foster's side when an outraged, privileged golfer shouts '*Fore!*' and drives a ball at his head only for him to yell '*Five!*' and start blowing holes in the man's stupid electric golf cart?

Foster, whether massaging an ice-cold, overpriced can of Coke against his face or complaining that the burger he bought looks nothing like the one in the photo, is the most memorable consumer rights advocate you'll ever meet.

Don't go thinking he's a victim, though, or that the brilliant pacing of the over the top *Falling Down* condones his attitudes and actions. He's simply an abusive, dangerous man floundering on a scrapheap. However, Douglas in meltdown mode is riveting from start to finish. It might just be his best movie.

Disclosure (1994)

Back in the 90s I used to be a newspaper reporter. I covered a lot of court cases, a fair chunk of which was sex stuff. My paper got wind of a guy employed by the cops who was up for sexually assaulting a colleague. He was a paper shuffler, rather than an actual police officer, but reporters love the whole idea of anyone remotely connected to law and order doing naughty stuff.

Anyhow, I covered the first day of his trial and couldn't believe the prosecution's piss-weak opening statement. Basically, the guy had brushed up against a colleague at work but insisted it was inadvertent. No dick out or tit grabbing or lewd remarks or sustained campaign of harassment or anything. I can remember thinking *poor bastard* and that the case should never have got to court as no jury in their right mind would convict on such feeble evidence.

I happened to be on holiday for the trial's second day, but when I returned to work the guy in question phoned me all upset. Turned out he'd been cleared midway through the second day but the paper hadn't sent anyone in my place to cover it. He wanted to know where the story was proclaiming his innocence.

Well, I didn't have an answer for the news desk fuckup, but I do remember his acute distress at firstly being accused of sexual harassment and then being the subject of front-page prominence. He made it clear it was a ghastly, life-altering process with some people muttering all the way that there's no smoke without fire. Innocent until proven guilty means jack shit in the real world. Or to use another metaphor: Mud's easy to sling and it sticks good.

These days things have probably got worse, especially with the internet's arrival and the prevailing narrative that men are bad. 'Victims' are routinely believed, no matter how old or flimsy their claims, and very few observers seem to consider they might be attention-seekers, avaricious, back-stabbers or malicious liars. Indeed, the media can't get enough of such reputation-destroying stories. Sure, it's still easier to be a man than a woman and a certain percentage of men *are* predatory shits, but that doesn't mean there aren't some dark sisters out there willing to use changing times to their advantage. After all, women are human and we know what those fuckers are like.

Disclosure plunges headlong into such incendiary material. It's definitely one of Michael Douglas' hot button masterpieces, a flick that remains scarily relevant when it comes to the fractious nature of male-female workplace relationships. This is a nuanced, thought-provoking and uncomfortable watch.

Douglas plays Tom Sanders, a former playboy turned *Fatal Attraction* everyman. He might've 'seen more ass than a rental car' but those days are long gone. Now he's settled with a loving wife, two cute kids and a nice home. He's also in line for a prestigious promotion at the tech company where he's worked damned hard for the last decade.

However, there are a couple of troubling signs. For a start his wife says: "Grandma used to have this expression: Don't climb up too close to God. He might shake the tree." Then a laid-off IBM worker tells him on the ferry he catches to work that he was earning one hundred and fifty grand a year before being 'surplussed.' Both comments suggest how quickly things change, how you can go from riding the crest of a wave to being dumped in a cesspit.

When Tom arrives at the office he catches a glimpse of a pair of bare legs going up the stairs and pauses to admire the swaying arse on top of them. It's not intimidatory or creepy, it's just an involuntary, healthy appreciation of the female form. He's a regular, red-blooded guy, all right.

Then he swats his attractive secretary's bum with a handful of manila folders. There's nothing even remotely sexual or power-based about it and she doesn't complain, but it's the first suggestion he might not be the most enlightened employee.

Tom, however, has more pressing things to mull over as news filters down that he's missed out on his long dreamed-about vice-president promotion. The job's not only been 'stolen' by an outsider, but given to an ex-flame by the name of Meredith Johnson (Demi Moore), a highly sexed woman he used to watch porn with, sodomize, bang in public places and use a dildo on. At a team meeting his male subordinates suggest she only got the plum job because she's attractive and sleeping with the big boss while the solitary female in the room rolls her eyes. "All I know is any woman has to be twice as good as a man and work twice as hard to get the same job," she says.

The first shot we get of Meredith is a close up of her shapely calves ending in black high heels as Tom passes by in the background, an unquestionably sexual piece of framing. Is he going to end up skewered on one of those alluring spikes? She invites him up to her office for an after-work drink, saying: "I remember how you liked a good bottle of wine. I'll get one."

During the subsequent meeting, which I'd argue is a classic scene of 90s cinema, the role reversal already hinted at is played out in full. I love how Meredith sits and pats the space alongside, indicating for him to park his cute little butt next to hers. "I like all the boys under me to be happy," she says before hungrily running her eyes over him and belittling his nourishing domesticity. "You've kept in good shape, Tom. Nice and hard."

Christ, it's fascinating upside-down stuff. Not long after asking him to massage her shoulders she launches an aggressive, cock-rubbing raid as he does his best to protest. "Why don't you just lie back and let me take you?" she pants. "I could've had anybody and I picked you."

Tom manages to abort the subsequent blowjob but when she starts pushing her finger into his mouth, he kicks against his submissiveness and finally becomes the 'man'. Tom's no saint here as he rips her blouse open and knickers off, but when he catches sight of his demented face in the window he comes to his senses and stumbles out of the office with telltale scratch marks down his chest.

"You get back here and you finish what you started," she yells after him. "You hear me? Or you're fucking dead!"

Wow. What a bloody great scene. Bold, graphic and a long way from black and white, but it's still clear the entitled Meredith has abused her power as his new chief. On top of that I've got so used to seeing Michael Douglas bossing others that it's a real eye opener to catch him in a passive role, eventually fleeing from a *woman* with his tail between his legs. Indeed, he spends most of the movie in a state of extreme discomfort as the poison of her ensuing sexual harassment claim spreads.

And fair play to Demi Moore, she nails her role as a ruthless, power-hungry corporate cow. Now I don't usually care for her (bloody hell, have you seen *Striptease* and *G.I. Jane*?), but she has her uses (*A Few Good Men*) and she's superb here. Every scene with Douglas is a corker. Meredith's a shell of a person, some sort of frightening prototype, a cold, humourless bitch, and ambitious for ambition's sake. I suspect if you scraped off her perfectly applied makeup you'd find cancerous sores. In the classic 70s movie *Network* Max Schumacher (William Holden) rips Diana Christensen (Faye Dunaway) apart by ramming home the 'shrieking nothingness' of her existence. Well, Meredith's the personification of shrieking nothingness, a status-obsessed woman who must win at all costs. There's no love in her, no warmth, no joy. She's Ilsa-lite: you'd better fuck her now and fuck her properly otherwise she'll rip your balls off.

Her only claim for sympathy is that equality has become a double-edged sword. I imagine many women feel pressurised into trying to have a successful career and attaining prominent positions, as if being a stay-at-home mom is some sort of 1950s throwback that lets the sisters down. It's a seismic shift that perhaps forces some of them to ape the aggression of men, both in bed and the workplace.

Meredith's teary, pale-faced recollection of her sexual encounter with Tom during the subsequent in-house mediation is nothing short of compelling. It's amazing how we *know* she's a bare-faced liar yet she still seems more credible than the flustered Tom, who has to recount the sordid events in front of his angry, humiliated wife. And who can forget Meredith smugly standing in an elevator as the doors ping open in front of Tom only for her to say: "Going down...?"

This is a prophetic movie, chockfull of snippets of dialogue that illustrate how the male-female pendulum has swung (as it needed to do) but is now more like a wrecking ball. I suspect men have grown intensely wary of working women (both above and below them) because it's clear anything can be twisted. A remark, a laugh, a non-verbal gesture, a shared history or even a gift can all play their part if there's a spiteful agenda to be served. An argument becomes verbal abuse, raising your voice is bullying, an overheard private remark is harassment, and a passing comment or a shoulder touch become inappropriate.

And sexual contact? Oh, boy. That sort of thing can be flipped as easily as a particularly rotten egg.

After *Disclosure* Douglas' ability to pick edgy scripts noticeably tailed off, resulting in so-so efforts like *The Ghost and the Darkness* and *Wonder Boys* and an outright dud like *Don't Say a Word*. Yes, 2000's *Traffic* was a good ensemble piece, but his conventional, mainly passive performance as a newly appointed drug czar (whose straight A teenage daughter becomes a junkie) smacked of contrivance.

Not that his decline into more standard stuff mattered much. With a Best Actor Oscar under his belt, numerous iconic roles, massive box office success, and a clear hatred of blandness, what did he have left to prove or achieve anyway?

Crawlspace (1986)

Director

David Schmoeller

Synopsis

A Nazified acorn doesn't fall far from the tree

Cast

Klaus Kinski, Talia Balsam, Barbara Whinnery, Kenneth Robert Shippy

Sometimes you want a movie to educate, move or inspire you.

And sometimes you just wanna watch that pint-sized Teutonic nutter Klaus Kinski collect eyeballs.

Now I'm not one to condemn actors for their off-screen behaviour or ill-judged Tweets. I don't really care what they get up to or what their political affiliations are. I just focus on the movies and have always found it pretty damn easy to separate person and artist. For example, Charlton Heston used to be president of that awful, borderline criminal organization, the NRA. Don't care. I still love *Planet of the Apes*. Sean Connery was in favour of smacking chopsy women. Not brilliant, but nowhere near enough to stop me pulling the plug on his tussles with Oddjob. Bollocks to all that Orwellian cancel culture shit. People make mistakes, sometimes serious ones, but pretending they no longer exist is *babyish*. Expecting artists to be saints or share the same outlook is really boring, immature and unrealistic. Don't you know they're often as messed up as you and me?

Saying that, sometimes familiarity with a star's life can amplify how you respond to their work. Look at Karen Carpenter, one obviously sad lady. Knowing about her pathetic, drawn-out struggles, in which she literally tried to fade from view, really adds to the melancholy timbre of a song like *Rainy Days and Mondays*. It makes the sentiment more authentic, you know?

It's a similar situation with Klaus Kinski. When he wasn't a ranting, bug-eyed madman radiating hostility, he was apparently preying on and terrorizing his daughters. This information definitely adds a *frisson* to his performances, especially if playing a murderous, Nazi-haunted voyeur.

Crawlspace is a key Kinski movie. Given the nature of his role as Karl Gunther, he's surprisingly restrained throughout, as exemplified by his serene expressions, lack of rants and fondness for open-necked shirts and cardigans. However, nothing can disguise the depth of depravity on display. This is one messed up little flick that doesn't seem to generate much respect in horror circles. Not sure why. It's a good, short watch and often displays imagination and inventiveness (catch the Newton's Cradle clacking away in a fridge full of rats). Indeed, its pre-credits opening is near-perfection.

We see a nervous, torch-carrying girl wandering around an apartment block's empty corridors and stairways. She comes to an open door. "Mr Gunther...?" she hesitantly calls out, switching on the flashlight while peering into the darkened room. The chattering of unseen rats can be heard.

Don't go in, girl. For fuck's sake, don't go in.

She creeps in, the flashlight revealing vaguely sinister clutter. The door swing shuts behind her and automatically locks. Her torch beam picks out a crop-haired female in a small cage on the floor, a prisoner who immediately becomes agitated and starts making incoherent noises. We see Gunther is also in the room. He switches on the main light, causing the girl to spin. "She can't talk," he says, pointing to his prisoner. "I cut her tongue out." Cut to a close-up shot of a severed tongue in a jar of formaldehyde. The girl backs away as a very relaxed Gunther adds: "What a shame. I really liked you." The girl swallows. "Liked...?" Gunther presses a button and a spearing device shoots out from the wall and impales her as the imprisoned girl beats her head.

Pretty good, huh? Certainly enough to hook me in, but director Schmoeller quickly outdoes himself by switching to an overhead shot of Gunther in a different room sitting at a table twiddling a scalpel. There's also a handgun, a solitary bullet and what looks like a blank piece of card in front of him. The camera floats down until we're level with that extraordinary face. He slices open a fingertip before wiping the blood on the side of a *personally engraved* bullet. He slips it into the chamber, spins it and puts the barrel to his forehead. He pulls the trigger to the sound of an empty click. Giving the weakest of smiles, he whispers "So be it." Then he picks up the card and flips it over.

It reads *Apartment for rent.*

Mein Gott, what a start! In four minutes flat, Schmoeller has doled out a plethora of warped information with less than twenty words spoken. It's a technical master class of *Show, don't tell.* We know Gunther's a landlord who builds murderous contraptions. We know he's a sadist and experienced, matter-of-fact killer. We know he's fascinated by death and flirts with experiencing it, suggesting guilt or at least a troubled conscience. Whatever the case, another victim will soon be lured into his lethal web. We also doubt he wells up if he happens to hear a Karen Carpenter song.

Gunther is the son of a Dachau concentration camp doctor, a man who was executed for crimes against humanity back in 1945. Gunther, a former Hitler Youth member, has also become a doctor, but it's fair to say he's long forgotten his Hippocratic Oath. For a start, nearly seventy patients under his care at an Argentinean hospital didn't make it through the night. Since arriving in America, he's been unable or unwilling to shake off his troubling addiction to death. Or as he writes in his diary: "Killing is my heroin, my opiate, my fix. It gives me a God-like sensation that goes beyond that special feeling doctors have because they can save lives. When you can take away life as easily as you can save it, that is a feeling very few people ever experience."

Crawlspace is not a sleazy, nasty movie, even though it concentrates on the worst kind of human behaviour. I wouldn't say it pulls its punches, but it mostly prefers black comedy and a tongue in cheek approach. For example, a prowling, knife-wielding rapist turns out to be role-playing while the amount of nudity (one pair of tits!) that a hardcore peeping tom would surely encounter is kept disappointingly low.

Unfortunately, Schmoeller does drop the ball when it comes to *Crawlspace's* other characters. In particular, he should've gone a lot more Kubrickian on his Final Girl. A Shelley Duvall-level of exhausted horror was needed, but she's just not up to the job. Not that it matters too much when you've got Kinski. He's the whole show here, typified by the scene in which he smears on lipstick Joker-style before slipping on a peaked army cap as black and white footage of the Third Reich flickers over his manic face. "I am my own God, my own jury and my own executioner," he barks while clicking his heels together. "Heil, Gunther!"

Well, if that doesn't whet your appetite, I dunno what will.

Ridiculous Deaths

We're all gonna die.

It's a sobering thought, but we cling to the hope it'll be relatively painless and perhaps even dignified.

But what if it isn't?

What happens if you end up like one of those Pan Am passengers in the 1988 Lockerbie Bombing perched atop a Scottish roof still strapped into a seat after a 30,000-foot freefall?

Or how about that guy in Brisbane who swallowed a backyard gecko for a dare? Man, that did not turn out well. His body reacted to the bacteria in the lizard's gut, went septic, swelled up and caused an excruciating checkout, an exit so god-awful that even his balls were the size of grapefruits. I wouldn't even wish that on Billy Ray Cyrus.

In the movies we've long been treated to absurd deaths, such as the teary downfall of chief scumbag Manny Fraker in the world-class *Death Wish 3*. Bronson makes sure he'll no longer be bothering the neighbours by firing a rocket launcher at him from six feet away, a fearsome blast that sends the former gang leader out the window and smeared onto the street for rubberneckers to gawp at.

Aah, God bless the heart-warming subtleties of cinema.

Bond's blowjob

Can't say I'm a big Bond fan.

It had its place, but any franchise that staggers on for more than six decades has gotta be stretching things, you know? Much like the *Carry On* stuff, I enjoy a twenty-minute burst on TV here and there but don't feel any need to keep watching. I think the moment I turned away was during one of the latter-day flicks in which Judi Dench called Bond a 'misogynistic dinosaur'.

Fucking hell, if a fantasy figure like 007 is getting slapped down for having a good time, then movie-making really is in bad shape. How long before Bond becomes monogamous and eschews violence in a bid to shake off all that toxic masculinity? Indeed, I wouldn't be surprised if he gets turned into a Muslim and given a mission to protect the world's mosques from custard pie throwers.

Anyhow, back to the days when Bond still amused me. *Live and Let Die* was Roger Moore's debut and is best remembered as the one with the voodoo and all the blacks. A black Bond Girl, a black villain, numerous black settings (such as Harlem and the Caribbean) and basically more blacks than you could shake a stick at. A fair few people see it as racist now because it has a plethora of drug-dealers, ghetto stereotypes and generally unsavoury types. They cry: Where are all the 'good' blacks?

Yawn.

The Bond movies have always perched near the top of the commercial tree and for the franchise to feature a black-heavy cast was an enormous step forward in terms of visibility and acceptance for the brothers. I don't see how it can be interpreted any other way. *Live and Let Die* represented an overdue barrier snapping, even if it is some distance from the much better *Spy Who Loved Me*. Still, it has good moments, such as the non-Adele title song, the lengthy speedboat chase, a pincers-wielding henchman, and Bond annoying PETA by running across the backs of those alligators.

I don't think *Die* ever catches fire, though, a deficiency emphasized by its daft final scene in which Dr. Kananga (Yaphet Kotto) meets his maker after displaying the usual lackadaisical, overcomplicated attempt to dispatch Bond. This time round he winches Bond and Solitaire (Jane Seymour) over an underground pool and tries to feed them to a shark but Bond manages to escape with the aid of a super cool buzz saw watch. He gets back onto dry land and has an unconvincing tussle with the knife-holding Kananga, resulting in the pair tumbling into the water. Kananga, for some reason, feels it's necessary to not only allow Bond to put a compressed gas pellet in his mouth but to swallow it as well, even though it's about three inches long. And so he surges upward accompanied by a wet farting noise before thumping into the cavern's roof in a bloodless, offal-free explosion. A shame, as I would've quite liked to see the dull Jane Seymour smacked in the face by a length of intestines.

Cue Bond to look rakish, brush himself down and deliver the requisite one-liner: "Take that, you fucker."

Oh, all right, it was something cleverer.

Horizontal dancing twelve meters up

Australia produced hardly any horror flicks in the 1970s, but at least it took a shot at its first vampire movie in 1979. Pity *Thirst* is such a toothless, anaemic effort. It's built on an interesting idea that manages to link one of history's alleged great bitches (Elizabeth Bathory) to a clinical take on vampirism, complete with 'blood farms' and the worldwide distribution of disease-free blood. There's also the notion that conditioning can play a big part in bloodsucking, an approach that brings to mind the psychological aspect of Romero's vastly superior *Martin*.

Ultimately, *Thirst* is too slow and nonsensical to be recommended, but at least it boasts a memorably silly death in its final half an hour. One of the bad guys decides to hang onto the landing gear of a departing helicopter (does that kind of shit ever go well in the movies?) and manages to get shaken off over high-tension power lines. He crash-lands on the wires and does a terrific little jig, the weight of his sizzling, thrashing corpse eventually causing them to snap. He bangs into the ground and we get a pleasing close-up of his blackened face.

Bigfoot bollocks

Before 1979's *Prophecy*, I don't think I'd ever seen a flick in which the main character is so irrelevant that he or she could be fished out without making any difference to the storyline.

However, this cheesy, quite mad slice of eco-horror starring Rocky's missus, Talia Shire, manages just that. Her pregnancy, fear of birth defects and abortion dilemma are introduced and... don't influence events in the slightest. The poor lamb has to console herself by occasionally playing the cello in the background while waiting for *Rocky II* to get things back on track.

Instead the action concentrates on her superhero hubby confronting a pollution-created, rampaging monster in the woods. As played by Robert Foxworth, he's a paramedic, scientist and environmental warrior, the sort of busy chap who saves rat-bitten ghetto babies in New York before dashing off to a Maine forest to tackle a bunch of dastardly big business types.

Prophecy is essentially an update on all those 1950s monster movies, sharing the same nonsensical foundations. Pollution is incapable of making animals oversized and super strong just like it's impossible for radiation to create the giant ants of *Them!* Call me a spoilsport, but both contaminants simply sicken and kill whatever life forms they touch. I dunno, it's almost as if the movies plain make stuff up for the purpose of entertainment. Still, if you're prepared to put aside commonsense, the straight-faced *Prophecy* does boast a big budget, a professional gloss supplied by *Seconds* director John Frankenheimer, and lots of laughs.

The best scene arrives when we meet a family of hikers who've bedded down for the night around a campfire. Little Johnny's asleep in a bright yellow sleeping bag with the zipper all the way up to his adorable chin, but for some reason its garish colour is not enough to deter a ten-foot tall, half-insane, mutated grizzly bear. Johnny does his best, though, and upon hearing the creature's terrifying roar, he's up on his feet. Shame there's no time to unzip the bag, leaving him in the unfortunate position of trying to hop away like a giant, condom-encased stiffy awkwardly backing off from some particularly rank pussy.

Hop, hop, hop... Go on, Johnny, you brave little boy, you can do it.

Then he's caught by a massive swipe and sent hurtling through the air where he *explodes* against a boulder in a mini-blizzard of white feathers. The camera lingers as the guts of his sleeping bag poignantly drift back to earth.

This comical scene is just one of the many reasons *Prophecy* fails, but it remains a fun watch with its duck-swallowing salmon, crazed raccoons, superstitious Indians, lovely scenery, and moping, extraneous wife.

Wakey! Wakey! Hands off, snakey!

All right, that amusing catchphrase might come from a different animal-flavoured horror pic, but the unfortunate Klaus Kinski would've done well to heed such sage advice in the hokey 1981 misfire, *Venom*. He's a naughty criminal aiming to kidnap a rich kid with his girlfriend, who's already working as a maid where the animal-loving boy lives. For some reason she's decided to seduce the family's burly chauffeur and rope him in as well. Trust a woman to complicate things. Anyhow, on the day of the kidnapping (in some unlikely pet shop mix-up) a deadly black mamba is wrongly picked up by the boy and gets loose in the house...

Doesn't sound too bad a premise, does it? Indeed, I feel this flick had the potential to be a corker with a cast that includes the high-profile nutters Kinski and Oliver Reed, British sexpot Susan George, and *Godfather* and *Strangelove* veteran Sterling Hayden in his last role. Unfortunately, the expected manly fireworks between Kinski and Reed (stoked by sexual jealousy over Ms George) don't really materialize as the pic deteriorates into a stodgy siege complete with boring British Bobbies bumbling around outside.

However, we do get a couple of daft deaths. Firstly, Ollie sweats buckets when the reptile fancies a jaunt up the leg of his strides, its cloth-clad outline heading straight for his no doubt very nervous crown jewels. Much, much better is Kinski's demise, an extraordinary two-minute sequence of sustained melodrama in which he opts against the immediate application of a tourniquet or that time-honoured movie tradition of trying to suck out the poison. Now I appreciate Herr Kinski is rarely known for the subtlety of his performances, but his overblown downfall simply has to be witnessed once in a moviegoer's life.

He's negotiating with the cops from an upstairs window when our slithering serial killer sneaks up behind a curtain, understandably attracted to such a prime slice of German ham. Once bitten it's expected that Kinski screams and staggers backwards, but it's somewhat of a surprise to see him fall over, roll across the carpet, get up, wrap the mamba around an arm, hold it triumphantly above his head like a boxer's belt, run around, and thump it into a table and a chandelier. *Flail* is not the word. Maybe his energetic tantrum is simply a delayed reaction to having passed on *Raiders of the Lost Ark* to star in this turkey.

But there's really only one question left: Is he going to start using the mamba as a lasso?

Coz he sure as hell ain't finished yet.

Somehow he's managed to get entangled in a blood-stained sheet that might be a curtain, tablecloth or the fucking Shroud of Turin. Suitably adorned, he smashes through a pair of balcony doors and whacks the snake three times against an outside wall, perhaps to give the watching coppers a laugh. Then he reels back inside. Nope, hang on, he's back outside again and this time he's got a gun. He bravely shoots at the snake's tiny, black-eyed head, but misses from three inches. Well, he is full of poison. Not to mention he's heard they're already planning a sequel to *Raiders*. I guess it's hard to shoot straight when you're shaking with rage at your career choices. Never mind. It's kind of irrelevant anyway as a police sniper has just put two slugs in his chest. You'd think such a rapid ingestion of high-powered bullets would stop the manic thrashing, but Kinski's managed to up the ante again by going into what appears to be a full-blown epileptic fit. At least he finally blows the pesky snake's head off in a close-up explosion of gore before (of course) plunging to his doom off the balcony.

Phew.

And I tell you what: That snake deserved an Oscar.

Slam dunk!

Most teenage boys are on an epic quest to get laid, but *Deadly Friend's* Paul Conway puts in more effort than most. Mother-drugging, vehicle theft, trespass, body snatching and experimental brain surgery are all utilized. Why? Because Samantha, the cute girl next door, gave him a peck on the lips and now he's got grandiose dreams of moving into the big time i.e. squeezing a tit.

Paul is a short, sixteen-year-old whiz kid. He's such an egghead that he's built a naff robot on caterpillar tracks and even teaches stuff about artificial intelligence and the human brain at university. He fails the cool factor, though, by not having a girlfriend. Luckily, Samantha's drunken father is an abusive asshole who inadvertently puts his downtrodden offspring on life support. With the news the hospital is about to pull the plug, Paul is determined that his one chance of a handjob before he's twenty-five is not going to slip away...

So, of course, he sticks the Commodore 64 brain of his pet robot into Sam's cranium. What else is a backed-up teenage boy s'posed to do? For a moment it looks like an upgrade bordering on genius in that he's replaced his bright yellow, burbling nerd machine with a busty, blonde hottie who will supposedly respond to his every command.

Unfortunately, like most teenage girls, Sam's become a fucking psychopath. Her murderous instability is best illustrated by an impromptu game of basketball with a grumpy old neighbour, who'd earlier confiscated the ball. Sam breaks into her house and hurls the orb with such force that her head explodes in a geyser of blood and brains. To top things off, the shortened neighbour then staggers around the living room like the proverbial headless chicken.

Not even sure a Harlem Globetrotter could replicate a crowd-pleasing trick like that.

Paul, meanwhile, is still not getting any tit action. Some genius. What he should have done is skipped the brain surgery and instead opted for a spot of necrophilia. At least that icky shit gives guaranteed results.

Deadly Friend is a tonal mess made by horror stalwart Wes Craven. Credibility-wise, it fares even worse than his other back-from-the-dead effort, the 1985 TV movie, *Chiller* (released a year beforehand). The painfully obvious writing features characters that might as well be introduced with signs above their head such as Bad Dad, Wacky Comic Relief and Bully Who Bites Off More Than He Can Chew. It's packed with coincidences and implausibilities, as well as a wonderfully absurd turn from Kristy Swanson as Samantha. Having established she's not the best actress in the movie's opening half-hour, she proceeds to play a *robotic* version of herself complete with pincers-hands. I kept expecting her to start body popping or at least have a go at the moonwalk. Honestly, *Deadly Friend* is a far-fetched treat. At one point a criminal's bag-snatching attempt is improbably foiled by Paul's Mark 1 robot, leaving the guy to muse: "What the hell was that?"

After watching this flick, you're likely to ask the same question.

Lawnmower suicide

Taking the piss out of 2008's *The Happening* is like firing fishy bullets into a barrel full of low-hanging fruit. It's staggeringly inept and fully deserves the derision heaped upon it, although it's tricky to put your finger on *why* it goes tits up from the first scene onward. In theory, there's nothing wrong with a flick focusing on an epidemic of plant-induced suicide. Plenty of scope for intrigue, heart-pounding drama and inventive deaths, yes?

And yet when the first bunch of people starts killing themselves (in this case a load of builders leaping off a roof) it's inexplicably *funny*. More Monty Python than Eric Steel's 2006 queasy suicide-porn doco, *The Bridge*.

It doesn't help when we later see our imminent self-destructors doing a funny little half-dance before their big moment in which they freeze and then take four or five steps back. This is an attempt to generate suspense. Nails are supposed to be dug into palms while you think *Oh no, it's about to happen again!* Ditto the endless shots of soughing trees. Not scary, not even remotely atmospheric. Neither does it help that at one point some of our heroes realize the suicide germ is airborne so they try to *outrun the wind* across a field. Then there's the dialogue ("It makes you kill yourself. Just when you thought there couldn't be any more evil invented"). Casting Mark Wahlberg as a sincere, tank top-clad science teacher was also a bad move. Games teacher, yes. Something involving actual qualifications and intellectual discipline? No. Sadly, he survives (despite a kowtowing, one-sided conversation with a plastic pot plant) when he surely deserved to swallow a gecko.

Or two.

So anyway, nothing works in Shyamalan's mega-turkey (which still made money and is already on its way to becoming a cult movie). However, I am fond of a woman showing Marky Mark phone footage of a doolally bloke at a zoo who's gone for a wander in the lion enclosure. Both his arms are quickly bitten off. "Mother of God," the woman says. "What kind of terrorists are these?"

Not sure, lady, but maybe (eek!) the type that dresses up as big cats...

The feline-fuelled fatality is an entertaining scene, but *The Happening* outdoes itself around the hour mark as our dismally uncharismatic hero watches a man fire up a ride-on mower. It starts phut-phutting around the front yard. Strange time to be concerned about the lawn but wait, oh my God, he's lying down in front of its whirring blades!

Marky Mark's eyes widen. He takes a deep breath. Surely this is too surreal to be happening...?

Now the unfortunate gardener is flat on his back, one arm reaching toward his looming, petrol-driven murderer, perhaps asking for a short back and sides. Almost as cool as the T-1000 bearing down on a hapless victim in *Terminator 2*. The machine bumpily trundles over him spitting out a red mist. Christ, who needs a liquid metal, shape-shifting cyborg when you can have a riderless lawnmower doing its best to wipe out humanity at one mile per hour instead?

Creepy Shit

I s'pose there's only one time I had the shit creeped outta me.

Granddad was in a nursing home and one night we got the call that he was on the way out. I went with dad and sat in a room as death came to play. Granddad was wired, unaware of his family alongside and instead fixed on something at the foot of the bed.

I mean, whatever it was, he could *see* it.

It didn't matter how much my distraught, helpless dad tried to calm him, granddad just kept staring at this invisible entity.

Then he began mumbling. We strained to listen, the words mangled in his cracked throat, and slowly we understood he was talking to his long dead wife.

"Elsie... Elsie... I'm coming to you..."

Well, the hairs on the back of my neck stood up. Hands down, it was a seriously fucked-up few minutes, so much so that I told dad I was leaving. He nodded and returned to the thankless task of trying to get his rapidly expiring father to concentrate on Earthly connections, even if only for a moment or two.

The next morning I got up to find dad numbly doing the washing-up while staring out the kitchen window. Granddad had died not long after I'd skedaddled. Amid a minor pang of guilt, I started trying to process what I'd witnessed. Now I don't believe in fairy tales like life after death, heaven and hell, and all that other absurdity that's been designed to provide the intellectually feeble with an ego-boosting alternative to the concept of nothingness. I'm afraid I have a rather unsentimental take on things: just like a cockroach, you die and that's the end of it.

But if that's the case, then what the fuck happened in that stuffy nursing home room?

Bit by bit, I came up with an explanation. Granddad's body was shutting down after ninety odd years. His brain was going haywire. Deeply embedded images and memories were in all likelihood being dredged up and replayed, fooling his eyes into believing they were reality.

Dying, after all, must scramble your senses.

Of course, if you are a religious or spiritual type, you can still reject such a rationalization. You can still believe my granddad is once again with his wife, busy ignoring her to gamble on the horses and smoke just like he did for most of their marriage. Whatever the case, I'm at peace with accounting for his frantic final few minutes.

Then again, I haven't forgotten that creepy shit and in a strange way I treasure it. Indeed, sometimes I wish it would come back. To be that close to death, to be peering into that twilight between this world and the possibility of the next. Shit, is this why I love horror movies?

So many, of course, concentrate on gore, violence and that modern curse, the jump cut. Fair enough, but conjuring up *eeriness* takes a lot more skill, often depending on mood, lighting, characterization, understated dialogue, nuance and camera angles. Now don't go thinking I'm gonna say the following flicks evoke the same sort of granddad-perishing strangeness I once experienced. Please don't think I'm *that* trite. However, I will say these movies are best watched on your own in an unfamiliar, darkened room with volleys of rain pellets occasionally rattling the windows.

Les Diaboliques (1955)

"What we need to be is very calm," one female teacher says while gripping her colleague's shoulders at a rundown Parisian boarding school. "Calm and coldblooded."

Cripes, what are they planning?

Murder, as it happens. Murder of an abusive, philandering headmaster who happens to be both husband and lover to the two Machiavellian femmes. "Kindness is a waste of time to you," he says to his divorce-demanding wife, underlining his point by doling out a couple of backhanders. This man is such a pig he even serves rotten food to the school kids to save a bit of cash.

Hmm, guess doing away with him is all right, then.

Now they say the road to hell is paved with the best intentions, but I reckon most of it must be paved with the *worst* intentions. And this possibility of eternal damnation is a very real one for the delicate Catholic, Christina (Vera Clouzot). Will she go through with the diabolical plan?

The creepiness of the celebrated and influential *Les Diaboliques* doesn't kick in until the last ten minutes, but it's worth the wait. Indeed, it leads to one of the all-time great endings before immediately fumbling it.

Oh, well.

Eyes without a Face AKA *The Horror Chamber of Dr. Faustus* (1960)

"I'll succeed," a renowned Parisian doctor tenderly tells his mask-clad daughter. "I promise you."

But at what?

We already know big trouble's afoot as the opening of this black and white classic has shown a corpse being dumped into a river. Then the obviously preoccupied doctor delivers a lecture on the latest development in skin grafts before popping off to the morgue to identify his missing daughter's remains.

But, hang on, if that corpse fished out of the Seine really is his daughter, who's the chick he's making promises to?

It's clear there's something not quite right about this Dr. Genessier (Pierre Brasseur). Barrel-chested and overly serious, he's also a bit stiff and standoffish. Arrogant, you might say. Soon we learn he has a private operating theatre at his secluded villa. That can't be good. Bit by bit, we see he's a single-minded man, driven by a toxic mixture of love and guilt, but not lacking in self-awareness or humanity. He is determined to put things right, though.

Even if that means making everything worse.

This is classy stuff, Grand Guignol at its finest. Check out *Face's* memorable atmosphere, all tolling church bells, cawing crows, moonlit graveyards and howling dogs. Then there's the carefully chosen victims lured to their doom, gruesome surgery, profound anguish and torment, and a prowling, birdlike woman living in a beautiful, mirror-free cage. If I had to make a criticism, I'd point to the occasionally jaunty and twee score not matching *Face's* creepy ambiance and poetic visuals. Otherwise, this is a great horror pic built on fascinating subject matter. The last few scenes are outstanding.

The City of the Dead AKA Horror Hotel (1960)

A key witch movie, this one features a young, lean, bird-killing Christopher Lee, bursts of *Omen*-style choral music, and an unexpected development that makes *Psycho* look rather less daring after all.

Nan Barlow (an alluring Venetia Stevenson) is an inquisitive history student determined to get a good grade on a term paper by doing some firsthand witchcraft research. She travels to Whitewood, a Massachusetts village with a history of burning witches, and checks into The Raven's Inn.

Not the best move as it turns out.

For a start it's next to a disused graveyard that contains the bodies of executed witches lying in unconsecrated ground. Secondly, it's run by the cold, black-clad Mrs. Newless (Patricia Jessel), a landlady whom you can bet won't be telling any jokes.

Asked what to do in town, Mrs. Newless replies: "I think you will find the church interesting. Unfortunately, it no longer has a congregation."

Now there's an understatement. It does have a reverend, though. He's an elderly, cane-tapping blind man who couldn't be more pessimistic about Whitewood's predicament. For this is a Godforsaken place where 'time stands still'.

City of the Dead is a short, briskly-paced flick with gleaming black and white photography. Whitewood's wooden buildings, loudly ticking clocks, rudely staring locals, mysterious hooded figures, disappearing hitchers and fog-shrouded streets are convincingly conjured up and linger in the memory.

It also has a nice sense of repetition, as if events have been playing out the same way for centuries, like some kind of satanic Groundhog Day.

The Innocents (1961)

This is such a goddamned classy movie with its great photography and evocative atmosphere that someone as grubby and lowbrow as me shouldn't even be allowed to watch it in the first place, let alone review it.

Deborah Kerr plays Miss Giddens, a 19th century mildly neurotic Christian governess who also happens to be 'a damned hussy, a damned dirty-minded hag'.

Well, that seems a bit harsh, but one thing's for sure: there's something not quite right with the genteel picture she presents. On the surface she's polite, sincere, and dedicated to looking after the two young children in her care at an isolated country estate. *Prim and proper*, I think is the phrase, but after five minutes in her company, you suspect deep down she's gagging for it.

Bit by bit she becomes fascinated by her immediate predecessor, Miss Jessel, a woman who got tangled up in a doomed, sadomasochistic affair with another employee, Quint. Giddens demands salacious details from the kindly housekeeper, details that reveal the cruel man died in a drunken accident before the heartbroken woman drowned herself.

"There are things I've seen I'm ashamed to say..." the blushing housekeeper divulges. "Rooms used by daylight as though they were dark woods... I don't know what the children saw, but they used to follow Quint and Miss Jessel, trailing behind hand in hand, whispering..."

Miss Giddens is transfixed by the sordid revelations, obviously wanting to vicariously wallow in such alien passions. She's desperate to know how Miss

Jessel was "hungry for him, hungry for his lips" as her panties start to smoulder.

But surely it's too much to suppose the children are now possessed by the pair's troubled spirits so they can continue their abusive sexual union?

For Miss Giddens this 'sickness' is one mighty puzzle, but she needs answers when it comes to the way her charges are now behaving. She might know diddly squat about hiding the sausage, but she does understand that a child under ten shouldn't be pashing her during a bedtime kiss. Or as he chirps: "Good children can be a bit boring."

This is a great hundred minutes of Victorian creepiness, a flick filled with billowing net curtains, foreboding candlelit wanderings along corridors, strange nocturnal animal cries, erotic dreams, distant apparitions appearing during bursts of sudden silence, and two angelic-looking children who like to watch butterflies get eaten by spiders before hurling tortoises through windows.

The children, played by Pamela Franklin and Martin Stephens, are superb, effortlessly creating the impression of telepathy amid a secretive, vaguely sinister world of play. Franklin later turned up half-naked in another haunted house flick, the brooding, well-directed but weakly written *Legend of Hell House*, in which the reason for the supernatural shenanigans would have to be the barmiest ever put on film.

Repulsion (1965)

As you can tell from *The Innocents*, I find repressed female sexuality fascinating. I just love the way some women are buttoned down so tightly that one day all those bottled-up but undeniable juices will start leaking, if not spurting out, in weird, unpredictable ways.

Carol Ledoux (Catherine Deneuve) is a prime example. She's a demure Belgian beautician working in London and the whole notion of women's lib is passing her by. She's not standing up for her rights or burning her bra. Nor is she enjoying any newfound sexual freedoms in the swinging sixties.

In fact, just like Miss Giddens, she's a virgin and likely to remain one for a long, long time. She's not only withdrawn, but often in a world of her own, a world in which men are most definitely barred.

Her older sister Helen (Yvonne Furneaux), however, is a lot more liberated. They share a flat, but the regular visits of Helen's boyfriend are a bone(r) of contention. For a start, he keeps leaving his toothbrush in her glass, as if that has some sexual symbolism. Then she has to listen to their lovemaking in the next room, excited nocturnal noises that make Carol chew her hair and clench her hands.

"I don't think Cinderella likes me," is the mocking boyfriend's verdict, but at least he suspects something is wrong.

Out in the street Carol fares no better. A leering, vest-clad layabout greets her with the slightly non-PC: "Hello, darling, how about a bit of the other then?" Meanwhile, a potential boyfriend is doing his best to get past her resolute defences. He's a nice guy, bewildered by her constant rebuffs. At one point he's amazingly permitted a chaste kiss, but it's an experience akin to pressing his closed lips against a mannequin. Plus, it doesn't exactly have the desired effect on Carol as it only makes her dash into her home and furiously clean her teeth.

The message is clear: men are dirty and must be avoided.

Even at work she gets lectured about the opposite sex. In one fantastic image she's standing at the head of a supine customer, her vision fixed on the middle-aged woman's upside-down mouth. "There's only one way to deal with men and that's treat them as if you don't give a damn about them," the customer tells her. "There's only one thing they want and I'll never know why they make such a fuss about it, but they do, and the more you make them beg for it the happier they are. They're all the same, just like children. They wanna be spanked and then given sweets."

It's all too much for the fragile Carol, especially when her sister takes a two-week holiday with the boyfriend and leaves her alone in the apartment. Beforehand she'd already been weirdly staring at her reflection on the kettle and brushing invisible things off her clothes, but now she sees cracks splintering the walls. Best of all is the way she hesitantly picks up her sister's discarded, post-coital slip off the bathroom floor and starts sniffing it. She then throws up, a marvellous moment that perfectly captures her fascination and revulsion with sex. You can tell this is seriously strange behaviour because any normal person would simply put their sister's underwear on and dance around in it.

Polanski's first great movie is a queasy, increasingly claustrophobic portrait of mental breakdown. It's rife with brilliantly staged hallucinations and paranoia, but is also notable for its withering depiction of men. Some idiots claim *Thelma and Louise* is an anti-men paean, but *Repulsion* is a much more convincing example of misandry.

And I love it.

Every man bar one is a sexist, sleazy, abusive pig whether they're propositioning Carol on the street, demanding sex in lieu of rent, or phoning her up to do the heavy breathing thing. Even if they're *absent*, they're still horrible. The great thing about *Repulsion*, though, is you don't peg Carol for the violent type, chiefly because of her ethereal beauty and downcast eyes. There's nothing in her behaviour, language or attitude to suggest she's capable of going to town on all those beastly men with a cut-throat razor. Deneuve is bloody tremendous and puts in a hypnotic shift in what I would label a textbook example of the Strong Female Role.

And remember: if you fancy a girl and happen to notice she's carrying a severed rabbit's head in her handbag, try to date her sister instead.

Don't Look Now (1973)

How many horror movies have been set in Venice?

Not enough is my bet, but I doubt any have made such great use of its location as this one. It's a wintry, shadowy place filled with crumbling brickwork, swimming rats, rust-stained balconies, labyrinthine alleyways, tolling church bells, flocks of fluttering pigeons, and of course, a diminutive, red-clad, scurrying figure.

Or as a blind psychic tells the grieving John Baxter (Donald Sutherland): "It's like a city in aspic left over from a dinner party and all the guests are dead and gone."

Now psychics happen to be one of my pet hates. They're revolting, bullshit-pedalling attention seekers, but I've no problem with them spouting their spooky bullshit in moviedom. Here we get one telling John's wife Laura (a ravishing Julie Christie) that she can see their 'happy' daughter sitting right next to them, even though the poor tyke has already drowned in a pond back in England.

There's more, though. The sceptical John needs to get out of the Italian city. Bad shit is coming. But he's obstinate, telling Laura: "My daughter is dead. She does not come peeping with messages back from behind the fucking grave."

With its premonitions, near-death experiences, and emphasis on water, breaking glass and the colour red, *Don't Look Now* has a strange, cumulative power that rewards repeated viewings.

The Stepford Wives (1975)

I know it's odd, but sometimes I get the impression I'm supposed to condemn this flick's serene goings on.

But why would anyone *tut-tut* that pan-scrubbing haven, Stepford? Men and women get on famously. There's neither domestic abuse nor even the slightest hint of an argument. It's just relentless pleasantness and fantastic sex. When that disruptive newcomer Joanna Eberhart (Katharine Ross) tries to get the resident ladies to focus on stuff other than shopping, keeping their houses spotless and pleasing their men folk, one replies: "I'm sorry to disappoint you, but I'm happy."

Stepford, you see, is a byword for *harmony*. The fact this harmony is built on murder and robotic doppelgangers just strikes me as nitpicking. I'd move there in a shot.

The Stepford Wives is based on Ira Levin's readable, but very short novel. It repeats his *Rosemary's Baby* trick of having a lone woman threatened by a sinister group after being betrayed by a weak, corrupt man who supposedly loves her. To be honest, although I enjoyed it, the book's details are so understated that it feels like a sketch. The movie improves things because it takes Levin's brilliantly subversive idea (cooked up during the height of feminism) and fleshes it out in a much more satisfying manner.

Still, its first half doesn't offer a lot to creep Joanna (or the viewer) out. It's just her womanly intuition has started to growl in the pit of her lovely, taut stomach. When she attends a lawn party and looks at the gorgeous surroundings and sumptuous display of food, she says: "I like it. It's perfect. How could you not like it? I just don't like it. Does that make any sense?"

Matters aren't helped by contact with the quietly unsettling members of Stepford's Men's Association. Or as one tells her while she fills the kettle: "I like to watch women do the little domestic chores."

The worrying signs feeding her paranoia keep building and it's great how a clean kitchen or a bulldozed tennis court can speak volumes about the looming threat to her identity, her very *existence*. "I just know something's wrong and my time is coming," she blurts out to a shrink.

Will Joanna survive? This is a slow-burning pic that eventually gets where it wants to go. To be sure, the final twenty minutes take place on a stormy night and offer a delightfully creepy soak.

Fantastic coda, too.

Invasion of the Body Snatchers (1978)

1978 proved a bumper year for creepy shit with the likes of *Coma* and *Long Weekend*. The creepiest of the lot, though, was Philip Kaufman's bloody brilliant sci-fi remake of the 50s classic... Oh boy, I love this one.

It's a movie in which a sinister vibe is often generated by the simplest things like a face pressed against a window, an office cleaner polishing the floor, or the mere act of falling asleep in a favourite outdoor chair. One by one San Francisco's residents are catching 'hallucinatory flu', resulting in loved ones becoming automatons. They're recognizable, all right, yet *unrecognizable*. The complaints and growing unease run along the lines of "Geoffrey is not Geoffrey" and "That not my wife." Suddenly it's a city full of secretive gestures, meaningful eye contact, clandestine meetings with strangers, and mysterious pods. Life's become so weird it's even got a cameo from Robert Duvall as a silent, staring priest not having any fun at all on a child's swing. And we haven't even got to the bit where a dog with a man's head is running around.

Donald Sutherland plays a none too popular public health inspector, which seems fair enough given his double crime of tash and perm. He's half in love with the delectable Brooke Adams, who tells him: "I keep seeing these people all recognizing each other. Something is passing between them all, something secret." Slowly the two of them begin to grasp what's going on, determined to resist ending up in the back of a garbage truck before being 'born again into an untroubled world' free of anxiety, fear, hate and anything resembling humanity.

Kaufman sets up his camera so that he seems to be surreptitiously watching events, if not *spying* on people. Then there's his fondness for distorted reflections or seeing things from behind a shattered windscreen. Something's not quite right with the pictures he's showing us, as if they've gone rotten underneath. It's fantastic stuff, and he holds his nerve right through to the brilliant ending.

The Sixth Sense (1999)

What to make of M. Night Shyamalan?

He's the modern day Tobe Hooper, a man who came up with an iconic, monstrously successful flick early on before spending the rest of his career exemplifying the law of diminishing returns. And, of course, I'll retract that assessment of Hooper if the lingering suspicion that Spielberg actually directed *Poltergeist* ever goes away.

But Mr. Shyamalan?

Despite his powerful imagination, he can't buy a good movie for love nor money. Still, as I've always said, I don't care if the bulk of an artist's work is below par or hopeless. Why focus on the negative if someone has given you one great thing? Celebrate its existence, I say, and be grateful for that artist's birth. You can scoff at *The Happening's* plant-based lunacy all you like, but *The Sixth Sense* remains a sublime achievement and it's hard to see Shyamalan ever topping it.

For a start (and you may have forgotten this) but Bruce Willis used to be a Genuine Movie Star. He's superb here, giving an understated, quip-free, and deeply melancholy performance that's devoid of smirking sarcasm and macho bullshit. Indeed, his only Brucey moment arrives when he mutters (unheard) to a potential love rival: "Keep moving, cheese dick."

Aah, poor Bruce. Perhaps (like me) he lost all his powers after losing his hair.

Anyway, *Sixth Sense* is a marvellously clever flick, much more so than its forerunners that include the initially decent *Dead and Buried* (1981), the admirably creepy *Carnival of Souls* (1962) and the terrific *Twilight Zone* episode *An Occurrence at Owl Creek Bridge*.

Shyamalan's re-tweak centres on Cole Sear (Haley Joel Osment), a nine-year-old boy who can see dead people. Apart from rendering him regularly terrified, this unnerving ability is also undermining his relationships, especially the one with his doting mum (Toni Collette). The last thing he wants is for her to regard him as a 'freak', but that's tricky when he draws pictures of people getting stabbed in the neck with a screwdriver. Then there's school in which a teacher's most innocuous question can lead to the little rascal scaring everyone by talking about mass hangings.

This is a movie about loss and the acceptance of that loss. "Sometimes people think they lose things," Cole says, "but they just get moved." There's an autumnal mood throughout, punctuated by some nicely judged shocks. Mainly though, Shyamalan adopts a subtle approach through his use of moving shadows, a disappearing palm print, a reflection in a polished doorknob, a thermometer showing the temperature falling, clothes pegs that snap open by themselves, and some strange *Omen*-style marks on a bunch of photos. It's a triumph of sustained eeriness. Or as Cole says: "You ever feel the prickly things on the back of your neck?"

The Others (2001)

Illustrating there's still spooky life in the old haunted house clichés, *The Others* is an intelligently written, smartly acted horror flick that also has the decency to show Catholicism's an excellent method for filling children's heads with poisonous shit.

I'm not much of a Nicole Kidman fan and can't think of any movie I want to see less than that Oscar-winning one where she dons the big nose, but I wouldn't deny her talent here. Pale, willowy and neurotic, she gives the impression of always being a few heartbeats away from a controlling outburst or full-blown hysteria. You know she loves her kids, but you can also tell it's a fucked-up kind of obsession.

"My children sometimes have strange ideas," she tells her new housekeeper in 1945 Jersey, "but you mustn't pay any attention to them."

Hmm, we'll see...

Set almost entirely within a gothic mansion, *The Others* creates a world of darkened corners, mute servants, foreboding dialogue, self-playing pianos, mocking whispers, slamming doors, overhead footsteps on hardwood floors, and misty, leaf-covered grounds that contain gnarled trees and a small, private cemetery. It's the sort of isolated, uncanny place where a long-missing husband can emerge out of the fog clutching his army kitbag.

The new housekeeper is obviously kind and patient, enduring her employer's brittle, unpredictable behaviour with barely a murmur of protest. However, she also appears to be trying to pass on something profound. "I think that sometimes the world of the dead gets mixed up with the world of the living," she says.

The Others is like *The Sixth Sense* in many regards, especially the way it also boasts excellent child performances. If you want to be picky about both flicks, you could argue they spell things out too clearly, but that's probably being a bit harsh, and I find them highly rewatchable. I like how *The Others* is infused with religious babble, photos of the dead, intense yearning, the pain of loss, echoes of a recently finished war, the lingering threat of disease, and a hell-bent refusal to cede territory.

Hey, who knows? Maybe one day I'll get to see it with granddad.

Fucked-Up Films #3: I Spit on Your Grave (1978)

Synopsis

Woman 4 Men 1

Director

Meir Zarchi

Cast

Camille Keaton, Eron Taber, Richard Pace, Anthony Nichols, Gunter Kleemann

What are these sick bastards doing? Bored by the prospect of going bowling yet again and the lack of choice at the local cinema, four men in rural Connecticut plump for a bit of fishing.

Oh, and rape. Lots and lots of rape.

How skuzzy are the men? Matthew's a camp, bespectacled half-idiot only good for delivering groceries on a pushbike while Stanley and Andy are bare-chested, jobless layabouts. Well, perhaps I'm selling Andy a bit short as he has learned to play the harmonica. In comparison, the group's de facto leader, Johnny, is a roaring success. He's a married father of two who runs a gas station.

During the aforementioned fishing trip, conversation runs along the lines of whether attractive women do indeed take a shit. Stanley's confident he can settle such a delicate matter. "Hey, all women shit," he says. "Women are full of shit."

Case closed, me thinks.

Stanley hasn't finished, though. Bolstered by having just outwitted a small fish, he's keen to share yet more wisdom. "One day I'm gonna go to New York

135

and fuck all the broads there," he says. In an instant, his optimism about the opposite sex has become contagious. "Yeah," Andy pipes up, "I'm gonna do the same in California."

Surprisingly, things don't pan out that way, especially after Johnny decides it's time to help 'fix up' the virginal Matthew with a broad.

And I think we all know what that involves.

How do the lovely ladies fare? Jennifer (Keaton) is a beautiful, willowy New Yorker who publishes short stories in women's magazines. She's rented a riverside cottage during the summer to write her first novel. She's obviously a nice person and treats people well. When she meets the groceries-delivering Matthew there's nothing condescending in her attitude toward his disability and she even gives him a sizeable tip.

In other words, she meets the stock requirement of such a movie: she's an innocent.

Still, it's tricky to think of another flick which puts its heroine through the wringer as nastily as *Spit*. She not only has her bikini torn off, but is repeatedly called a bitch and slut. She's kicked, punched, raped at least three times, and violated with a whiskey bottle ("That's what I like in a woman," Stanley tells her. "Total submission.") Her fledgling attempt at a novel is then mockingly read aloud before being torn to shreds. It's only gross incompetence and rank cowardice that prevents her murder.

Curiously, Jennifer never considers going to the cops, even though she knows her attackers and where they can be found. She doesn't talk to any friends about her ordeal. Instead she lets herself physically heal, dons a black outfit and goes to church. As an organist plays, she kneels between the empty pews beneath a giant wooden crucifix, crosses herself, and asks for forgiveness.

She's asking for forgiveness? *Uh-oh*, I think more trouble's afoot.

Would the violence make a vicar faint? No reputable tea-drinking vicar would be able to get through his cucumber sandwiches during this one. Perhaps elderly imams, who charmingly labelled Bengali women 'war booty' from their mosques in Pakistan during the genocidal rapes of the 1971 Bangladesh Liberation War, might like it, though.

Apart from the graphic sexual violence, we also get a hanging, a castration, an axe in the back and an underwater disembowelment. The special effects, particularly the first spurt of blood during the castration, are impressive.

Groovy.

How fucked-up is this film? Rape fantasies are common, although, of course, none of us are going to admit that. Still, whether you're a man or woman, there's a massive difference between fantasizing about rape and actually wanting or trying to make it happen. I would suggest the brilliantly titled *Spit* taps into such fantasies and that might partly explain the way this movie has not only endured, but produced sequels and a 2010 remake. There's a *demand* for such exploitative fare, you see. Even so, most so-called video nasties have faded into the obscurity they deserve. Why? Because they're boring and inept. *Spit*, however, is nicely paced, creates tension and is more than capable of generating heated debate. It's certainly outlived its chief detractor, Roger Ebert, while its notorious reputation as the video nasty *par excellence* remains undimmed after nearly half a century.

It's the ultimate rape-revenger.

Still, after watching Jennifer's 25-minute degradation it's hard to walk away and think anything other than rape's a Really Bad Thing. *Spit* does get this across well. There's no blurry *Straw Dogs*-style ambiguity that she's enjoying it because this is what a woman secretly wants. It's a gruelling watch and if it turns you on then you've got some issues. I must admit I was quite pleased I experienced no trouser stirrings. There's hope yet I can form a mature relationship with a female.

The rape does go on for too long, though. It reminded me of the feeling I got while watching that Jew-hating piece of Christian propaganda, *The Passion of the Christ*. From memory about half that flick concentrated on beating the living shit out of a deluded man. Now I'm all for violence and a bit of rape in my movies, but I don't want to watch someone being degraded for the best part of *half a fucking hour*. Hitting the same note is never a good idea. Just give me a few lackadaisical minutes of abuse and I'm happy. In short, *Passion* takes all the fun out of violence while *Spit* does the same with rape. Bloody hell, I can't believe I just made a rape joke. As *Blazing Saddles* proved with its *I like rape* bon mot, that sort of thing is never funny. Even if it does make you laugh.

Saying that, I was surprised upon my second viewing by how well Zarchi's low-budget directorial debut has lodged in my memory. Perhaps that's because it's a fair bit better than its (often rabid) critics give it credit for.

Yes, the audio sucks, but the direction is more than competent. Zarchi is capable of coming up with some striking images. Look at the well-composed shot amid tree trunks of Jennifer draped face-down over a large rock as her rapists depart. I also like the scene following the castration in which Jennifer dons a sheer white gown, sits in a rocking chair, and listens to opera with a faraway look in her eyes as her victim screams in the locked bathroom that he can't stop the bleeding. Then there's the image of her on the sun-dappled river powering forward in a speedboat with its bow in the air as she holds an axe above her head zeroing in on a hapless victim. Indeed, Zarchi does well in repeatedly using the motorboat's ugly engine noise to convey disturbance in the natural equilibrium.

As for the cast, I guess the mildly retarded Matthew is a troubling aspect, especially as it could be argued he's also a victim. He's initially none too keen to dip his wick and even helps Jennifer to her feet after the first rape. Still, the coercing of a gang member into rape does seem a staple for this kind of flick (see *Savage Streets*). He's continually taunted with stuff like: "Wanna be a man, don't-cha?" Despite becoming a rapist, it's not enough to save him from the group's ongoing contempt and you can understand why he later tells Jennifer: "You brought nothing but bad luck with you."

Acting-wise, the four yokels do OK. Tabor comes out best as the gang leader. He manages to capture a sense of casual cruelty quite well, especially when he walks toward Jennifer's bloody and battered form blowing his nose. He's into the whole victim-blaming thing, insisting her provocative dress sense was the reason for everything. *Spit* is not big on humour, but I must admit I laughed aloud when she later orders him to strip at gunpoint and he blurts out: "You don't have to force me."

However, has an actress ever put in a braver shift than Keaton? She's pretty damn good here, using her eyes to convey a strong sense of numbed rage, particularly after the first rape in which she wanders naked and mud-spattered through the woods accompanied by birdsong. I'm less sure about her continued nudity after the rapes. It's pretty screwy (and not very believable) how she engages her pussy to lure at least half of the gang to their doom. The experience of playing a rape victim obviously didn't bother her too much, though, as she not only married the director but was back playing the same in the little seen *Savage Vengeance* a few years later.

Now I wouldn't go thinking there's any point to this movie, apart from illustrating through its starkly simplistic approach and the refrain 'Suck it, bitch!' that violence begets violence. Perhaps that's enough to justify its existence so I would recommend seeing it once. Yes, it's a visceral, deflating experience and I sincerely doubt any rape victims have ever behaved like this in real life, but *Spit* does have that certain quality of *je ne sais quoi* to it.

On a final note, I did know a rape victim in the days before mobile phones. She was a colleague and her five-year relationship with her boyfriend was breaking down, partly because she planned to move to the other side of the country to pursue a new career. We became friendly and she spent the night at my place, although very little happened. Problem was, she hadn't told anyone where she was, leaving her conservative parents frantically ringing around everyone they knew. Once she got home, all hell broke loose with the boyfriend delivering his jealous verdict by fucking her up the arse a day or so later. I had no idea any of this had happened until she came back to see me. She said the boyfriend had always wanted anal sex but she never had. As for her immediate plans, she had no intention of reporting the crime and just wanted to focus on her new job, especially as her parents were fond of the ex-boyfriend. Of the rape she said: "Nothing prepares you for the terror of it."

As you can tell, I've never forgotten those words.

Early Days

I've met a handful of folk who insist old movies are boring. They don't like stuff from cinema's greatest decade, the 1970s, because it's slow or the special effects aren't as good or the hairdos are silly. Anyhow, after I've stabbed these ignoramuses and they've begun to recover from the shock, I make them a nice cup of tea, bring out the Kit Kats and gently explain why they're wrong.

Take something like 2018's *Ready Player One*. It might be technically impressive, but it's a frantic, soulless pastiche that feeds off the past. It's not so much a movie as a series of fast-moving images strung together, the equivalent of watching a computer game being played. Put simply, it is not an upgrade on *Raiders of the Lost Ark*.

But old movies...?

Aah, now we're talking. Old movies, you see, have *verve*. They're also free of the artistically crippling taint of political correctness. What's more, by having some knowledge of 20th century flicks, it provides context and enables a viewer to judge things like originality, merit and influence. Hence, it's handy to know where and when cinematic staples originated.

Old is good, I get my recently punctured acquaintances to repeat as we mop up any remaining blood. *Old is good*. Oh yes, that's a fine mantra to live by, especially when settling back to enjoy a blowey from a toothless, geriatric hooker as the opening credits of something like *Network*, *Wages of Fear* or *Double Indemnity* unfold.

Flesh-eating Zombies

Hammer Films broke new ground with 1957's massively successful *The Curse of Frankenstein* by showing the monster not only getting shot in the face, but bright red blood spurting out from behind its raised hands. Horror movies had just got *gory* and from that moment on they only got gorier.

142

Alas, innovation like that proved increasingly hard for the studio to come by, despite churning out four or five flicks a year through the sixties. Now I certainly enjoy some of these, such as the kiddie-fiddling *Never Take Sweets from a Stranger* and that monumental badass bitch in *She*. However, too often Hammer got stuck in a rut, exemplified by a bored-looking Christopher Lee shoving plastic fangs into his gob every couple of years. Eventually Hammer tried updating their approach with topless lipstick lesbos and some piss poor kung-fu. It didn't work and the blood-smeared writing was on the wall. Hammer could no longer cut it and by the time things reached their cheesy nadir with *Dracula A.D. 1972*, most horror fans were sick of the vampire obsession, the rubbery bats, the fake-looking blood, the lack of chills and the desperately tired scripts.

A shame, really.

Take 1966's *Plague of the Zombies*, the first time Hammer did a zombie flick. Here the zombies are used as slave labour in a Cornish tin mine, rather than hunting down the locals and pulling out their guts to munch on. It's among Hammer's better efforts in that it has some handsome production values, a certain amount of imagination and three or four decent scenes. Still, it was only a small, voodoo-tinged step in the right direction and not enough to save the company's fading fortunes. Of course, hindsight is a wonderful thing, but it was up to the father of the modern zombie movie, George Romero, to give the undead a much-needed kick up the arse. With *Night of the Living Dead*, he rudely grabbed hold of a minor sub-genre and took it in an exciting new direction, delivering a death blow (compounded by the polished class of Polanski's *Rosemary's Baby*) to Hammer's future. It's arguably one of the most influential films of all time and it'd be interesting to know how many moviemakers have fed off its rotting carcass.

Saying that, *Night* is not perfect. Despite its groovy, non-bloody graveyard opening ("They're coming to get you, Barbra!"), it sags in the middle and the score's not up to snuff. However, such criticisms are small potatoes next to its strengths, such as the eerie monochrome photography, a pioneering black hero, a nude female zombie, the introductory concept of a contagious bite, a more pronounced sense of danger, and a worried newsreader announcing at the forty-minute mark: "Murder victims show evidence of having been... partially devoured by their murderers."

New ground, all right.

Despite the paltry two-year gap between *Plague* and *Night*, Hammer's effort feels staid, especially when the latter kicks into life with its final twenty-five minutes of offal-gnawing nastiness. It's deeply unsentimental stuff, typified by the zombified kid finishing off both parents, as well as that abrupt ending ("That's another one for the fire.")

Night may have depicted Yanks saving the day through their pronounced gun fetish, happily banding together to blow holes in heads, but a new breed of zombie was up and running.

Or shuffling, anyway.

The Gangster's Rise and Fall

It's not unusual to stumble across best gangster movie lists that include 1931's *Little Caesar*.

Hmm, don't think so. It's a pre-Code turkey that manages to be both stilted and hammy.

I think cinephiles speak up for it because of the failure to appreciate the difference between a historically significant flick and a fucking good one. *Little Caesar* is the former, but something like 1971's *Get Carter* is the latter. *Caesar* is noteworthy because it was the first to offer the structure that the likes of Michael Corleone and Tony Montana were doomed to follow, but its simplistic writing and woeful acting are embarrassing.

The pocket-sized Edward G. Robinson plays our cuddly hero, Rico, a small-time hood going nowhere with his more arts-inclined buddy, Joe (Douglas Fairbanks). Rico's got a case of Napoleon complex, though. "Money's all right, but it ain't everything," he tells Joe as they sit in a diner dreaming of the big time. "Be somebody. Look hard at a bunch of guys and know they'll do anything you tell 'em. Have your own way or nothing. Be somebody!"

Well, fine, no problem, but during the next Chicago-set couple of scenes Rico waltzes into the main gang (despite no one bothering to check him out) while Joe is busy *dancing* at a club and falling in love. For fuck's sake, have you ever known a gangster flick in which one of the main tough guys is torn between packing heat and mincing around on stage with a girly?

Now I like Mr. Robinson, but he's as unconvincing here as everyone else. He's supposedly the ambitious, snarling, trigger-happy type, but I never bought it for a second. Whereas shortasses like James Cagney and Joe Pesci were able to convince me they were out and out nutters in *White Heat* and *Goodfellas*, Robinson never does. In fact, he carries on like a petulant teenager with a gun. I just wanted to smack his little botty and send him to his room without supper.

Old is good? What idiot said that?

Redneck Hillbilly Scum

Deliverance certainly wasn't the first flick to depict civilized city dwellers encountering unfriendly rural locals. Off the top of my head, I can think of a one-armed Spencer Tracy stepping from a train at an isolated spot in 1955's *Bad Day at Black Rock*. However, John Boorman's magnificent survival thriller did define a certain kind of deranged backwoods fuck. You know, the sort of guy who thinks he looks good in dungarees, distils brain-eroding moonshine, perves on his sisters, humps whatever four-legged animals are in the vicinity, and votes Republican. You can draw a straight line from *Deliverance* through *Texas Chainsaw*, *The Hills Have Eyes*, *Rituals*, *I Spit on Your Grave*, *Southern Comfort*, *Cabin Fever*, and even Aussie and British stuff like *Wolf Creek* and *Eden Lake*. Such is *Deliverance's* monumental influence, it's clear that line is going to keep being drawn for a long time yet.

Four Atlanta businessmen plan a canoe trip along a soon-to-be-dammed Georgian river. "There any hillbillies up here?" the not very likable Bobby

(Ned Beatty) asks during the opening credits as their cars slink around a dirt road's bends.

"Yeah, there's people up here ain't never seen a town before," Lewis (Burt Reynolds) replies. "Those woods are real deep."

Stopping to get gas and arrange for their cars to be driven to a rendezvous point, we soon realize how patronizing if not outright prejudiced Bobby is. Surveying the shacks and surrounding piles of junk, he says they may have arrived at 'the end of the line'. There's no other way of interpreting this than as meaning the end of civilization, prompting Drew (Ronny Cox) to warn him not to upset 'these people'.

But 'chubby boy' Bobby hasn't finished. "People...?" he shrugs. "Talk about genetic deficiencies..."

His mate Ed (Jon Voigt) is a lot more cautious. In fact, he already seems to have the heebie-jeebies. "Let's go back to town and play golf," he suggests.

Not that the suspicion and contempt isn't replicated. These hillbilly types don't exactly roll out the red carpet for their urban visitors. Comments from the less than friendly natives include "You don't know nothing", "What the hell you wanna fuck around with that river for?" and the obviously scornful refrain "City boy".

The Duelling Banjos sequence is, of course, legendary, although I'm not sure you'd get away with it today. The intellectually-challenged must be portrayed in a positive light these days whereas Banjo Boy is one quietly sinister fucker. With his slit eyes, weird young/old face and remarkably blank expression, he's the last sort of beau you'd want your daughter to bring home. The musical interchange, however, is brilliant at capturing a spontaneous but deceptive moment of connection within a chasm. Once the duel is over, Banjo Boy refuses a handshake, looks away and doesn't want to play another.

Apparent solid ground has just collapsed.

Later he's seen gazing down at the canoeists from a wooden bridge. Drew waves and indicates for him to start strumming again, but it's like they've never met. Instead Banjo Boy keeps staring, the unused banjo left to dangle near his no doubt six-toed feet. It simply isn't possible to have the slightest idea what's going on in that cuckoo's head.

Then there's the rape scene, one of the most memorable episodes in American cinema. The two sweaty hillbillies are fantastic villains with their chillingly loaded glances, obscene threats and god-awful teeth. Both are so convincing you really buy into their inbred, borderline insanity. It's also fascinating how they see Bobby as a female, firstly ordering him to take his 'panties' off and calling him a 'sow'. Still, it takes two to tango for a scene to emblazon itself upon memory, and Bobby is a brilliant victim. Just look at the mounting fear in his eyes as one of his unshaven suitors casually reaches out to stroke his jowly, anxiety-ridden face. Then there's his cluelessness concerning what's going to happen, even after being ordered to drop his pants. "What's this all about?" we hear him ask. It's a fair question because their amorous intent is so far off his radar that it wouldn't even form part of a nightmare, an uncertainty undoubtedly matched by the average viewer in 1972.

The hillbilly as scary motherfucker had arrived.

The Urban Vigilante

Before Bickle, before Kersey, there was... Joe.

Who's he? A big, bald bloke who hates blacks, dole scroungers, commies, gays, hippies and 'nigger lovers'. Just having long hair or saying the word 'groovy' is enough to set him off because all these types are 'pissing on America'.

The guy's so fucked up he even respects Nixon.

Chances are, you haven't heard of John G. Avildsen's *Joe*, a blistering pic that hails all the way from 1970. It's definitely not your traditional slice of vigilantism in which the main character is wound up like clockwork and then set down for a spot of bullet-spraying vengeance against the criminal lowlifes who've directly wronged him. *Joe* is much more nuanced and thought-provoking. It's a queasy, long-simmering outpouring of bile that clearly laid down the foundations for *Taxi Driver*. I'd say it's not only a great 70s flick, but a great movie full stop.

Joe is introduced sitting in a bar (called American Bar and Grill) shooting his mouth off: "The niggers! The niggers are getting all the money. Why work? You tell me. Why the fuck work when you can screw, have babies and get paid for it? I sweat my balls off in front of a fucking furnace for forty hours a week and they get the same money I do. For nuttin!"

Now Joe might be a bigot but he's no psycho-loony. He's not a man on the edge with apocalyptic visions of wiping the streets clean of scum. Not once does he pump iron or have an aggressive conversation with his reflection. Sure, he's a foul-mouthed crashing bore after a few beers, but that's not quite the same as being a Hinckley or Chapman type.

Talk is cheap and all that.

No, and perhaps this is *Joe's* strength, Joe's a bog-ordinary, blue collar guy who served his country fighting against Japanese tyranny. Marriage, a couple of unappreciative kids, the odd steak dinner, a bit of bowling with workmates, and routine frustrations occupy most of his time. Sure, he's bloody uncouth and increasingly resentful ("It's the kids who are screwing us up") but you don't get any sense he's going to explode. Surely he's just an average Joe? Then again, he does have a 'well-balanced' gun collection...

Meanwhile, Bill Compton (Dennis Patrick) is having problems with his beautiful daughter, Melissa (Susan Sarandon). She's mixed up with an unlikeable junkie hustler and living in a shithole, a classic example of a confused rich chick slumming it. After she ends up in hospital, Compton confronts the guy who's hooked his daughter on drugs and spontaneously beats him to death. He then stumbles shell-shocked into a bar and meets Joe. Joe belatedly latches onto the crime but instead of turning the killer in or trying his hand at a spot of blackmail he expresses admiration.

Oh boy, the way these two strike up such an unlikely, toxic, but *believable* alliance is a treat. Separated by wealth, class and education, they still somehow find common ground, the main one being they're both deeply flawed, hypocritical bastards.

Compton can barely stop his head spinning at what he's done, but is also experiencing other emotions. "I get this... I've had it a couple of times lately..." he tells Joe. "A feeling of pleasure... satisfaction..."

"Yeah, yeah!" Joe enthuses. "Like in the war. You remember how you felt in the war sometimes after you'd killed a few of them? You'd feel bad and good at the same time."

Compton can only express his bewilderment to his wife at the mess he's in, desperate to keep Joe on side and yet weirdly starting to like him. "The crazy thing about Joe is that," he tells her, "it's as if he shared in it, as if he killed that boy, too."

Director Avildsen is a long way from the future wholesomeness of *The Karate Kid* here. This is a fascinating exploration of counterculture tensions and radically changing times, complete with references to the ongoing Vietnam War and Desmond Morris' *The Human Zoo*. It's a time capsule, a state of the nation address, and an examination of patriotism. After forty minutes I had no idea where it was going, but could already tell it was both worrying and funny. The characters are exceptionally well-drawn, although it's tricky to know whom you're supposed to root for. There's a huge amount of grit and edge, exemplified by its tremendously coarse and memorable dialogue. Listening to Joe ignorantly rant ("You ever get the feeling, your whole life, is one big crock of shit" and "Forty-two percent of all liberals are queer. That's a fact") is plain great. Both leads are superb, especially Peter Boyle, a man you might know better as a singing, dancing monster who occasionally puts on the Ritz.

Joe also features a very young, longhaired and skinny Susan Sarandon. Those goddamn bewitching eyes are reason enough to watch, but about thirty seconds after meeting her she strips off and climbs into a bath. God bless the 1970s.

Joe is astonishing. And apart from everything else, it's got one of the best climaxes in cinema.

The Vietnam Vet Running Amok Back Home

I've never been to America and I don't know any Americans so I feel that puts me in a commanding position to make profound, incontestable judgments about the place. Indeed, my knowledge of South Canada is so comprehensive that I am familiar with the taste of Coca-Cola and even know who Arthur Fonzarelli is. Now Yankland probably was a reasonable sort of place at one time, but those days appear to have long gone. If I had to rank countries in terms of mental health, I have little idea of the U.S.' exact position, but I'm sure it wouldn't be anywhere near the top.

As far as I can tell, three key events are responsible for rattling this nation's psyche. Did I say *rattle*? I meant inflicting such traumatic wounds that they have turned into festering sores. These three little beauties are Pearl Harbor, the Vietnam War and 9/11. Lob in a few high-profile assassinations and the country's ongoing inability to get to grips with race and you end up with one toxic Yankee Doodle cocktail.

This is why Americans have become such a suspicious, paranoid, gun-loving bunch of confused flag-wavers. They're so fucked up that a sociopath can become president, religion continues to hold too much sway, Chuck Norris was allowed a movie career, basketball and baseball are considered watchable sports, and misguided parents believe it's fine to name a newborn *Randy*, *Newt* or *Rip*. The poor lambs have regressed so far that if they wanted to casually dismiss the irrefutable points of my stellar argument they wouldn't even understand it's grammatically wrong to say *I could care less what that asshole Dave says.*

Anyway, back to a cataclysmic event like the Vietnam War. Now most wars are unjustifiable, but Nam might very well be the *piece de resistance* of indefensible military mistakes. *Why's that?* I hear you ask. Well, Vietnam was a country that simply wanted to get rid of its colonial masters. It hadn't attacked America. Or anyone else.

No matter.

America was too busy losing its shit with its 20th century witch hunt (otherwise known as the Red Scare) to make any rational assessment of events. Communism had to be stopped, especially in an irrelevant, backward country on the other side of the world. For Christ's sake, the warmongers argued, if Vietnam fell, how long before the countries around it toppled into the same goddamn evil pit?

And so those 'military advisors' arrived and the B-52s started flying overhead and My Lai was just around the corner and... oh, fucking hell, what a despicable, heartbreaking, *avoidable* mess. There was also no escaping this one, with Vietnam becoming the first conflict to be beamed nightly into people's homes, enabling even the most myopic of supporters to be soaked in every putrid drop. America was on the verge of tearing itself apart.

And, of course, the joke is after all that Herculean effort, gargantuan expense and everything else, America lost. The world's greatest power had its arse kicked by a bunch of undersized, rice-eating peasants in cute conical hats. Despite the chattering M16s, the rocket-firing Hueys hovering over the jungle, the tons of napalm fired at villagers, the carpet-bombing of a neighbouring country, and America's unshakeable belief in its military prowess, those gung-ho Marines were forced to slink away in the mid-70s with their tails between their legs.

And the jokes kept coming. After kicking its criminal invaders out, Vietnam went fully commie anyway. Not that the surrounding countries noticed. So much for the Domino Theory. Fast forward half a century and Vietnam remains a dirt-poor threat to no one.

All that savagery... for nothing.

It wasn't over for America, though. The vets had to come back with their rearranged bodies, broken minds and seesawing emotions to face their own deeply divided people. My audio Nam bible, Paul Hardcastle's *19*, tells me that none of them received a hero's welcome. "According to a Veteran's Administration study, half of the Vietnam combat veterans suffered from what psychiatrists call post-traumatic stress disorder," Mr. Hardcastle reliably informs us. "Many vets complain of alienation, rage, or guilt. Some succumb to suicidal thoughts. Eight to ten years after coming home, almost eight-hundred thousand men are still fighting the Vietnam War."

Now I don't think the toe-tapping veracity of a three and a half-minute chart topper can be disputed, an anti-war view that is clearly backed up by the movies. It was only a matter of time before the spectre of Nam started appearing on the silver screen. What better place to give things a whirl than the horror genre? In 1974 *Deathdream* (AKA *Dead of Night*) updated the old *Monkey's Paw* story by depicting a family left desolate by the reported death of their enlisted son/brother, Andy (Richard Backus).

The shell-shocked mother simply can't accept the news, leaving her husband to get up in the middle of the night to find her sitting in the dark cradling a candle. "You're alive," she keeps saying. "I can feel it. They lied. You will come back."

Sure enough, the baby-faced Andy turns up in his uniform the next day. Problem is, he's not the same happy-go-lucky guy who left. Pale, non-blinking and listless, this version of Andy barely speaks, doesn't eat, and dislikes company, especially cute doggies. He doesn't so much smile as the corners of his mouth start crawling up his face. When his dad asks "Pretty rough over there, eh son?" he gets the classic blank reply: "Over where...?"

Deathdream is a pretty good mash-up of zombiism and vampirism. I like the way there's no supernatural reason or voodoo hijinks for the combatant's return, just a mother's overwhelming love. It has an excellent, fast-moving opening, maintains an eerie tone throughout, and is complemented by a minimal but effective score. It also nicely captures a sense of dislocation with its focus on family breakdown rather than the wider effects of the war. Indeed, the references to the conflict are fleeting and sometimes oblique. Andy doesn't deal with protestors or get called a 'baby-killer'. When the father says he never acted 'that way' after returning from World War Two, it suggests Nam was a more traumatic event for its soldiers. I also enjoyed a waitress dismissing Andy as the chief suspect in the murder of one of her well-liked customers by paradoxically blurting: "I can't believe a soldier would do a thing like that!"

Better known movies, such as *The Exterminator, First Blood* and *Jacob's Ladder* would emerge in the ensuing years, but *Deathdream* was the first to deal with the fucked-up vet. Its message was unmistakable: those half-crazy war chickens were on their way home to dole out a firsthand taste of the conflict's fifteen-year-long agony.

Blaxploitation

As you probably know, I likes me a bit of blaxploitation, even though much of it was an unashamed rip-off of whatever whitey was up to. Westerns, horror, crime, comedies... the blacks always had some sort of crappy facsimile to hand as typified by the likes of *Blacula* and *Black Shampoo*. Well, everyone's gotta start somewhere, a perfectly acceptable excuse for enabling decent actors, directors and writers to get a foothold in a hitherto not exactly welcoming industry.

Now I'm still building my knowledge of this exploitation sub-genre, but my initial rooting around into its first wave hasn't been a roaring success. Sometimes it's near-impossible to get past the fashion e.g. just take a gander at the titular pimp's array of brazen outfits in *Willie Dynamite*. At other times an excess of dancing, anti-drug finger-wagging and deeply dodgy acting proves fatal (1979's amazingly incompetent *Disco Godfather*). Having said that, I often enjoy blaxploitation's jive talk, funky music, racial tensions, depictions of ghetto life and yes, the stereotypes. Occasionally I even get a sense of the cast thinking *Ain't this great? We're finally doing our own thang...* Plus, there's really nothing wrong with the uncompromising grit of *Across 110th Street*, the entertaining lunacy of *Three the Hard Way* and the sheer unrelenting horror of *Mandingo*.

But where did blaxploitation start? Apparently, 1970's buddy cop flick *Cotton Comes to Harlem* is a good bet. It's a weird, not entirely successful blend of comedy and action that never finds a consistent tone, although it did well enough to produce a sequel two years later. Its strengths include a shit load of outdoor filming (that provide a vivid portrait of the borough), decent acting, a lively approach and a naked chick telling a bamboozled police officer: "They say the badder the woman, the better the smell. Come sniff." Bloody hell, why don't women ever say things like that to me?

Charismatic preacher and poncy show off Deke O'Malley (Calvin Lockhart) has been busy raising money to buy a ship that will help Harlem's blacks relocate to Africa. At a well-attended outdoor rally he tells his cheering people: "Goodbye rats and roaches... Goodbye having to live on white man's welfare. We are going home!"

Now my knowledge of black history might be lacking here, but did blacks really want to piss off to Africa in the late 20th century? I know Harlem had significant problems, such as crime, poverty, racism and drugs, but surely it was a helluva lot better than Nigeria or the Congo? And anyway, how would the whole residency/citizenship thing work? You can't just rock up to a new country on the basis you don't like the old one.

Then again, I guess that's a side issue. Back to the movie. At the rally a bunch of armed masked men steal the eighty-seven grand Deke has raised. Bummer. Two black cops, the unlikely-named Coffin Ed and Gravedigger (Raymond St. Jacques and Godfrey Cambridge), are handed the task of finding out what went down. It's a question of whether Deke's in on the rip-off, but considering he's already happily revealed he's an ex-convict and that God told him in a dream to build an ark, I'll let you figure it out.

Cotton is not a dull watch as it chucks in whatever it can find, such as the subgenre's staples of racial mistrust, police brutality and religion. It lacks coherence, but it does have a decent car chase, a funny watermelon-eating gag, a hot black chick running around naked and a not so hot honky male cop running around naked. Sometimes the comedy is grounded, sometimes it's pure farce, but people getting shot to death, phrases like 'nigger pig cop' and women being belted don't sit brilliantly with its overall knockabout manner. Still, any movie featuring Rock Ridge's future mayor can't be all bad.

A year after *Cotton* came out a cocksure private dick by the name of John Shaft was filmed strutting around a different part of Harlem in his black leathers, accompanied by an Oscar-winning theme tune. Blaxploitation was about to explode.

The Mad Doctor/Scientist

Who doesn't love a bloke with a fevered ego in a white coat self-experimenting or flat-out killing folk in a bid to advance the frontiers of medical knowledge? Such a demented archetype has given us a plethora of fantastic flicks that include *Re-Animator*, *Eyes Without a Face*, *Island of Lost Souls*, and 1986's *The Fly*.

The most famous, Frankenstein, came along in 1931, but there was also another mad doctor plying his trade the same year. His name was Dr. Jekyll (the Oscar-winning Fredric March). This guy's as ambitious as they come, faintly contemptuous of conformist, lily-livered colleagues and most definitely sexually frustrated. Not that he advertises his flaws. Indeed, to the outside world he's a saint, helping crippled children walk and operating in his own time on charitable cases. He loves his fiancée and even has a sense of humour.

But he's a restless man, not wanting to wait for anything, whether it's knowledge or his girl's virginity. He wants the future *now*. Listen to him giving a lecture to his esteemed associates: "Gentleman, London is so full of fog that it has penetrated our minds and set boundaries for our vision. As men of science, we should be curious and bold enough to peer beyond it into the many wonders it conceals."

Uh-oh. I think it's gonna be a case of curiosity killing the cat. Jekyll's impatience grows worse when he intervenes in a street brawl and ends up carrying a working class girl to her bedroom. Suddenly he's in a different world where the locals speak funny and are a lot earthier. Not to mention the rescued girl saucily tossing garters at him and placing his hand on her bare thigh... No wonder the reluctantly departing Jekyll remarks: "It's the things I can't do that always tempt me."

The subject matter of *Dr. Jekyll and Mr. Hyde* remains timeless in the way it taps into our perennial frustrations at having to be nice guys and play the game as expected. Keeping up appearances and so on. Surely most of us want to occasionally yell *Fuck it!* and knock back that frothing, psyche-dividing potion? I mean, look at what it does to Jekyll. One moment he's kowtowing to his prospective father-in-law about marriage plans, the next he's shaking a fist and staring at the simian Hyde in the mirror: "Free! Free at last! You hypocrites! You deniers of life! If you could see me now, what would you think?"

Toxic Masculinity

I have a theory that we're not too far off seeing the day when men start growing breasts. Indeed, I feel the western world's commitment to lefty feminization makes this tragic prospect inevitable. Men are bad, you see. We're sexual predators. Thugs. Sexist wankers. I dunno, we eat too much red meat or something, and need to be a bit more civilized and considerate. Tone our behaviour down. Then we might understand that everyone and everything must be respected. It's amazing, really, that some of us still haven't grasped that banter is wrong, even when happily reciprocated. For Christ's sake, put an end to those piss-taking songs at the footy. Curb your drinking. Stop with the macho antics. End the insensitive pranks. Shave off the chest hair, you bloody caveman. Go and change that diaper. Don't you know saying stuff with a tongue in cheek or a twinkle in the eye is no longer a defence against being labelled something nasty that ends in *phobe* or *ist*?

Well, enough is enough.

It's time men started behaving like men again. It's time we reclaimed our manliness. Please get in touch if you wish to set up a fight club, a punishing yet liberating arena to reassert our innate, blood-spattered aggression. Of course, I won't be taking part in any such brutal displays of hyper masculinity as I'll be too busy working on my B cup, but I am prepared to heartily cheer on the brave participants and hand out halftime refreshments. Are you in?

Anyway, I have no idea when the term 'toxic masculinity' gained currency, but it's clearly become a popular stick to beat men. Movie-wise, it's got a fair old tradition and is easy to spot in such classics as 1993's *Once Were Warriors* and my fave, *Wake in Fright*. Back in 1960 we can see its origins in the ace kitchen sink British drama, *Saturday Night and Sunday Morning*. Based on Alan Sillitoe's vivid novel, it focuses on a handsome, self-centred working class lad who slaves away at a lathe all week before bursting butterfly-like into glorious life once the factory whistle's blown. Except this butterfly's a bruiser. Within a few hours he'll have necked ten pints, smoked forty fags, upset at least a couple of pub-goers with his physical and verbal carelessness, had a fight or two, banged a workmate's wife, and fallen blind drunk down the stairs.

Not that he's likely to apologise the next day.

"I'd like to see anyone grind me down," he boasts. "That'd be the day. What I'm out for is a good time. All the rest is propaganda."

Arthur Seaton, as played by the fantastic Albert Finney, doesn't take shit from anyone. This means he's in a sulky state of near-perpetual conflict. At the mechanized hive he calls work he dislikes 'brownnosers' and the foreman, a man who has 'a fat gut and lots of worry'. Cowed old-timers have wasted their lives. His harried mum and tea-drinking, TV-watching dad are 'dead from the neck up'. As for women, he's got an angling analogy: "Never bite unless the bait's good. I won't get married till I'm good and ready."

As you can probably tell, Arthur is one of those mouthy guys who see traps everywhere. He's brilliant at knowing what he *doesn't* want, but not so great at figuring out what he's after. He might talk big, he might ruffle a few feathers, but reality does tend to intrude on the heroic, anti-authoritarian picture he paints of himself. For this is a man who rides a bicycle to his monotonous job, catches the bus and lives with his parents. To be fair, viable options do seem limited for such a bright, aggressive chap, summarized by a mate who tells him: "All you can do is go on working and hope something good'll turn up." In the meantime (before he makes his big move) there's always Saturday night, a time of hedonistic escape. Or as that disco-dancing god Tony Manero concisely put it seventeen years later: "Fuck the future."

Saturday Night conjures up a wonderful world of working class life, replete with terraced houses, kids playing on cobbled streets, washing lines strung across alleyways, headscarf-wearing, gossiping housewives, sing-a-longs in smoke-filled pubs, gruff blokes in flat caps, industrial accidents, backstreet abortions, fishing at the canal, and people calling each other 'duck'. Can our brusque, deceitful, vaguely cruel hero escape living out the rest of his life in such surroundings or is he going to meekly settle down, lose the toxicity and grow a lovely pair of breasts?

The Slasher

As far as I can tell, people enjoy watching slashers for four reasons: the gory or inventive murders; young women getting their just desserts for stupidly daring to be attractive, naked, half-naked or sexually active; the whacked-out reason for the slayings; and the whodunit aspect. I guess some fans also enjoy the choice of weapon. This might include a hammer, a scythe, a javelin or a kebab skewer (although I feel it's a pity no killer has tried his luck with razor-sharp sarcasm).

Now although I spent a good deal of my lamentable, glue-affected youth consuming slashers, I don't care for them. The vast majority, especially from the 80s onward, are pretty damn tedious. Some, however, remain well regarded, if not cult favourites, such as *The Prowler, My Bloody Valentine, Just Before Dawn, Happy Birthday to Me* and *The Burning* (which would've been immeasurably improved if fledgling producer Harvey Weinstein had been set on fire instead). Still, I have little idea why fans give these movies any more than a cursory viewing. Sure, there's the odd decent kill, and I am partial to Cropsy rearing up from that canoe and gleefully slicing off those campers' fingers, but it's never long before such simplistic, plodding flicks collapse under their own absurdities.

Slashers peaked in the early eighties when it seemed we were getting one every couple of weeks, a production line of homicidal havoc sparked by

Halloween's gigantic success in 1978. Nothing replicated that flick's commercial high tide, but *Friday the 13th* two years later did a helluva lot better than most by raking in sixty mil worldwide.

Fuck knows why.

It's a dull, nonsensical, poorly directed ninety minutes, even if we are treated to the sight of young Kevin Bacon's buttocks. In fact, *Friday* demonstrates many of my pet peeves with the sub-genre in that the killer often possesses superhuman strength (despite being a middle-aged mom), as well as one of those interminable back from the grave endings. Or am I just being nitpicky and failing to enter into the spirit of things?

Well, surely you'll agree that Jason Voorhees is a damned sight less interesting than his sweater-wearing mom. Fucking hell, how many times did that hockey mask-clad numbnuts bumble through one carbon copy of a movie after another? I think I quit after four instalments, which was about three too many. Jesus Christ, I think Jason even ended up in *space*.

At any rate, around the time of *Friday the 13th's* release, slashers had become increasingly controversial with their explicit gore. Many ran into trouble with the censors, a prime example being 1982's *The New York Ripper*. Here we get a masturbating woman watching a live sex show, an oblivious mutt happily retrieving a severed hand, a female nipple being sliced through with a razorblade, a pathologist talking about 'good, efficient butchery' and the unbelievable decision to have the police-taunting killer quack like a duck. And not even a level-headed sounding duck, but one that comes across like it's been inhaling helium.

Ripper is a monotonous trawl through mechanical depictions of sleaze, managing to lack atmosphere, tension and scares. It just lurches from one implausibility to the next before ending with a predictably bonkers attempt at an 'explanation'. I mean, the whole point of stuff like this is to give you a visceral jab. Supposedly one of the nastiest slashers out there, all it made me do was try to find the discipline to get up and give my lawnmower an oil change instead. Nice location work, though.

So, in summary, I don't like slashers, but there are exceptions to their blunt, vaguely depressing mediocrity. Now while it's difficult to define a pure slasher (as so many horror movies like *Psycho* and *Peeping Tom* have a hefty dose of slasher elements), I'd argue that the best of the fucked-up bunch are 1974's *Black Christmas* and *Texas Chainsaw*, *Halloween* and 1984's *Nightmare on Elm Street*. Pinning down the origins of such movies is not easy, though, but I'm going to plump for Mario Bava's 1971 offering, *A Bay of Blood*.

Not that I'm a fan of Italian horror, either. It's too ill-disciplined for my taste. The titles are often lyrical and bloody great (*The House with Laughing Windows*, *The Red Queen Kills Seven Times*, *The Bird with the Crystal Plumage*), but the actual movies are little more than a few imaginative kills adrift in a sea of incoherence. I always appreciate plausibility (a very difficult thing to pull off in horror flicks) but the antics of *giallo's* black-gloved killers often run expressly against such an old-fashioned notion.

A Bay of Blood (also known as *Twitch of the Death Nerve* and about five different other titles) is no different. It has an excellent, unexpectedly inventive opening in which a killer gets killed. Unfortunately, herein lies the problem: this might be flashy and attention-grabbing, but it's also deeply contrived.

However, there's no doubt *Bay* is a prototype slasher. And so the members of a small group are picked off by a prowling murderer who only has the vaguest (if any) connection to them. All the typical ingredients are present and correct: a local resident warning of doom ("There will be tears shed over the bay"), an array of fun-seeking, characterless young people to act as knife fodder, snatches of voyeurism, honeys in a state of undress, gruesome, explicit murders, shots from the killer's POV, the superhuman strength (as shown by a spear being driven through two bodies), red herrings, and a flimsy, if not bloody silly reason for the mass of bodies.

Still, *Bay* remains a significant horror movie that boasts a fine location, as well as above-average direction, cinematography and music. Some of the splatter work was so good that the *Friday the 13th* franchise was obviously happy to copy. I wouldn't knock its first forty minutes, but I still feel it's operating on a basic level that can't match the imaginative and subversive extremes of the best horror. The longer *Bay* goes on, the more cracks in its construction appear. By the hour mark, it's gone *insane*.

I did like the writhing squid on a corpse's face, though.

Naziploitation/Women in Prison

When it comes to directing, Lee Frost is a long way from a household name, but the low-budget exploitation stalwart sure gave us his best shot. There wasn't a grimy subject he wouldn't roll around in whether it was roughies, head transplants, disfigured bikers, castration or witchcraft. And then, of course, there was 1969's *Love Camp 7*, a pic that not only got Naziploitation up on its jackbooted feet but also launched the perennially popular babes-behind-bars sub-genre.

However you look at it, that's some sort of cinematic achievement.

Shame *Love Camp 7* is such a dreary, repetitive, cheapo state of affairs. It centres on a hush-hush plan to send two undercover women into a military brothel to extract sensitive info from a female scientist (who somehow knows about advanced jet engine manufacture). "Both are experts in the field of guerrilla warfare, hand to hand combat and karate," their boss says. "In addition, they speak French and German. I feel confident these women can handle the mission."

Yeah, but do they look good unclothed?

Hmm, I shouldn't joke. This is an explicit, really quite unpleasant pic that features lengthy bouts of rape, whippings, a lesbian orgy, enforced boot licking, and bashful officers keen to maintain the dignity of their rank by refusing to take their trousers off in the presence of *Untermensch*. Our chief bad guy is a black-clad commandant, a combat-avoiding coward who does appear rather short and tubby to be a representative of the so-called master race. His personality veers between disdain, sarcasm and screaming fits of rage. Never mind, I'm sure he's nice to his kids.

"I cannot guarantee that you will love Love Camp 7," he tells the latest bunch of unfortunate (but shapely) inmates, "but I can guarantee you will love in Love Camp 7. You have been brought here for one purpose, and one purpose only, and that is to please the front line officers of our army... To please will be your only function."

His best scene involves his subordinate goons holding down a spread-eagled naked prisoner on his desk as a scarred female doctor does the rubber glove thing. "I understand that your father was a banker," he muses as the sexually violated inmate writhes and grimaces inches from his face. "I should imagine what with the war and everything that the banking business isn't what it used to be. Certainly, the interest rates are down, ya?" It's a nice piece of disassociation that might have served as the inspiration for Bret Easton Ellis' sociopath prattling about Huey Lewis and the News while carrying out his abominable acts of violence.

But that's about the only good thing I have to say about *Love Camp*. I didn't enjoy it anywhere near as much as the equally nasty, but much more campy, ridiculous and inventive *Ilsa, She Wolf of the SS*. In that pic at least it was a bunch of Nazi vixens overwhelmingly dishing out the abuse, but in *Love Camp* it's the men so it feels ten times more ugly and misogynistic. There's no energy in the direction, the sets are a joke, the acting ranges from mediocre to poor, there's never any sense of events taking place in the early years of the war, and you can tell the whole shebang is nothing more than a flimsy excuse to humiliate women.

Saying that, I wouldn't underestimate how many mutated, retarded and ultimately loveable children *Love Camp* birthed.

Fucked-Up Films #4: Deep River Savages/ AKA Man from Deep River (1972)

Synopsis

A Club 18-30 holiday for the most ardent of sadomasochists

Director

Umberto Lenzi

Cast

Ivan Rassimov, Me Me Lai, Pratitsak Singhara, Sullalewan Suxantat, Ong Ard

What are these sick bastards doing? I don't think I caught the hero's name, but given his wondrous flaxen mane I shall refer to him as Blonde Magnificence. Really, his flowing tresses are on a par with Klaus Kinski and Rutger Hauer. No idea if this dude graduated to playing a Nazi but, believe me, he would've been a shoo-in at portraying Aryan supremacy. Anyhow, he's a photographer doing a job somewhere on the Thai/Burmese border. He hires a guide and goes far upriver to see what delights he can find. Basically, this means tits, dangling skulls, blow darts, true love, a tracheotomy and cockroach consumption. He's soon caught by the none too friendly natives (who call him 'Fish-Man' because he's wearing flippers) and put on display in the village square suspended in a net. "I'm a human being like you!" he wails at them as they daintily cut out the tongues of a couple of rival tribe members.

Is the villain any good? We get one constantly frowning tough guy whom I think is the witchdoctor. He's got an elaborately painted face, but still manages to look like a heavily suntanned, constipated Bjork. Somehow I was a little disappointed he never once belted out a cover version of her excellent *Army of Me*. Unfortunately, he doesn't really develop as a character, leaving us with no main villain. Rather, the enemy is the tribe's superstition and barbarism. It's simply a question of whether Blonde Magnificence is going to have his bollocks cut off, lightly roasted and eaten.

How skuzzy are the men? Some are cannibals which I guess is a hard pastime to justify in polite company. Others are rapists which I guess... Oh, you get the idea. Mind you, these are the sort of blokes who chop off the top of a monkey's skull and eat its raw brains in the belief it will give them wisdom. When you consider such a practice, it does suggest they doubt their own intellectual superiority.

How do the lovely ladies fare? As you'd expect, this is a patriarchal world. None of the women wear pantsuits, demand to be called *Ms* or expect their hubbies to stay at home to raise the kids. Luckily, the chieftain's fucking gorgeous daughter wants Blonde Magnificence as a slave, which hopefully means *fuck toy*. I have to say she's remarkably well-groomed for living in the middle of the jungle. Perhaps our western ladies could learn a trick or two from whatever her vigorous beauty routine involves coz she has lovely skin, lustrous long hair and flawless white teeth. And yes, she does get fully nude, as do plenty of the other frolicking babes. At first, it's difficult to get a handle on this Love Interest as she orders Blonde Magnificence to strip in the hot sun and do strenuous work before tying him back up and licking his tears. Still, I suppose all courtships have their quirks.

Elsewhere, the women don't fare so well. After one husband gets crushed to death in a work accident, he's cremated. Fair enough, but the next day his naked widow lies on her back in his recently cooled ashes and is fucked by all the other guys as she's now 'available'. I remain unsure if I would like this eye-opening funereal custom adopted by westerners because it does seem somewhat hasty and disrespectful. On the other hand, the widow is a bit of a hottie.

Later, we get a gang rape. Well, I call it that, but the attackers clearly haven't perfected the art. The first guy starts off promisingly by clambering on top with panache but then reveals himself to be a rank amateur by only lasting *three* seconds. I'm not even certain such an ill-disciplined prod qualifies as a sexual violation. Surely any presiding judge would write that one off as little more than a tickle? However, I should say the tickling does give way to murder and cannibalism. This is obviously terrible as I can't imagine the consumption of raw human flesh doing anything other than leading to the most traumatic indigestion.

Would the violence make a vicar faint? Yes, it bloody well would. The gore is generally well-done and utterly fucking gruesome in places. We get the aforementioned tongue amputations and gang rape, as well as a chopped-off hand and a fair bit of death. Worst of all are the real-life animal killings. There's one sudden slaughter of a tethered goat that (through an admittedly good piece of editing) made me swear aloud and turn away. Unfortunately, it seems par for the course that the less intelligent species don't get treated well in this kind of exploitative trash. This was a deplorable trait that stretched throughout the seventies and eighties, probably reaching its nadir in 1980's boring, disjointed and inept *Cannibal Holocaust*. And it wasn't just the wops trying to give an edge to their movies by incorporating such lamentable shit, either. Even towering classics like *Apocalypse Now* (a water buffalo hacked to death) and *Come and See* (a cow hit by bullets) were tainted this way.

Yeah, well, *boo* is the only thing you can say. If filmmakers really do need to include real-life butchering of the lower life forms to add grit and authenticity to their art, I suggest using Justin Bieber fans or Muslims.

How fucked-up is this film? Hmm, yeah, it's definitely not pc. It is, however, consistently engaging. There's a lot of outdoor filming that really captures the local colour, such as curious kids, stomach-churning cuisine, Buddhist statues, kickboxing, and exotic, teeming wildlife. All of this is complemented by decent acting, full-frontal nudity and competent direction. It's a fast-paced story packed full of sadistic twists and turns.

I also liked *Deep River's* unpredictability. The tribe that Blonde Magnificence gets sucked into isn't without honour and has its own code, but there's no way of knowing what whacky shit its members are gonna come up with next. On the whole the flick frequently displays an off-centre, wonderful inventiveness, such as a hole in the wall mass groping that beats any western-style notion of dating hands down. Apart from the dismal animal killings, this was far better than expected.

I loved it.

Old Fuckers

At the beginning of *Rocky IV*, Rocky and Apollo dance around the ring throwing mock insults but essentially admiring each other's physiques. It's one of moviedom's gayest starts, especially with lines like "I'm gonna whip your butt" and "You really look good for an older guy." To be honest, it's a bit of a surprise they don't just embrace, lock lips and fall in soft focus to the canvas.

Nevertheless, before they start lovingly pummelling one another, Apollo utters a key line: "It's too bad we gotta get old, huh?" It's jokingly said, but so well delivered that you can pick up on a tinge of sadness and fear. Apollo, you see, *is* afraid of aging, having become increasingly aware of his profession's brutal reality: being in your late thirties means you're way past your best. And if you can no longer fight at the highest level, then you're one step closer to death. That's why he takes on the monstrous, terrifying Drago. It's his attempt to slay the dragon, to reverse time, to bring back the glory days and, ultimately, to give death the finger.

And, of course, although Apollo says the line to Rocky, he's speaking for all of us. It is 'too bad' the clock is ticking. You don't have to be an ex-professional boxer to worry about your body and mind degenerating. Let's face it: no one is looking forward to buying their first hearing aid. And once you've popped such a device into your lughole, how long before you end up a frail, semi-abandoned joke in a nursing home?

Aah, the nursing home. No matter how they try to disguise those places, no matter what euphemistic language is employed, we all know what they represent. For example, I recently bought my house from an eighty-two-year-old OAP, who was about to move into a nursing home. I heard through the real estate agent that she was in tears in the hours before leaving, partly because it had been her home for nearly three decades, but also because she must have understood what the relocation meant. The last stop on life's journey. The end of the line where the Grim Reaper clips your ticket.

Too bad we gotta get old, huh?

Nursing homes appear to be a curiously Western invention. In many parts of Asia they don't exist or are in their infancy. Old folk there are looked after by family, a noble, heart-warming tradition which has long fallen out of fashion over here. We seem *embarrassed* by physical and mental decay, and do our best to push it away. Hence, the enormous growth of aged care facilities, places where a visitor might only have to come into contact with the ravages of time once a month instead of daily. Some Asian people I've met abroad can't believe Westerners treat their older family members so cruelly.

But that's how things are overwhelmingly done. We shunt geriatrics off to a home. What else can we do? Well, after being wowed by *Terminator 2's* nonstop action back in the early nineties, the world's greatest-ever stand-up, Bill Hicks, mooted a possible solution. He argued there was no way to top such stunts unless we started using terminally ill people. "Put them in the movies," he insisted. "You want your grandmother dying like a little bird in some hospital room, her translucent skin so thin you can see her last heartbeat working its way down her blue veins? Or do you want her to meet Chuck Norris?"

Bill then imagined a rapid-fire interchange between a concerned relative and the movie director. 'Hey, how come you've dressed my grandmother up as a mugger?' 'Shut up and get off the set. Action! Push her toward Chuck.' 'Wow! He kicked her head right off her body!' 'Did you see my grammy?' 'Son, she's out of her misery, and you're about to see the greatest film of all time.'

I'm sure you'll agree, it's a tantalizing proposal. Meanwhile, here are seven old fuckers in a conspicuously youth-orientated industry who managed to shine without having their heads actually kicked off.

Professor Marcus Monserrat and Estelle Monserrat in *The Sorcerers* (1967)

Altruism.

What a wonderful thing.

Wish I had some.

Still, at least Professor Marcus Monserrat (Boris Karloff) has it in spades. It doesn't matter he's living an impoverished life with his wife, Estelle (Catherine Lacey). The professor used to be a renowned hypnotist, employing his subtle skills to help rid patients of everything from anxiety to nicotine addiction. Things started going wrong after a muck-raking newspaper ran an exposé, but he's hung in there and kept trying to make life better for others.

Now he's invented a machine that can not only hypnotize, but enable the hypnotizer to *feel* whatever the patient does. Marcus sees this breakthrough as a way to help old people, enabling (for example) infirm nursing home residents to have vicarious holidays. Estelle, however, wants to use the machine for a different purpose, a much more selfish and dangerous one...

Like a lot of horror flicks, *The Sorcerers* shows older folk preying on the young. However, it's more intelligent than most and built on fascinating subject matter, one that directly taps into our love of power over others. It might also demonstrate how older folk routinely envy the young's hedonistic opportunities, especially in swinging London.

The Monserrats pick up a bored clubber, Mike (Ian Ogilvy), and bring him back to their apartment. "For forty years I've been acclaimed as one of the world's greatest hypnotists," the professor tells him. Mike sarcastically claps and says "Bully for you, mate", perfectly encapsulating the vague contempt the young so often have toward their elders. Undeterred, they offer "dazzling, indescribable experiences" and "ecstasy with no consequences," but this is a straightforward fib. Poor Mike's not gonna get anything of the sort, just a series of future blackouts.

It's great to watch the downtrodden Monserrats come back to life by simply sitting at a dining room table feeling long-forgotten sensations as their plaything Mike takes an illicit night-time dip in a hotel swimming pool with his posh French girlfriend or hammers along the highway on a stolen motorbike. Estelle, in particular, gets hooked on her virtual-reality drug, displaying a near-orgasmic excitement at being pseudo-young again. It's all quite creepy, especially when Estelle starts enjoying the danger. "We all want to do things deep down inside ourselves," she says, "things we can't allow ourselves to do..."

Both Lacey and Karloff (in a late career renaissance that would include the remarkably prescient *Targets* in 1968) put in good shifts. I like the way they convey old age as a growing sense of desiccation; of new experiences, respect from others, excitement, pleasure and hope all having dried up and long ago blown away.

Wunderkind director Michael Reeves, who went on to make the nasty as fuck *Witchfinder General*, does a good job in capturing dark impulses, bursts of horror and the groovy, mini-skirted vibe of the swinging sixties. Sadly, he never got to experience old age, or even middle age, dying in his mid-twenties.

Grandpa in *The Texas Chainsaw Massacre* (1974)

Grandpa must be one of the feeblest fuckers ever put on film. According to his enthusiastic PR team (the slightly biased members of his family), he used to be the 'best killer there ever was', but now he's such a dribbling spaz he doesn't even have the strength to *hold* a hammer, let alone bash someone's brains in.

We first meet the old coot being carried down the stairs by Leatherface and the Hitcher. He's well-dressed and even looks a touch debonair, but his bald, bright white head does suggest something's amiss, partly because it makes him resemble the senile older brother of *Salem's Lot's* chief vampire, Barlow. Grandpa's also a bit spaced out. The Hitcher's obviously a good grandson, though, and does his best to involve him. "Look, Grandpa!" he says, showing him a recently captured, trussed-up girl. "Look!"

Grandpa doesn't perk up. Somehow I don't think he's gonna be the life and soul of the imminent blood-soaked party. To be honest, I believe this elderly gentleman would be better off placed under immediate medical supervision.

Meanwhile, Leatherface is patting his frail shoulders and kissing the top of his head, the only time he shows any affection in the entire movie (excluding that for his trusty chainsaw). Perhaps some sustenance would enable Grandpa to take a livelier part in proceedings. Leatherface cuts the girl's finger and sticks the bleeding digit into the senior citizen's mouth, causing her eyes to widen as he starts enthusiastically sucking. Suddenly both arms are off his lap and swaying with excitement. There's life in the old dog yet!

It's a false dawn. Later we see him slumped at the head of the dinner table. Just like Grampa Simpson, he seems to have nodded off at an inappropriate time. The boys put their heads together and decide it's time to get rid of the female, perhaps tired of her near-constant screaming. Who better to do it than Grandpa? "Hey, Grandpa," the Hitcher says, pointing at the thrashing girl, "we're gonna let you have this one."

As they move him in his chair toward her, the Cook reminisces about Grandpa's legendary cattle-killing skills in the abattoir. "Why," he soothingly tells the girl, "he never took more than one lick, they say. He did sixty in five minutes once. They say he coulda done more if the hook and pull gang coulda gotten the beefs outta the way faster."

She's then forced onto her knees with her head over a big metal bucket as Leatherface tries to get Grandpa to clasp a hammer. It keeps falling to the floor. I do believe this is *Chainsaw's* attempt at levity.

"Come on, Grandpa," the Hitcher urges, obviously disappointed at the dearth of head-splitting action. "Hit her! Hit that bitch!" The Cook is also doing his best with an impromptu cheerleader impersonation that involves clapping and jumping up and down. "Get her, Grandpa! Get her!"

It's not happening though. The hammer's in the bucket now. Leatherface fishes it out and uses Grandpa's hand as a proxy, finally managing to draw some of the red stuff with a half-decent whack. Problem is, everyone knows it's a cheat. Grandpa can suck blood, he might even be able to slurp, but *killing*? Don't think so. He's officially washed up. Oh, bloody hell, look

172

what's happened now. That crazed girl has just jumped clean through the window.

Sorry, grandpa, it's off to the nursing home with you, good sir.

Lou in *Atlantic City* (1980)

Both *Unforgiven's* The Schofield Kid and English Bob were memorable bullshitters, but I have a particular fondness for Burt Lancaster's aging, ex-small time gangster in Louis Malle's fine drama.

Lou might dress well but he's clearly past his prime, if he ever had one. Now he makes ends meet running the numbers in a decaying coastal city. Oh, he's also a paid lackey for a demanding hypochondriac called Grace (Kate Reid), whose deceased gangster husband used to employ him. She's not above needling Lou with taunts of 'Mr. Ten Most Wanted' and it's easy to see he's fighting a constant battle to hang onto his temper while dealing with her shrill, endless orders that include rubbing her feet and exercising her pampered poodle.

None of this fits in with his self-image, you see, the image he likes to project of having been an important face back in Las Vegas. Just look at the way his demeanour changes when he starts reminiscing about rackets, whores and guns with anyone dumb enough to listen. Suddenly he's a man again, someone who knew the likes of Lucky Luciano, not some present-day downtrodden minion at the beck and call of a dried-up flower.

But are any of his tales true? Or was he actually a wannabe, a cowardly joke given the nickname 'Numb Nuts'?

Whatever the case, it's not long before he meets a loser who's run off with a bag of Mob coke. A deal is hatched to regularly supply an illegal gambling den, enabling Lou's yen for fantasy about the good old days to step up a gear. "Sometimes things would happen and I'd have to kill a few people," he tells his new 'partner'. "I'd feel bad for a while, but then I'd jump into the ocean, swim way out, come back in feeling nice and clean, and start all over again."

Lou's in the ascendancy. With a chunk of change in his pocket and the chance to consort with hoodlums again, the pictures in his head of who he is and the way he can go about doing things have magically aligned. Now he's a man about town flashing the cash. Christ, he's even found the confidence to stop perving on the gorgeous, dream-filled Sally (Susan Sarandon) and start wooing her with a nice bottle of wine at a fancy restaurant. And when she leans forward to say "Teach me stuff..." you can tell it's music to his ears.

Of course, such a facade can't last. Reality's bound to intrude. Just look what happens when two hoods on the trail of the missing coke come calling, barely pausing for breath as they rough up both Lou and Sally on the street. In a few brain-scrambling seconds it's laid bare he's no tough guy, no commander of respect. Even Lou knows it, as evidenced by the marvellous prolonged close-up of his shaken face. His self-delusion has been dynamited in much the same manner as the rundown old hotels making way for the gambling-fuelled regeneration of Atlantic City. For perhaps the first time in decades this chivalrous, pathetic old fucker is standing on levelled ground.

So what's Bugsy Siegel's ex-cellmate gonna do?

Hobson in *Arthur* (1981)

Can you imagine having a butler or valet?

I can't, even though I'm the laziest bastard on the planet. It's just beyond me how some people pay a dogsbody to run a bath or fetch an umbrella or open the front door. I guess it's all to do with subtly demonstrating wealth and power, but I'd be *embarrassed* to ask an employee to do such mundane and trivial tasks. After all, what are mothers for?

The duty-obsessed Stevens in *The Remains of the Day* would have to be my favourite cinematic butler, but *Arthur's* acid-tongued Hobson (John Gielgud) is a close second. Hobson surely has one of the highest hit rates for quality lines given to any supporting character in movie history. Nearly everything that pops out of his erudite, disapproving and occasionally vulgar mouth is funny or on the money. Listen to his putdown of the shoplifting, garishly dressed Linda (Liza Minnelli) after watching her cause a kerfuffle on a Manhattan street: "Usually one must go to a bowling alley to meet a woman of your stature." And his elegant parting jab? "Good luck in prison." It's this constant flow of bon mots, and the way they're couched in such wonderfully deceptive politeness, that makes the ultra-sarcastic Hobson such a treat.

Introduced standing ramrod straight holding a breakfast tray as the elevator doors open into Arthur's sumptuous bedroom, it's not hard to tell he's a prim and proper English gentleman of the finest pedigree. "Please stop that!" he barks upon seeing his playboy employer cuddling a floozy in bed. "Hi," she groggily manages through a hangover, prompting Hobson's best lemon face. "You obviously have a wonderful economy with words," he replies. "I look forward to your next syllable with great eagerness."

Arthur (Dudley Moore) is, of course, the son Hobson never had. For decades he's been trying to get the 'spoiled little bastard' to grow up, but hasn't made much progress since the days of playing hide and seek. Now he treats Arthur like an overgrown child, routinely telling him to sit up straight or not to forget to wash his armpits while promising ice cream if he accomplishes anything of the mildest importance. Not that the immature Arthur ever stays on track for very long, mainly because he's a bored pisshead. Still, the impeccably dressed Hobson isn't beyond giving Arthur some home truths or doling out a backhander whenever his patience runs out.

But underneath it all there's deep affection. Mind you, who cares about that soppy shit? Much better to dwell on the guy's seemingly endless sarcasm, such as when Arthur states he's going to have a bath.

"I'll alert the media," comes the ever-courteous reply.

Buck Grotowski in *Monster's Ball* (2003)

Racism is an interesting subject to explore, especially if done with verve and imagination as *Blazing Saddles* and *Planet of the Apes* managed. However, one of my pet hates is a movie that shows a character learning Racism Is Wrong before abruptly turning over a new leaf. Take Maggie Smith's character in 2011's god-awful *Best Exotic Marigold Hotel*. She's an elderly bigot that travels from London to India for a cheap hip operation. A fair chunk of the time she's spewing hate, banging on about Indians with their 'brown faces and blacks hearts, reeking of curry'. Of course, such an attitude does beg the question of why she's placing her health in the care of these people in the first place, but by the end of this thoroughly unrecommended flick she's done a one-eighty. Those brown-skinned chaps are apparently all right after all.

Fuck, I hate such a facile handling of a complex, uncomfortable subject.

Racism is a pretty damn difficult ailment to rid yourself of, especially if it's been drilled in from a young age, and most racists never accomplish it. Instead they learn to manage it, to try not to act on it or to keep it hidden, mainly because they know there can be serious consequences for any outbreak. They're still prejudiced; they just don't show it. Like alcoholism, the malady sits within, perhaps suppressed, perhaps cowed, but always biding its time.

So, yeah, I find any movie with an about-face approach to racism trite. I much prefer flicks that show racism to be *self-defeating*. This is where *Monster's Ball* scores big. Back at the turn of the century this capital punishment-flavoured drama caused a splash, mainly due to Halle Berry's energetic sex scene ("Make me feel *good*!") and the fact she went on to become the first black woman to nab a Best Actress Oscar. Well, I'm not gonna complain about her nudey gyrating, but I will say *Monster's Ball* is weakened by its substantial implausibilities.

However, the one thing it does get right is Peter Boyle's contribution. Thirty-three years after his hateful turn as a bigoted everyman in the sleeper hit *Joe*, he's back playing a mean sonuvabitch by the name of Buck. In *Joe* he started sitting in a bar ranting about blacks. He does the same here sitting at a window after spotting two 'porch monkeys' cutting across his rural Georgian property.

"There was a time when they knew their place," he tells his equally fucked-up son, Hank (Billy Bob Thornton). "Wasn't any of this mixing going on."

Right, we've got the measure of this unsmiling patriarch, a man who probably couldn't even spell 'Southern hospitality' let alone practise it. Now it's just a case of how far he's gonna push things. Quite far as it happens. In his best scene Hank's new girlfriend Leticia (Berry) comes calling with the gift of a hat only to find Buck alone in the house. Buck pesters her for a ciggy, slips on the headwear and makes some complimentary remarks about its quality. Is the old fucker softening? And then he fixes her with a dead stare. "In my prime," he says, "I had a thing for nigger juice myself. Hank just like his daddy. Ain't a man till you split dark oak."

Buck, of course, is unapologetic when Hank discovers he's been up to his old tricks. "I'm your father," he says, as if Hank's behaviour is disgracing what's left of his family. "Remember that."

But his little faux pas proves to be the straw that breaks the camel's back. This poisoned oak tree, whose wife and grandson both 'failed' him by committing suicide, is condemned to live the rest of his barren life in a nursing home.

Alone, disorientated, and still devoid of any insight into his life-long curse, we leave him sitting on an unfamiliar bed staring into space.

Harry Brown in *Harry Brown* (2009)

Art's a strange old thing.

As we know, there's nothing new under the sun. Nothing illustrates such an adage better than a vigilante flick like *Harry Brown*. Christ, this shit has been done so many times beforehand it's almost funny. Do I really need to tell you Michael Caine plays a decent, ex-army guy trying to keep out of the way of the ever-growing scum clogging up his little corner of the world? I mean, is it any surprise the cops are useless and his bullied, terrified best mate gets splatted? You know what happens next, yeah? I guess the 'twist' here is that Harry's an emphysemic, widowed pensioner. A sheep in sheep's clothing.

C'mon, this is about as stale and silly as it gets, right?

Well, no, not exactly.

Like I said, art's a strange old thing. I guess it's all about the *way* you do it. *Harry Brown* has an undeniably tired plot (in which the dots can be joined by a retarded child) but it still manages to work. In fact, it's an entertaining, surprisingly nasty watch. Events unfold with a pleasing economy, typified by its chaotic opening that covers gang initiation, drugs, profanity, mindless machismo, an inadvertent killing and a motorbike crash in two minutes flat. All the visceral confrontations, fights, shootouts and killings are well-handled. The hoodie-clad gang members fizz with a sour energy and are convincingly skuzzy, especially in the police interview room with their obscene sexual threats. They live on the usual rundown council estate, only this one's situated next to a motorway. To say the place is lacking in charm and community spirit is somewhat of an understatement, although it does provide nightly entertainment. Who needs HBO when you can look out the window to see law-abiding citizens getting beaten up?

Caine wanders through this urban shittiness in quite a subdued way. I'm not even sure he ever raises his voice. He certainly doesn't rant about reclaiming the streets for decent folk or start trotting out the quips once his hands get bloody. He might put a couple of toes on a soapbox at one point but he soon removes them. However, I like the way he reveals his inner steel in a plausible, unhurried way. Thank God we don't get any obvious stunt doubles or age-defying, plausibility-undermining bouts of strength and speed. Indeed, at one point he pursues a baddie only to collapse from exhaustion and end up in hospital.

Caine has made a lot of movies and I doubt he's given them all one hundred per cent, but you can tell the old fucker's into this one. Best of all is his electrifying confrontation with a bare-chested Sean Harris in a hideously unpleasant drug den. With his badly self-drawn tattoos, heroin habit, indifference to human suffering and fondness for making rape videos, I reckon even scabies would think twice about hanging around with this dude. Caine's mildly bewildered expression at someone choosing to live in such a manner is priceless.

In short, *Harry Brown* might be a warmed-up rehash but it still succeeds with its credible portrayal of a none-too-sprightly vigilante. Funnily enough, it's the youthful, ultra-polite Emily Mortimer respectfully on Caine's trail of mayhem who hits the movie's only bum note. She has to be Britain's least convincing detective-inspector.

Zev Guttman in *Remember* (2015)

We all have regrets. We all imagine a different past from time to time. Some of us probably even fantasize about being someone else. Hell, I'm certainly guilty of wondering what it'd be like to be Raquel Welch ambling around a prehistoric landscape in a fur bikini. Perhaps one day we'll invent machines or come up with a drug that'll enable us to do things like that at the drop of a hat.

In the meantime, we've got nature's sly old beast, dementia, and its supremely fucked-up older brother, Alzheimer's. These two afflictions usually get the worst of raps but they do provide ample opportunity for mental escape. A nice little break from that big boo-hoo called reality. Who knows what horrible shit its lucky recipients are erasing? Who knows where they're popping off to?

Take my mum's favourite, Christopher Plummer, in *Remember*. This guy's so out of it he keeps forgetting his wife's no longer alive. One minute he's married, the next he's a footloose and fancy-free widower. He can be cognizant, then take a nap and (just like me after two whole pints of beer) have no idea where he is or what he's doing. Never mind, a fellow Jew in his nursing home has just given him a letter, a letter that provides instruction for tracking down and killing a former Auschwitz guard who murdered both their families.

And so our elderly, gun-wielding assassin starts putting one doddery foot in front of the other. It's a fascinating odyssey in which he's mainly able to remember his deadly mission but often gets lost in a thick fog of confusion. Every unpredictable encounter with receptionists, taxi drivers, customs officials, security guards, fellow passengers and especially *Breaking Bad's* Dean Norris is so well done that the flick never loses momentum, despite its protagonist only being able to move at a quarter of a mile an hour.

It's marvellous, Nazi-tinged stuff, both a vivid depiction of a failing brain and the way in which monstrous evil is capable of creating ripples that can keep travelling outwards for decades.

Ulzana's Raid (1972)

Director

Robert Aldrich

Synopsis

Merciless killers chase merciless killers across a merciless desert

Cast

Burt Lancaster, Bruce Davison, Jorge Luke, Richard Jaeckel, Joaquin Martinez

Some films don't appeal.

They might be a huge hit, win a boatload of Oscars, and get cracking reviews and yet... I'd rather read the Koran than take a gander.

Maybe you feel the same. Maybe there's a flick or two that the prospect of sitting through leaves you cold.

Dances with Wolves fits this category for me, partly because I regard Kevin Costner as little more than a competent, blandly handsome actor, but mainly because I suspect it's a super-earnest flick served with a hefty dose of gag-inducing political correctness. Now you might find my next comment slightly askew, but I prefer the people in my Cowboy and Indian movies to behave horribly. I want Indians to slaughter and get slaughtered coz, you know, that's the sort of thing that makes a movie *fun*. Why would I wanna learn about the richness of their culture? If I fancy that, I'll get a library book out.

Perhaps I'm being grossly unfair. Maybe Sioux courtship rituals or the intricate skill needed to make a tepee are a much more interesting watch than whitey getting scalped. After all, I haven't seen *Dances with Wolves* so it's dumb to have a pseudo-opinion on it. Maybe if I do ever get around to it,

I'll love its illuminating three hours. Who knows? I'm just saying it *doesn't appeal*.

Robert Aldrich's *Ulzana's Raid*, however, is a different, bullet-riddled kettle of racist fish. This is exactly the sort of gory shit I want my unenlightened, unreconstructed antagonists to get up to. Here the cowboys never consider they're invaders who've stolen the Apaches' land while the fucked-over Indians get to indulge, of course, in some awesomely mean payback. And so we're treated to arson, torture, blind racial hatred, a helpless woman getting shot between the eyes, suicide, a liver being ripped out of a still warm corpse, gang rape, naked terror, and not one trace of Costner anywhere. Even beloved pets don't make it out of this one alive.

Marvellous.

This is no tawdry piece of exploitation trash, though. In fact, it's got a tremendous script, top-notch acting, wonderful cinematography and masterful direction. For all its violence, the story couldn't be simpler. The granite-faced, near-silent Ulzana (Martinez) and fifteen or so other bucks break out of an Arizonian Indian reservation, sending a collective shiver of fear through the local white folk. At a nearby army post the young, inexperienced Lieutenant Garnett DeBuin (Davison) is given the job to warn anyone in the marauding war party's path, as well as track down and deal with the aggressors. Helping out is an aging, laconic scout, McIntosh (Lancaster), and an Apache tracker, Ke-Ni-Tay (Luke).

Realism's the name of the game here and boy, does *Ulzana's Raid* nail it. The bursts of intense action are expertly staged, especially any stunt work involving the horses. There's also a fantastic attack on a wagon-riding woman and her young son in which the defending trooper, obviously knowledgeable of how Apaches like to amuse themselves, makes the most chilling, instantaneous decisions I think I've ever seen.

However, at the movie's heart is an attempt to understand, explain or at least come to terms with the nauseating savagery. Mackintosh respects and fears the Apache, but crucially doesn't hate them ("Be like hating the desert coz there ain't no water on it"). This is in stark contrast to the rest of the seething troopers whose clamour for reprisals grows ever fiercer with the discovery of each atrocity.

The idealistic DeBuin is caught in the middle, convinced a 'lack of Christian feeling toward the Indian' is at the root of the problem, and apparently unaware of his creed's long history of cruelty committed against individuals, groups and even countries.

"Why are your people like that?" he asks Ke-Ni-Tay after finding a pinioned homesteader with charred feet and a dog's tail sticking out of his mouth. "Why are they so cruel?" The Apache tracker is unapologetic about his brethren. "It's how they are," he replies. "Always been like that."

Pressed further, Ke-Ni-Tay explains Ulzana has lost power while being kept in the reservation and needs to reinvigorate himself by 'taking power' from every man he kills. The more a man suffers, the more power Ulzana takes. "Here in this land, man must have power," the tracker adds.

It's an explanation, but not enough to satisfy the troopers' growing thirst for blood. Soon they're mutilating an Indian corpse, an act of barbarism that causes the outraged lieutenant to drag them off. The watching McIntosh offers a typically pithy observation.

"What bothers you, lieutenant," he says, "is white men behaving like Indians. Kinda confuses the issue, don't it?"

Ulzana's Raid would have to be among the best Westerns of the 70s. You can find a Vietnam War allegory hiding within if you want, but I just think of it as a supremely tense slice of cat and mouse nihilism.

The Amusingly Bonkers

There are plenty of people who take enormous pleasure in hooting through terrible movies. The so-bad-it's-good crowd.

Fair enough.

I must admit I enjoy *The Exorcist's* craptastic sequel, a flick that regularly ends up on lists of the worst ever made. I also heartily respond to the mammalian madness of the *Jaws* knockoff *Orca: The Killer Whale*, a seafaring venture that sets sail for the port of insanity and nimbly manages to dock there ninety minutes later.

I guess I'm a fan of clueless flicks that have talent both behind and in front of the camera. I like a decent budget, well-known actors and a daft script. This type of setup usually results in floundering A or B-listers who really should know better, as opposed to the no-budget ineptness of celebrated dogs like *Reefer Madness, Glen or Glenda* and *The Creeping Terror.* Well, sorry, I don't get the appeal of terrible acting, lifeless direction and dreadful special effects. Indeed, laughing at the talentless Ed Wood's stuff just seems a bit mean, akin to sniggering over adolescents with learning difficulties putting on a school play.

For me, the enjoyment derived from a bad or whacked-out movie is little different from a good one. Both have to *flow.* They can't be dull, the worst crime a movie can commit. Here are half a dozen that make me smile.

One Million Years B.C. (1966)

A squabble-heavy, almost dialogue-free mix-up of ape men, superimposed live animals, stop motion animation, warring tribes and volcanic eruptions that illustrates little more than the old adage cavemen prefer blondes. What's not to love?

The story: Not much, really. A macho bloke gets kicked out of his unenlightened tribe and bumps into the statuesque, much more civilized Raquel Welch. Some might call that a stroke of luck.

185

The characters

Tumak (John Richardson): A born thief and fighter. Somewhat lacks people skills, although handy if you need a warthog killed in an enclosed space. Hates his dad. And brother. And everyone else. Unsurprisingly, it's not long before the Rock Tribe ousts him. Gets taken in by Raquel's Shell Tribe, whose members appear to have come up with the world's first hippy commune. Tumak struggles to adapt to the good life. Hell, laughing is an alien concept to this dude, let alone hospitality. Bemused by cave paintings and jewellery-making, he's noticeably unimpressed by their artistic temperament. How long before this off-kilter bunch light joss sticks, serve herbal tea and charge him for a bout of New Age crystal healing? Suffice to say, he receives another eviction notice. Raquel tags along as he wanders through a monster-dominated landscape that's even more forbidding than a Welsh Valleys town after chucking-out time.

Loana (Raquel Welch): A goddess in a fur bikini. Perhaps bored of all the Shell Tribe's nice, respectful boys, she opts for a bit of rough. And with his dreadful table manners, mistrustful stare and penchant for theft and violence, Tumak's obviously the one. Not that she's beyond flexing her claws. Watch out for her victorious catfight, although those annoyingly well-made fur bikinis stay in place.

Why it's bonkers: I actually feel a bit bad starting off with this childhood favourite, especially as it contains some of the best work of the master, Ray Harryhausen. There's an awful lot to enjoy, such as its casual brutality, effective score and a scintillating fight between a Ceratosaurus and a Triceratops, but you can't get away from its disregard for sticking dinosaurs and mankind together. Not only that, but its title doubles down on the blatant error. Dinosaurs had been extinct for *65 million years* before Jesus popped up, although their existence (unlike the Son of God) has amusingly never been in question.

I Don't Want to be Born AKA The Devil Within Her (1975)

How on Earth did *Dynasty's* Joan Collins survive the 1970s to become a worldwide star?

During this decade she notched up movies that included an ill-fated *Alfie* sequel, derided, erotic money-spinners like *The Stud* and *The Bitch* (which are not so much soft-core as *mushy*-core), the amazingly bad *Empire of the Ants*, and about fifteen others that made very little impression whatsoever.

Still, I have a soft spot for Ms. Collins, a woman who clearly paid her dues, kept herself in fantastic shape and has obviously led a colourful, interesting life. Part of my affection rests on her yen for the macabre, as exemplified by her handful of horror movies. Hard to pick a worst, but the nonsensically titled *I Don't Want to be Born* might be the one.

The story: An amorous, dancing dwarf is rejected by a middle-aged stripper and so curses her womb(!) Somehow this outpouring of bile works and she gives birth to a possessed, super-strong baby who's invariably decked out in a cute jumpsuit.

The characters

Lucy Carlesi: In a cinematic first, Joan plays a rich woman. She's the aforementioned stripper, having moved on from a less than saintly past after meeting and marrying a wealthy Italian. Childbirth doesn't prove much fun and her first attempt to cuddle her hefty newborn results in a scratched face. Things go steadily downhill and it's not long before she's intermittently seeing the dwarf's face instead of her baby's.

Gino Carlesi (Ralph Bates): I'm not sure why Ralph Bates was contractually obliged to have the same side-parted hairdo in every movie and TV show he ever made, but at least he tried to danger things up here by attempting a European accent. Not that he uses it too much. It just comes and goes, a bit like his wife's clothes. As Lucy's hubby, he blandly does his best to reassure her about their 'very violent' offspring so it's not much of a surprise he ends up stepping into a dangling noose in the garden and being hauled up to his doom. That'll teach the bastard for not once reading a bedtime story or singing a lullaby.

Dr. Finch (Donald Pleasence): Supposedly the voice of cool scientific reason, this is a paediatrician who advises against breastfeeding and doles out drugs to sedate a newborn. Helpfully explains that a baby bloodily scratching its mother's face is the result of cuddling it 'too tightly'. Tasked with offering explanations for the baby's increasing aggression, he toys with the possibility of epilepsy and psychiatric intervention. It's a shame the latter wasn't utilized. For in a movie of this stature a baby lying on a leather couch being quizzed about its, er, childhood would've fitted in just swell.

To be fair to Dr. Finch, reasonable solutions do seem to be in short supply, particularly as the malicious mite has literally begun throwing its toys out of its pram. For as he wisely states: "A doctor can't write out prescriptions against evil and violence."

Tommy Morris (John Steiner): A Cockney Sean Penn lookalike who used to employ Lucy at his none-too-classy strip club/cabaret joint. Talks tough, but has no answer when punched in the face by a baby.

Hercules (George Claydon): They say hell hath no fury like a woman scorned, but what about a portly, sarcastically-named dwarf? "Maybe I egged him on," Lucy confesses to a friend at one point. "I thought it was just a game." Well, no, Joan Collins, the heartfelt emotions of little people are not 'just a game'. There can be serious consequences in failing to let them down gently or declining a request for a handjob.

Mind you, perhaps Hercules needs to polish his seduction technique as it seems to involve wearing a jester's three-pronged hat, looking manic and pawing the scantily-clad goods from the rear. He does have a novel response to rejection, though, and one I'm willing to try the next time I'm passed over: "You will have a baby, an evil monster conceived in your womb, as big as I am small, and possessed by the devil himself!" Then again, I'd probably skip the colourful language and offer the protesting chick a tenner instead.

Where there's a will and all that.

Nicolas the baby: Nicolas. Geddit? As in Old Nick. Or in this case Very Young Nick. The star of our shit show. Weighing in at almost twelve pounds

(5.4 kilos), he's a 'lovely big boy' with a yen for spitting, hair-pulling, biting and nursery-wrecking. He will put a dead mouse in your mug of tea, but I have to admit this suggests a fondness for pranks rather than a desire to establish a satanic kingdom on a cowed Earth.

On the plus side, he does hate nuns. See below.

Sister Albana (Eileen Atkins): Lucy's sister-in-law, a nun that works in animal pathology at a 'medical research unit'. Huh? Since when do these Catholic whackjobs get up to this kind of malarkey? I thought their jobs tended to involve filling school kids' heads with garbage about guilt and sin before rapping their knuckles with a ruler. Sister Albana, however, prefers torturing animals in a lab. Bless her. Well, presumably this scientific stuff has got something to do with the plot then?

No, not in the slightest.

Unsurprisingly, she goes up against our evil, eighteen-inch-long foe armed with a bible, a crucifix, a bad Italian accent, and a steely willingness to confiscate every diaper in sight. Somehow, though, a baby's grizzling is not quite as unsettling or memorable as a pubescent, heavily scarred, levitating girl demonically bellowing: "Your mother sucks cocks in hell!" Instead of a violently shaking bed we get a wobbling crib. Amazingly, Very Young Nick opts not to puke in Sister Albana's face, even though it's well-known all babies do this, whether possessed or not.

Why it's bonkers: *I Don't Want to be Born* was obviously a knockoff designed to cash in on the success of *Rosemary's Baby*, *The Exorcist* and *It's Alive*. Everything from its directing and editing to its script and score are amateurish, yet this London-based tale of a brutal bambino has an easygoing charm with a decent body count. I can't abide bad acting, but that's not the case with the likes of Pleasence and the blind psychic from *Don't Look Now* onboard while Joan certainly does her best. Apart from that, we also get a Vaseline-smeared dream sequence, some T & A, a suggestion that the baby's anti-social nature might be down to 'mafia blood', and a wonderfully whacked out strip club/nursery room exorcism finale.

Of course, it's never explained, or even hinted at, how Hercules has the power to throw a curse. Can all dwarves do this? And why would he hex Lucy's future baby anyway? To be nitpicky, this doesn't seem fair as the (not yet conceived) baby hasn't wronged him.

Anyway, the kills are terrifically funny, particularly an unsuspecting nanny getting shoved into a lake. And because the villain's a baby we never get to see him *do* anything, such as wield a spade or smash through a window, which is a bit of a problem in a horror movie. We just have to take his violence and murderous actions for granted. Not that the director doesn't try. There's always a close-up of Nicolas after each bout of mayhem, but I'm afraid I was unable to detect a malevolent glint in his eye, a cackle or a gleeful rubbing together of hands. Instead it's one shot of a sweet little face after another.

No wonder this kid's acting career fizzled out. Couldn't even do the fucking basics.

Switchblade Sisters AKA *The Jezebels* (1975)

Normally if a movie contains knife fights, rape, pimping, drug dealing, nudity and shootings, you can safely assume it's a drama. Not *Switchblade*. It's pure comedy from start to finish. It's so OTT there's not one ounce of dramatic tension to be found, but wander into its overheated, oestrogen-fuelled territory seeking a snigger fest and you'll be fine.

The story: The stability of a fearsome high school girl gang is threatened by a sassy, resourceful new member, especially when its associated boy gang goes to war with a larger gang. Soon there's blood on the streets. Homework is never done. Hey, everybody's gotta be in a gang.

The characters

Lace (Robbie Lee): Introduced to the tune of *Black-Hearted Woman*. As an R&B singer on the soundtrack ominously belts out *Evil as a man can be/ Never gonna be as evil/As the devil in a woman*, it's clear this is our main Bad Girl, especially as she looks like a prettier version of Johnny Rotten. She's the leader of a ten-strong pack of teenage vixens called the Dagger Debs.

So what's she up to? As it happens, sitting at a dressing table sharpening her switchblade. Good. Dabbing on some perfume. Not so good. Standing, slipping on a black denim jacket and... admiring her figure in the mirror. *Uh-oh*, doubt Steven Seagal ever did this. How long before she starts swooning over some guy and writing love poetry? As it turns out, about twenty minutes. At least she refers to her boyfriend's cock as 'junior'.

Patch (Monica Gayle): Our Iago figure. Yes, really. Lost an eye in service of the gang. No one's been able to find it. Has anyone looked down the back of the sofa? Spits out one of the flick's best lines in response to a cop's frisking hands: "Get your hands off the fruit, faggot!"

Maggie (Joanne Nail): The new girl in town. Favours tight denim shorts. Not gang-affiliated. Can look after herself, though. She immediately beats up the knife-wielding Patch with nothing more than a soda-filled straw, but is then accused of fighting dirty. Doesn't object much to being raped, later telling her rapist: "I like you."

Dominic (Asher Brauner): Lace's boyfriend, who looks to be pushing thirty but is still at school. He's a self-proclaimed bastard and president of the Silver Daggers. So mean that he refuses to pay for his burgers at the gang's diner hangout. He does have a considerate side, though, by only raping girls who 'ask for it'. Perhaps he could get meaner by working on his insults. For example, when the bow-tied school principal suggests a rival gang share the Daggers' territory, he says: "Why don't you stick your head up my ass? *Sir*." Surely his possessive adjective use is confused here? Unless, of course, he *wants* the principal's head up his arse. Luckily, the rest of the gang let the grammar slip go and don't immediately instigate a bloody *coup d'etat* because their leader's gone seriously homo.

Crabs (Chase Newhart): An over-cocky, medallion-wearing rival gang leader that gets transferred into the Daggers' school. Despite being an alleged schoolboy, Crabs has a Sean Connery-level of chest hair. Appears to base his gang's look on a cross between the 70s glam rockers Slade and Rupert Bear. None too enlightened when it comes to the ladies. Breast-ogling, arse-grabbing and abduction off the street for a spot of gang rape all form part of a busy day's misogyny. Wins points for calling Dominic 'Dumb-minic', a fiendishly clever level of goading in anyone's book.

Muff (Marlene Clark): A friend of Maggie's who happens to be a man-hating, militant commie black with a pudding bowl afro haircut. She hates 'capitalist gangsters' and believes political power grows out of the barrel of the gun. I think we all know such a type. Handy to associate with if you want to get your hands on Mao's Little Red Book or an M16. Oh, and an ad hoc armoured car.

Mom Smackley (Kate Murtagh): An overweight, predatory lesbian jailer sporting an unconvincing curly wig. Drawls like Clint Eastwood. Calls Maggie 'cutie pie' and grabs both her arse cheeks, but is labelled a 'fat pig dyke' in return. Never mind. Mom's got two blonde lackeys and a pair of rubber gloves.

Why it's bonkers: *Switchblade* is female-centric but a long way from feminist, typified by its lack of female role models, a couple of grumpily accepted rapes and the way Dominic pimps out the members of the Dagger Debs to his horny fellow high schoolers for $5 a pop. Most of the time the girls are referred to as 'little beavers'. Still, I guess our ladies eventually gain control, even if they do prove themselves just as groan-inducingly stupid as their male 'cripple-dick' counterparts.

For the record I will never buy into females physically pushing guys around, especially when played straight as it is here. Whenever the girls indulge in their macho swagger the movie, credibility-wise, falls flat on its tits. Then again, I'm not sure director Jack Hill was aiming for such a notion. In fact, fuck knows what he was aiming for with his scattershot approach. Take a mass shooting at a roller rink that results in a fair few deaths. We're talking about teenagers with semi-automatic rifles blowing the shit out of anything that moves. Surely such a major event would have resulted in part of the city being locked down and an intensive hunt for its perps? Instead a cop wags a finger at Lace, complaining that 'a couple of people got beat up at the roller rink. We don't like that. It don't reflect well on us.'

You *what*?

Whatever the case, *Switchblade's* a barmy romp, despite all its nasty (but non-graphic) elements. It wants to depict urban grittiness, but that's a tough ask when it's awash in unintentional humour. I particularly enjoyed a washroom catfight that results in Mom Smackley being transformed into a *male* stunt double who's finally subdued by a toilet plunger on the face. Indeed, the ladies magically change gender whenever a physically demanding fight is needed, a directing decision that does suggest a lack of faith in females being able to convincingly fight. It's almost as if Hill were worried they might end up looking like Silly Girlies.

Saturn 3 (1980)

Ambition can be a dangerous thing. Ask Macbeth. Or take a look at Farrah Fawcett's career. After one season of *Charlie's Angels* and an iconic red swimwear poster shoot she was a massive star. Hollywood was surely the way to go. So she went and started making one dud pic after another. By the turn of the new decade she was still managing to nab top billing, but the $10million *Saturn* pretty much put the kibosh on things until her 1986 Golden Globe-winning (brief) comeback in *Extremities*. Frankly, I'm surprised anyone gave her a lead role again, but no one emerges from this extraterrestrial turkey looking good.

The story: It's the distant future and, as usual, Earth's fucked. Saturn 3 is an 'experimental food research station' where Fawcett and the none-too-young Kirk Douglas are busy playing chess, drinking, skipping rope, patting their dog and taking showers together. No wonder Earth is starving if it's relying on these two lazy bastards to kick start things again. Meanwhile, a rogue, half-mad captain (Harvey Keitel) fails some sort of exam. Instead of wearily sharpening his pencil again and retaking it, he kills the legitimate candidate, steals a space shuttle and goes out to see our lackadaisical lovers, perhaps to join in the skipping. Gotta be easier than passing exams.

The characters

Alex (Fawcett): An archetypal Silly Girly. Forever flinching, getting flustered, fainting, screaming and running away. I don't think she comes up with one idea or proves to be any practical help whatsoever when things go awry. Makes up for her rampant silliness by briefly going topless.

Major Adam (Douglas): He's in charge of Saturn 3 which means he's the boss of Alex, a pet dog and some pot plants. Worries about becoming 'obsolete' but already seems to have achieved that with aplomb.

Captain Benson (Keitel): At this stage in his career Keitel had notched up plenty of quality fare, such as *Mean Streets*, *Taxi Driver*, *The Duellists* and *Blue Collar*. All good things must come to an end and you'd be hard pressed to find an actor looking so desperate to be anywhere else. Sporting a little gay ponytail, he's terse, non-blinking, unsmiling, and even speaks in a monotone. His expression does not alter throughout. I guess his pronounced lack of enthusiasm isn't a huge surprise when he's required to do stuff like hoist a dog in the air and look up its arse. Then there are his attempts to seduce Alex: "You have a great body," he says to her. "May I use it?"

No idea why he commits murder to get out to Saturn 3, but once there he takes his boyhood love of Meccano to another level by building a demigod robot that incorporates a 'non-born human brain'.

And, of course, this robot also wants to fuck Alex.

Hector: Our dog-hating, eight-foot tall, randy robot. Its weedy head is nothing more than a pair of eyes on a telescopic arm, somewhat undermining its sense of malevolence. Not a patch on *Robocop's* Enforcement Droid Series 209 and is more like Metal Mickey than the T-1000. However, it does put in a slightly more animated performance than Harvey Keitel. As do the pot plants.

Why it's bonkers: I think I'm honour-bound at this point to make a tired joke about *Saturn 3* not being as good as the first two instalments. Anyway, in 1980 Douglas was in his mid-sixties while Fawcett was thirty-two. I know the movies like to pair an older man with a younger lady but sheesh. Yes, Douglas is in terrific shape (the gnarly old fucker lived till he was 103), but it's hard to think of a more unconvincing, mismatched screen couple. Then again I guess Alex is marooned in space and not exactly stuck for choice.

To be fair, there's not much else to scoff about during *Saturn's* opening half an hour. It has decent special effects, typified by its *Star Wars*-like opening of a gigantic spaceship taking an age to pass overhead. The film also boasts a suitably grandiose score while the space station is well created.

Bit by bit, though, it goes off the rails. Sometimes it's minor stuff like a very visible cut on Benson's forehead shifting from left to right in successive scenes, but mainly it's the half-baked story. Nothing makes any sense, especially after the surly Benson arrives. He's the key character but his motivation and goals are lost in the murk. A cardboard cut-out of Keitel could've done the same job. No tension whatsoever is generated by the love triangle (or should that be love *rectangle* considering Hector wants in on the action?) Benson also acts like a rapist in waiting which, for some reason, fails to turn the happily monogamous Alex on.

Then, of course, we get consistently funny scenes like Hector making indignant whirring noises when coming under scary attack from a couple of hurled plastic buckets or a jet of dry ice. My favourite bit, though, would have to be Benson barging in on Adam and Alex in bed. "Doesn't it disgust you to be used by him?" he asks Alex. "To be touched by an old man?" Moments later we're treated to the sight of a nude sexagenarian leaping onto his spacesuit-clad critic and wrestling around the floor.

Poor Harvey. I don't think he ever set foot in space again.

Who Dares Win AKA *The Final Option* (1982)

I was a kid during 1980's Iranian Embassy siege in central London, which was resolved by the SAS kicking some serious terrorist butt. During the raid the soldiers abseiled from the roof, smashed through the windows and knocked out every baddie in about a quarter of an hour. All on live television! Not only that, but the vast majority of hostages were rescued unharmed.

Unsurprisingly, the SAS' reputation as the planet's best trained, *deadliest* bunch of super soldiers skyrocketed to the point of mythology. There was nothing these lads couldn't do. Each one was John Rambo except, of course, a Green Beret was a fucking wimp in comparison.

The triumphant SAS raid also had an immediate effect on me and my schoolmates. At playtime we became hard-as-nails paratroopers, forever bursting into the staffroom to hurl stun grenades and rescue hostages until the principal wrote to our parents insisting we stop, especially as Mr. Walker, the Games Teacher, was getting very, very tired of being abducted and waterboarded.

Two years after that daring Iranian Embassy mission, it wasn't much of a surprise that the Brits got a film up and running about this elite unit's legendary exploits. Mr. Walker probably didn't go to see it.

The story: An undercover SAS captain infiltrates a radical bunch of peace-loving loonies who want a nuclear missile fired at Scotland. Christ, I know Haggis Land is a bit grim, but this seems awfully harsh.

The characters

Captain Peter Skellen (Lewis Collins): Introduced pretending to be a hostage during a super-tough training exercise as his SAS buddies burst into a room with guns ablazing. Doesn't flinch once. This is obviously a Real Man who could kill you with a karate chop from ten feet away. Immediately backs up his unquestionable masculinity with heroic feats of strength, such as beating up two hooded, hogtied captives, leaping onto a departing ferry, riding a motorbike for a short distance in a straight line, and jumping off a slow-moving bus. Disapproves of the theatre, especially if the male performers wear tights and dance. This is not what Real Men do. Claims to be very knowledgeable about nuclear war. "I know more about nuclear devastation than you ever will," he tells the chief baddie. As he's too young to have lived through Hiroshima or Nagasaki and this movie is set four years before Chernobyl, I'm not sure how he's obtained this information. Doesn't do much else, except glower and use a portable shaving mirror at night to communicate an amazing array of information to his superiors.

Frankie Leith (Judy Davis): A bad attempt at a Strong Female Role, Frankie is a rich revolutionary and leader of the People's Front. Not sure why anyone wants a revolution or a nuclear explosion when they've inherited a lovely house and a tidy sum. Personally, I'd plump for things to continue as they are. Then again, Frankie is thick. Really, really thick. Despite knowing a major operation is on the cards, she thinks there's nothing fishy about being picked up by a man in a pub who quickly reveals he's ex-special forces. The next day she offers Skellen a five-hundred quid a week job with the People's Front and moves him into her place, even though he hasn't been investigated and fucks 'like a man just out of prison'. [This is slander: all SAS men are amazing lays]. When presented with credible photographic evidence and eyewitness accounts that Skellen is working for the other side, she insists his 'expertise' will prove invaluable. As for her commitment to nuclear disarmament, she believes the best way to achieve this noble goal is to atomize Scotland. "We want the world to see what one bomb can do, not in theory but in *fact.*"

Colonel J. Hadley (Tony Doyle): Skellen's immediate boss and the SAS' main PR mouthpiece. Usually seen with his beloved soldier boys in the background as they abseil into burning houses, assault terrorist-riddled trains, run across gangplanks between buildings, set off controlled explosions and generally go through their super-fit paces. I think this is supposed to give the impression that the SAS' training never stops. You're sleeping and they've cracked yet another way to kick our radical foes in the balls. "When the SAS is called upon to do what we're trained to do, it has been likened to a surgeon cutting out a cancer," Colonel Hadley says while stroking his engorged penis and blowing a kiss at a passing paratrooper. "It's a filthy and difficult job, we don't like doing it, but it is our duty."

Secretary of State Arthur Currie (Richard Widmark): On hand in a brazen attempt to appeal to the American movie-going public. Not impressed by Frankie, and makes the mistake of trying to talk to a zealot. "Miss, why don't you go out and hijack an airplane?" he says after her bout of machine gun-wielding tomfoolery has interrupted a formal dinner at a colleague's residence. "It's a lot more fun. Little kids can hijack a dinner."

Yeah, mate, but can they blow up Scotland?

General Ira Potter (Robert Webber): Another unimpressed dinner guest. Slightly less diplomatic than the Secretary of State, as when offering his verdict on Frankie: "She's a fucking lunatic."

Why it's bonkers: After *Top Gun* there was apparently a big surge in drooling blokes wanting to slip on aviator sunglasses and become closeted homosexual navy pilots. Well, four years before the cocktastic Cruiser strutted his pert pecs, Lewis Collins did pretty much the same by starring in a two-hour advertisement for the SAS. *Who Dares* is undoubtedly a load of right-wing, flag-waving, jingoistic bollocks that a fair few idiots somehow pegged as anti-CND, even though the film makes it clear the terrorists have infiltrated the group to use it as cover. Not that their camouflage plays any role in the proceedings.

Indeed, this clumsily written flick doesn't make a lick of sense. The People's Front is an anti-nuclear protest group. Its express aim is to prevent nuclear explosions so its fanatical goons *try to do the exact opposite* by getting a US nuclear missile launched at a submarine base. I mean, it would be like those humourless Nazis in PETA deciding the best way to get their anti-cruelty message across is to start slaughtering animals on live TV.

Mad Frankie can justify it all, though. "We want this to be done in the name of peace," she says, giving the authorities a generous eighteen hours to disperse the Scottish natives. "We want everyone, every nationality, all the billions of us, to be reminded of the devastation of a nuclear explosion."

Why does she think anyone has forgotten what Little Boy and Fat Man did?

Oh well, at least we get a half-decent catfight.

***Body of Evidence* (1993)**

A perfect example of why the so-called erotic thriller is derided. Released ten months after *Basic Instinct's* gigantic success, *Body* apes that vastly superior flick's opening as a camera prowls around a mansion toward a bedroom. We can hear fucking, there's a shot of nipple clamps, and a TV screen is showing a video of a naked Madonna, black bush out, riding an older dude on a bed in the reverse cowgirl position.

Classy.

Hang on, now there's a dead dude on the bed viewing himself balls deep in our panting heroine. It's the same guy! I think he expired watching himself doing the nasty which, of course, is almost as ideal a way to cark it as dying *while* fucking.

Man, this is mind-bending stuff. Less than two minutes in and we've already had nudey num-nums, pervy sex toys and death. I suspect my childlike sense of wonder is gonna be stretched to the max by this little beauty.

The story: A blonde strumpet is accused of using her super-heated snatch as a weapon of war against a coked-up old man with a dodgy ticker. Why? Coz she's the main beneficiary in his $8million will. Blonde ambition, me thinks. She's put on trial, charged with inconsiderate lovemaking and mediocre acting. Much solemnity ensues.

The characters

Rebecca Carlson (Madonna): Liberated and confident, she thinks people who don't use drugs and handcuffs during sex are conservative hypocrites. She's the boss in bed and always fucks on top, although she doesn't mind a bit of anal rape. Such is the advanced state of her nymphomania she can't even pop to the pharmacy without ending up naked. Insists she's innocent of the state's charge, although we soon learn of her criminal tendencies when she confesses to repeatedly stealing strawberries during childhood. Spouts constant, hard-fought wisdom e.g. "I fucked you," she tells one conquest. "I fucked Andrew. I fucked Frank. That's what I do. I fuck." Specializes in blank stares, especially on the witness stand where you can almost see her sex-obsessed brains leaking out of her ears.

Frank Dulaney (Willem Dafoe): Rebecca's straight arrow lawyer who predictably can't control his cock. It's twitching from the moment he meets her grieving at the funeral of her ex-lay, but instead of clamping on an icepack he starts chasing the gold-digging tart up the stairs of her luxurious riverside home and tearing her dress off. Beaver munching ensues but before long he's getting dragged into more kinky, sexually adventurous shenanigans. "Are you scared?" Rebecca asks before tipping some hot candle wax onto his bare chest.

Big deal.

Rebecca fancies herself as an uncompromising S&M advocate, but back in the UK I can remember reading about a bunch of gay blokes who enjoyed nailing each other's cocks to planks. Eventually the crown's attempt to prosecute them fell apart because it was a case of consenting adults. No victims whatsoever. When you realize how some people get their kicks, the stuff Frank endures at Rebecca's behest (such as leaning back on some broken glass) seems... well, a bit *gay*. To be honest, I'm disappointed Frank didn't end up tarred and feathered and crucified upside down with a live eel up his arse.

Anyhow, he rightly believes the state's case against Rebecca is ludicrous. "What're you gonna do?" he taunts the district attorney. "Tag the body as a murder weapon? Exhibit A? It's not a crime to be a great lay."

Nuff said.

Robert Garrett (Joe Mantegna): The D.A. Obviously wants to fuck Rebecca, but as that's impossible he deals with his blue balls by trying to throw her shapely arse in jail for twenty years. Incapable of saying anything sensible. "She is a beautiful woman," he tells the jury, "but when this trial is over, you will see her no differently to a gun or a knife."

Joanne Braslow (Anne Archer): The dead man's duplicitous secretary, whose main contribution is to call Rebecca a 'cokehead slut' and sport some sort of awful, backcombed mullet.

Sharon Dulaney (Julianne Moore): Frank's wife. The wronged woman. In a dog of a role she offers nothing, except another bad hairdo and the sight of her sweaty, naked breasts during a deeply unerotic, nay *awful*, sex scene.

Judge Mabel Burnham (Lillian Lehman): A stern, no-nonsense stickler who likes to bang her gavel, warn counsel, clear the courtroom, and keep a rod up her arse in the movie's sole non-sexual insertion. A shame as this movie was crying out for a piss-taker. "I can't change the titillating nature of this trial," she says on its opening day, "but if I had wanted to work in a circus, I would've learned how to ride a trapeze." Unfortunately, trapezes, clown cars and bearded ladies all fail to appear as the judge keeps an iron control over proceedings. At one point she even reminds a witness of being under oath and the need to 'take it seriously.' Thanks for clarifying that, judge, because I had no idea murder trial participants were supposed to go about things 'seriously'.

Won't someone please put a whoopee cushion on her chair?

Why it's bonkers: The concept alone in this tit-heavy travesty is enough to justify such a tag, but there's also the dialogue. Jesus Christ, it's one long stream of po-faced howlers. Even eleven-year-old boys come out with stuff like: "Can you really screw someone to death?"

Or how about a clueless crime scene examiner being told the sex toy he's just picked up is a nipple clamp. "How does this thing work?" he asks. Fucking hell, mate, how about we leave you alone for five minutes and you try to work it out?

Later a doctor testifies that banging a coked-up man with a heart condition is 'the same as shooting a loaded gun' at him. Hmm, don't think so. And what about Rebecca posing this nugget: "Have you ever seen animals make love?"

The performances don't help with Madonna being our main offender. I'd say she's an improvement on Elizabeth Berkley's wretched overacting in *Showgirls,* but (despite the similar blondeness and fantastic body) definitely a poor man's Sharon Stone. The flat chemistry between Madonna and Dafoe is also a million miles from the fireworks generated by *Body Heat*'s Kathleen

Turner and William Hurt. Not that this half-courtroom drama, half-bonkfest doesn't try hard with its licking, shirt-ripping, bondage, and impromptu groping in an elevator. Indeed, it puts such an emphasis on sex that (like *Showgirls*) everything becomes ludicrously unsexy.

Perhaps the worst scene is when Frank storms around to Rebecca's house after she's ruined his marriage and shoves her to the floor. Her response? To stick a moistened finger down her panties and start flicking the pea. About a minute later she's still rubbing away as he stands with his back to her trying to walk out, his twitching nose obviously scenting warmed-up pussy. Boy, it's crass, awkward stuff, released just a few months after Madonna's equally obvious (but hugely successful) coffee table book, *Sex*. I suggest you don't flick through that tome's pages and then watch *Body* because you might start finding it a tad tricky to separate character and person.

I dunno. Sometimes I think it's a bad idea all round showing lengthy, detailed sex scenes. Maybe movies ought to take a leaf out of *The Graduate's* book. Discretion can work very nicely, you know.

Body did not do well at the box office, proving to be another unfortunate misstep in Madonna's acting career that followed the equally panned *Shanghai Surprise* and *Who's That Girl*. No need to worry, though, coz *Swept Away* was still to come.

Oh.

Fucked-Up Films #5: Wolf Creek (2005)

Synopsis

Australia. The outback. And you thought venomous snakes were scary.

Director

Greg McLean

Cast

John Jarratt, Nathan Phillips, Cassandra Magrath, Kestie Morassi

What are these sick bastards doing? Actually, Ben, Kristy and Liz aren't sick bastards. They're lovely guys partying on the Western Australian coast who are about to undertake an eleven-hour drive inland to see the world's second biggest meteorite crater. One of *Wolf Creek's* great strengths is the steady way it builds up these three backpackers. They are the antithesis of the gormless knife fodder usually found in slashers. There's no attempt to make them wacky, dumb or unlikeable. They're simply ordinary, believable kids goofing around, sharing a joint and recovering from hangovers on what may well be the trip of a lifetime. Director McLean excels at capturing their anticipation, spontaneity and hedonism whether it's gazing at a glorious sunset that borders on the mystical or jumping drunk into a hostel swimming pool.

In short, they're young and this is what young people are supposed to do. They don't deserve to meet Uncle Michael with his rainwater from the Top End.

Is the villain any good? Yeah, Mick Taylor is one of the 21st century's best. With his mutton chop sideburns, thick, slicked-back hair, flannel shirt, necktie, iconic hat and politically incorrect chat ('Sydney, poofter capital of Australia'), he's like a mash-up of those loveable larrikins Steve Irwin and Mick 'Crocodile' Dundee. This is not an educated, sophisticated or enlightened man. In fact, Mick is as rough as guts, a man who will give you all the details you could ever want to hear about slaughtering vermin. At best he's a character, playful and humorous at times, but both his appearance and chat are all part of the act. Only the occasional penetrative stare gives a clue to the underlying psychosis.

Like any serial killer who's been around the block, he's developed a modus operandi that borders on the slick. This is a man who will scope you out, disable your car in a remote spot and then play the reluctant Good Samaritan. It's no surprise he catches flies with such a sophisticated trap, one that may have netted him a dozen victims. He's obviously cunning, confident and decisive. That's why his trophy cabinet is so full of trinkets and his killing pit gives off that appalling whiff. Indeed, when he gets down to business, he's as terrifying as any villain you'll see in the movies. This racist pig hunter is sadistic beyond belief, often keeping his naked, pinioned victims for months on end.

Fair dinkum, mate.

How skuzzy are the men? Ben is pretty much the only decent bloke on show. Now the movies frequently tell us the Aussie outback male is not among the most evolved of the species, but when Ben buys a shitbox car from a second-hand dealer in Broome even the salesman is a tool. Or as he opines of Ben's female travelling companions: "They get real easy on their travels. Loosens 'em up. Mate of mine reckons he picks 'em up all the time."

Later at a roadside fuel stop, the trio bumps into a hairy bunch of knuckle-draggers who want to know if Kristy and Liz 'would be interested in a little bit of a gangbang'. Is the Aussie male more misogynistic than in other parts of the western world? Probably not, but McLean seems keen to suggest you're likely to bump into one on your travels.

How do the lovely ladies fare? Mick's sole interest is women, although he's happy to spend a bit of time watching any male bycatch being fed to a ravenous dog. He is a sexual predator who enslaves women until they end up in his killing pit. He enjoys rape, physical abuse, and psychological torture. In other words, I wouldn't recommend this one to the ladies. There's no empowerment here. *Wolf Creek* is far too believable to be anything other than a supreme head-fuck.

Would the violence make a vicar faint? Sure. The sexual violence of *Wolf Creek* is carried out off-screen, but McLean doesn't shy away from showing severed fingers being scattered across the floor. Indeed, the whole 'head on a stick' sequence is memorably horrible, as is Mick's skill as a sniper.

How fucked-up is this film? I firmly believe every viewer brings his or her emotional baggage to a movie. And so if you've been a victim of rape, you will react to a movie about rape differently to someone who hasn't. It's the same with a war flick if you've seen combat. Even a terrific comedy like *Office Space* will resonate a lot more with those who've experienced its infuriating, cubicle-dwelling absurdities than say a plumber or a builder.

Luckily, I have little experience of life and have pretty much wasted it sitting alone in a room staring at movies. This means I can indulge in a rare degree of flippancy when it comes to the subjects they tackle. However, in an out-of-character lapse, I did once manage to backpack Oz. I drove around visiting isolated spots like Wolfe Creek. I picked up hitchhikers and sometimes ended up testing the kindness of strangers. In other words, it's straightforward for me to identify with the poor fuckers in this nerve-shredding flick.

What's that saying? There but for the grace of God go I.

It's not often a flick gets under my skin like *Wolf Creek*. I found it deeply unsettling and can still remember a heavy feeling settling on me when I first watched it at the cinema. That feeling took a few days to lift, something I've never experienced with any other movie. I think this means McLean (who wrote, directed and produced) did his job well. Australia is both beautiful and menacing, *Creek's* wonderful cinematography almost on a par with *Razorback*. The four leads are excellent. The first fifty minutes are a triumph of suspense (although some find it dull). McLean obviously puts a great deal of effort into making us care about these ordinary kids before dropping them headfirst into unimaginable agony. *Wolf Creek* is a window into hell, one of the best outback movies, and a white-knuckle ride that once it gets going is as insistent and unnerving as the roar of Leatherface's chainsaw.

Tina! Bring Me the Axe!

Cinema is littered with ridiculous turns, most of them delivered by Nic Cage. Talented as he is at scenery chewing (as anyone who's seen *Con Air* or *The Wicker Man* remake will attest) I still don't think his frequent hammy excesses can ever reach the level of Faye Dunaway in *Mommie Dearest*. This 1981 travesty will always get my vote for containing the most over the top performance of all time.

Building the hysteria from behind a pair of distinctively sculpted eyebrows, Dunaway embarrasses herself to such an extraordinary degree that I have to recommend at least one viewing of *Mommie Dearest*. She plays the Oscar-winning Hollywood actress Joan Crawford, although this choppy, unconvincing biopic is more concerned with her private life than career.

Unable to have kids, she gets her hands on a couple anyway, and in the process manages to make child abuse pretty damn funny. In particular, she treats her young daughter Christina to her full range of demented maternal tics. One moment she's throwing her a lavish birthday party, the next she's hacking her hair off. During a backyard swimming race Joan treats it ultra-seriously, telling the blonde poppet after her easy victory: "No one ever said life was fair, Tina. I am bigger and faster. I will always beat you."

Joan, in other words, is like an amped-up combination of a Chinese mom and *The Fast Show's* Competitive Dad. Worse is to come. Witness Joan freaking out in the garden during a nocturnal, rose-lopping frenzy before taking an age to chop down a small tree. It's beyond camp, akin to C-3PO politely applauding an Oscar Wilde play at the theatre. Then there's the notorious (but much loved) wire hanger scene which morphs into Christina being forced to clean the bathroom floor in a billowing cloud of Ajax. Bemused and shaken, the seven-year-old child speaks for all of us (after the enraged Joan has flounced off) by muttering under her breath: "Jesus Christ."

In virtually every scene Dunaway is screaming, hurling drinks, being OCD, throwing her weight around, and indulging in unhinged reactions to the tiniest infringement. At one point she even yells: "I'm not acting! I'm not acting!"

Yes, Faye, we can see that. The question is: what the fuck are you doing?

Everything is turned up to eleven, but what makes it all so glaringly daft is she's mainly bursting blood vessels opposite a *child*. This spins everything on its head, giving the impression Joan is the ultra-petulant brat and Christina the sober adult.

Weirdly, Dunaway was no amateur at this point. She couldn't blame a lack of experience for this fiasco. Indeed, she was a hugely talented, hugely successful actress who'd starred in quality fare such as *Bonnie and Clyde*, *Chinatown* and *Network*, but it's startling to witness her lack of self-awareness. Ditto the director when it came reining in her hideous overacting. Her career was never quite the same again.

So, Faye Dunaway sits atop my mountain of ham. Plenty of others have jostled for her lofty position in their time.

Oliver Reed in *The League of Gentleman* (1960)

When you think of tough, manly occupations, acting doesn't usually spring to mind. I'm pretty sure I could've won a fist fight with Charles Hawtrey. I might even be able to kick Hugh Grant's arse. However, you could never accuse a thespian like Ollie Reed of being a pansy. He was a barrel-chested, underrated actor, a proud Brit who refused to move to Hollywood at the height of his early 70s fame. Despite some decent roles, such as the sexually magnetic priest in *The Devils* and the fading, betrayed strongman in *Gladiator*, he became increasingly famous for his boozing, brawling and off-screen behaviour, especially when his alcohol-soaked career nosedived into the toilet. This was a Rolls Royce-destroying, trouser-dropping, unreconstructed hell-raiser who (according to the quietly sad doco *The Real Oliver Reed*) once drank 104 pints in 48 hours.

At his 56-bedroom home he drunkenly challenged fellow drinkers to dangerous duels with broadswords or obliterated kitchen clocks with shotgun blasts. He created havoc on and off film sets. Very few women (at least in the early days) could resist his astonishing good looks. He remained a man's man, free of pretension and bullshit, until his burning the candle at both ends lifestyle resulted in a predictably early demise in 1999. For most of his life the charismatic bastard carried a dark sexual charge and genuine air of burly threat, the sort of danger that most of today's actors couldn't even dream of.

So it's a bit of a surprise to witness his speaking debut in the well-regarded but overlong British crime caper, *The League of Gentleman*. No animalistic brute here, folks. Instead we get an outrageous, eye-opening cameo in which he plays a shrewish Nancy-boy at a theatre being told he's got the wrong room as he looks to rehearse *Babes in the Wood*. With a hand on a hip and a drawn-out *charming*, he flounces off in a minor whirlwind of lisping, eye-rolling and dedicated mincing. He's such a queen he should be wearing a tiara.

I guess we all have to start somewhere.

Leslie Nielsen in *Day of the Animals* (1977)

I can remember going to the cinema in 1988 to see the quite amusing *The Naked Gun*. This was probably my introduction to Leslie Nielsen or at least the one that stuck in my head. From *Naked Gun* onward I grew used to seeing the guy star in one bad parody after another (*Repossessed, Spy Hard, Dracula: Dead and Loving It*), a parasitical approach that saw originality drain away and cake on the floor.

So he did comedy. He deadpanned. His films were ridiculous damp squibs that rarely made any money.

But at least he had a recognizable onscreen persona.

It was only later in the day I realized he didn't start off with all this piss-taking. In fact, during the first half of his career he avoided comedy, spoof and slapstick like the plague. Until 1980's *Airplane!* he played things straight for twenty-five years, such as his po-faced turn as the doomed captain in the megahit *The Poseidon Adventure*. Occasionally, however, he did nasty, an approach exemplified by his batshit mad performance in *Day of the Animals*. This is an enjoyably nutso eco-horror movie that features the wondrous sight of him bare-chested and foaming-at-the-mouth while wrestling a grizzly bear in a thunderstorm.

I shit you not.

He plays Paul Jenson and it's pretty easy to describe his character: he's an obnoxious prick. Well, he does work in advertising. Even so, he still puts in a terrific amount of effort annoying the other outdoor-loving, inappropriately dressed characters during a holiday hike down a Californian mountain. There's his racism, often referring to the Indian guide as Kemosabi while making limp jokes about reservations and medicine men. "You're an Indian," he tells the guy at one point. "That's nothing to be ashamed of."

Thanks for the insight, Mr. Jenson.

However, he spits out most of his contempt at the group's leader, Steve Buckner (Christopher George). Increasingly vocal about the man's perceived lack of competence, whether it be reading a map, finding food or protecting them from a range of savage animal attacks, Jenson calls him 'hotshot' to his face *twelve* times. Saying that, some of his relentless criticism does seem justified in that Buckner has failed to bring along a two-way radio or any form of weapon. This is absurd. These are Americans and, as such, I expect them to be armed to the teeth when going to the bathroom, let alone tramping around outdoors surrounded by coyotes and wolves.

Anyhow, it doesn't take Jenson long to turn mutinous, leading a splinter group back up the mountain toward a ranger station. Ten minutes later he's gone stark raving mad, a sea change that pushes an already deeply absurd, unintentionally funny movie into the realm of camp.

At this point I should tell you that during *Animals'* opening we're informed the reason for nature striking back is the damaged ozone layer. It's letting in too much ultraviolet light and 'adversely affecting all living things.' This environmental catastrophe explains Jenson's sharp left turn into bonkersville.

Fine, but why is no one else affected? Or is it just chopsy advertising execs that are particularly susceptible to a strong dose of UV?

Whatever the case, we know something's up when we find Jenson hiking along topless. Now it's starting to rain and he's attacking vegetation with his trusty walking stick, threatening to throw a 'cockroach' child off a cliff and fighting the boy's protective mother. Christ, he seems to think he's helming a WW2 death march.

"You lily-livered punk," he snarls at one bloke objecting to his unorthodox leadership style as the rain pours down his enraged face, "I'm running this camping trip! I take what I want and I give you what I wanna give you. And right now, I want that."

That? What's he ranting about? Oh, I see. The man's wife. Leslie Nielsen is gonna have a go at rape. This is... unexpected, a bit like switching on an Arnie pic to find the big guy pirouetting across the screen in a pink tutu. Meanwhile, Jenson has seized his intended victim. "Come on, baby," he reassures her, "you're gonna have a real man."

Unsurprisingly, this tantalizing promise does not cause the hubby to stop objecting. Seconds later their marriage is over, given that Jenson has just impaled him on the end of his stick. Shirley, you can't be serious? Now Jenson's bellowing at the lightning-crisscrossed sky. "My Father, who art in heaven, you made a jackass out of me for years. It's never been you for me. Melville's God, *that's* the God I believe in. You see what you want, you take it!" Time to have another go at rape. Hang on, a grizzly bear is intervening, obviously in a divine attempt to save the woman's blushes. Who says there's no God?

"Bastard," Jenson says as he wearily gets up and staggers toward the great shaggy beast.

Now that's what I call a fitting final word.

Gary Oldman in *Leon: The Professional* (1994)

Leon has about as much credibility as a drunken, pregnant nun in a brothel. It's a take-your-brain-out thriller, demonstrating all the inherent flaws and lapses in logic that I have come to expect from director Luc Besson (see 2014's *Lucy*, not so much a take-your-brain-out thriller as a take-your-brain-out thriller and stamp-it-to-mush while marvelling at the shining, rampant idiocy of one of the dumbest movies in existence).

Leon may not reach *Lucy's* loopy heights, but it is a consistent head shaker. It's full of incompetent, panicky, badly dressed gangsters/cops who don't have a shred of poise between them, all outwitted by a mentally subnormal, illiterate, milk-drinking hit man who appears to be part spider, part gymnast.

Now this might sound like I'm not a fan of *Leon*, but I've always argued the worst thing a movie can be is dull. *Leon* is never dull. It barely contains one iota of believability, but it sure is entertaining bollocks and I wouldn't have a problem with anyone loving its farcical, high-octane nature.

Its main absurdity rests on the shoulders of bent, drug-fuelled DEA agent Norman Stansfield (Oldman). How this bug-eyed guy has become an agent, let alone be allowed to continue when he's obviously as homicidally demented as Idi Amin is anyone's guess. Harvey Keitel's Bad Lieutenant pushed things pretty bloody far, but at least that fucked-up nutter was operating within some framework of masturbating plausibility.

Not our unshaven, tieless Stan.

He doesn't interview suspects in a bid to find the truth, he *sniffs* them. He takes drugs on the job, although he's such an exhibitionist he can't even swallow them discretely. Instead he does this overcomplicated thing in which an overhead camera watches him throw back his head, wrench it to the side and pull a tortured face like he's about to transform into a werewolf. And why not? Why not pretend he's a werewolf cop who doesn't recognize the laws of man while in the grip of one of his less amiable moods? That would be as good an explanation as any for his wildly OTT, tic-saturated behaviour.

After all, this is a man who launches a full-blooded assault with his equally corrupt crew on a strangely deserted apartment block in the middle of New

York City. Now we're used to the likes of Dirty Harry bending and even breaking the rules, but Stan finds it impossible to follow *any* recognized legal procedure in his professional life. He murders women left, right and centre. Not that he's content to merely shoot them in the bath or blow holes in their back with a pump-action shotgun. Oh, no. He has to pretend he's listening to Beethoven at the same time, waving his arms like a conductor.

He even keeps trying to kill you after you're dead.

When a bespectacled old dear wanders into the hallway to query what's going on, he loosens off a round at her, shattering a glass partition. No other tenants or passersby bother showing the slightest curiosity. It's like this raid is going down on a different planet, one that looks like Earth, but where it's actually not that unusual to slaughter a family in broad daylight. Ten minutes later we hear the wail of police sirens. Stan leaves behind a dreadlocked subordinate, who understandably questions what he's gonna say when the cops find a bloodbath in which unarmed women have been shot in the back. "Tell them we were doing our job," Stan replies.

All this to get their naughty hands on a solitary bag of coke?

During the subsequent inquiry, Stan is taken back to the murder scene to have a go at an explanation but is flippant, dismissive and once again, obviously mad. You don't have to be a shrink to see that his theatrical sighs, exaggerated face rubs and blank stares mark him out as a raving loon. And how the hell is he still on the job? Don't civilian-annihilating offenders get time off, needing to be cleared of wrongdoing before they can strap on a gun again? "I haven't got time for this Mickey Mouse bullshit!" he shouts at one investigator. Five people dead, including a cop and a toddler, and he's carrying on like they're pulling him off an important case for a parking ticket misdemeanour.

Did I say Dunaway put in the hammiest performances of all time? Maybe I need to rethink.

Tim Roth in *Rob Roy* (1995)

With a feather-adorned hat, shoulder-length curly wig, cravat, powdered makeup and effete manner, the English aristocrat Archibald Cunningham (Roth) is your archetypal dandy. A committed fop. An 18th century New Romantic who looks like he might break into a lengthy rendition of *Girls on Film* at any second.

Nothing scary about him, then?

Hmm, I think this is what they call misdirection.

Turns out this show-off is an expert swordsman, murderous rapist and total badass, although he prefers his poofter act to lull opponents into a false sense of security. It *amuses* him, you see. Take his duel early on with a gruff Scottish bastard. The man's got terrible hair, terrible teeth and probably couldn't even spell *fashion* let alone practise it, but at least he's a proper man. The bookie's favourite, too. Archie, meanwhile, is mincing around as the crowd jeers his every self-affected move and theatrical intake of breath.

Well, who do you think is gonna win?

Roth's florid take on the character in this mediocre, overlong period piece grows wearisome after a couple of minutes. Yes, he has his moments dealing with the ladies ("Think of yourself as the scabbard and me the sword, Mistress MacGregor, and a fine fit you were, too" and "Love is a dunghill, Betty, and I am but a cock that climbs upon it to crow") but overall his attempted encapsulation of limp-wristed Evil is way too much. The mock deference, the insincere expressions, the simpering, the over-articulate speech, the little flourishes in stark contrast to his rank callousness and abundant savagery...

Fucking hell, give me Jake the Muss any day.

Fucked-Up Films #6: Ilsa, She Wolf of the SS (1975)

Synopsis

Mein Gott! It's Nazisploitation!

Director

Don Edmonds

Cast

Dyanne Thorne, Gregory Knoph, Tony Mumolo, George Buck Flower

What are these sick bastards doing? Obviously inspired by Dr Josef Mengele's 'pioneering' work in Auschwitz, this is a flick that concentrates on the more extreme Nazi obsessions. Ilsa (Thorne) is a 'fraulein doctor' in charge of a small medical experimentation camp that at first glance looks like a converted garden centre. She's aided by one other doctor, a handful of nurses, two magnificent blonde SS subordinates and five or six male guards. "There is no need for you to be afraid," she reassures a bunch of new female arrivals, all of whom are suspiciously pretty and busty. "This is no Dachau, no Ravensbruck. We are doctors. We are here to help you. Your stay with us will be short, but in it you will be helped to serve the Third Reich. That is your destiny."

As you can see, she effortlessly does deceptive courtesy, straightforward lies and the odd euphemism. In time, she will jam an electrified dildo up each and every one of them.

Is the villain any good? Ilsa is introduced fully nude in her bedroom riding a supine man in much the same way as Catherine Tramell all those years later. Both are nymphos who like to be on top, but although Tramell's a psychotic super-bitch who's a dab hand with an ice pick she's a rank amateur next to Ilsa when it comes to inflicting agony and death.

Two things drive Ilsa's wholehearted destruction of life: the failure of men to satisfy her in bed and a fanatical devotion to the Fatherland. Straightaway we grasp the first motive when her latest lover suffers a bout of premature ejaculation. "You should have waited," she grumbles in a masterly bit of understatement. Not long afterwards he's dragged off by her magnificent blonde subordinates to be castrated. Well, that'll teach him for being a dud lay *and* a member of an inferior race.

Ilsa is no paper-shuffling bureaucrat a la Himmler. She likes to be right in the thick of the action and never shies away from the chance to mutilate. However, although she enjoys unquestioned authority within the converted garden centre, sorry, concentration camp, she's not always taken seriously by her Berlin superiors.

Those stupid *men*.

For a start, they're unimpressed with her meticulous private research into pain endurance. She's hell-bent on giving them 'documented proof' that a carefully trained woman can withstand pain better than any man. Frankly, I'm a little puzzled how this is going to help the war effort, especially as I thought childbirth was already ample evidence. Christ, if guys had to go through genitalia-wrenching shit like that, the human race would stagger to a halt within a couple of generations.

Anyway, it's an extraordinary performance by Thorne. She really does have a ball (or should that be *balls*?) as the sex-crazed commandant. With her expressive eyes, flaxen mane, long painted fingernails and awesome chest, she also looks bloody great in her jet-black uniform. She's a decent actress, has a fair stab at the Teutonic accent and can do a great *Heil Hitler* salute. Most of all, she's camp as hell. There's usually a twinkle in her eye, especially when she's doing the more outrageous stuff like tonguing the end of her horse whip while watching an orgy. Strangely (and despite the huge array of bush on show) she keeps hers hidden. It's the only time she's bashful in the whole shebang.

How skuzzy are the men? I guess it's a bit unusual in an exploitation flick for the men to be a lot more likable than the gals. Of course, the guards indulge in drunken gang rape, but apart from such small indiscretions they don't do much more than strut around and get shot when necessary. There is a male doctor called Binz (exploitation regular Buck Flower) but he's a timid non-entity with stooped shoulders. He usually only speaks when spoken to and wears a faintly quizzical expression, as if he's not quite convinced of the need to shave a prisoner's pubes off until the blood runs. Most of the time he's moseying around in the background, perhaps confused why he's the only Nazi not getting any pussy. He doesn't appear manly enough for Ilsa to fuck, nor intelligent enough to grasp that her disinterest happens to be an enormous blessing in disguise.

It isn't until a strapping blonde German-American prisoner called Wolfe (Knoph) turns up that we get a sympathetic male character. Ilsa sinks her claws in straightaway, loosening him up with a sophisticated bit of foreplay that includes stripping him naked in public and staring between his legs. "That's not the build of a true Aryan," the demented dominatrix sneers.

Well, the road to true love is never smooth, but luckily Wolfe has a fantastic secret: He's a sex god. Or as he tells a 'half-man' prisoner, who's already been on the sharp end of Ilsa's no-nonsense response to carnal disappointment: "I can hold back for as long as I want. I guess you could call me a freak of nature, a sort of human machine that can set its controls to fast, slow or never."

Once he gets between Isla's shapely legs (in a scene that should have been accompanied by the *Theme from Shaft*) we find out he's no bullshitter. He really can perform under the most extreme pressure, quickly transforming Ilsa into little more than a giant quivering vagina. Indeed, he's so good she even starts fantasizing about having his children. "They will be beautiful," she muses in post-coital reverie. "Strong!"

Bloody hell, the cougar's morphed into a kitty-cat.

I have no idea what it means that she becomes more feminine, more recognizably *human* after getting some proper cock. Is this the best way to stop the future equivalent of real-life monsters like Ilse Koch and Irma Grese? To fuck them well?

The only other significant man in this cult classic is a terrific appearance by a seemingly refined and composed SS general. He turns up to appraise Ilsa's gangrene-inducing work. "I see the reports of your charm and beauty were not exaggerated," he says after stepping out of his staff car and kissing her hand. For a short while his superior rank results in Ilsa being submissive. However, it only takes a few hours in her company before he's revealed to be a self-loathing little boy who crumbles before her highly polished jackboots in a brilliantly funny denouement.

How do the lovely ladies fare? Terribly. There wouldn't be anything wrong with subtitling this one *Lovely Lady Armageddon*. As already mentioned, Ilsa is helped by two immaculately dressed, blonde subordinates. Now these gals really are something, dishing out the sensual sadism with every chance they get. However, such enthusiasm does result in their military discipline occasionally slipping, best illustrated in the scene in which they've removed their tops to flog a pair of misbehaving prisoners to death. (Maybe I should give them the benefit of the doubt in that they didn't want their beautifully pressed uniforms splashed with blood). We never learn their names but I enjoyed their vigorous, sexually insane tomfoolery almost as much as The Countess, The Empress and The Princess in that bonkers bit of blaxploitation *Three the Hard Way*.

As for the prisoners, I have to say they have less fun. One teenage ginger chick doesn't want to remove her clothes for an initial examination in public, confessing she's ashamed.

Ilsa understands. "We have to see you in order to know what work to assign you," she explains, convincing precisely no one in the room.

But the prospect of acute embarrassment is the least of these girls' worries. The lucky ones are sterilized and sent to field brothels, but any that catch Ilsa's eye might be infected with syphilis, typhoid or just hung upside down naked.

Saying all that, the strange thing about this flick is that (despite the relentless degradation of women) it prompts unsettling questions for a bloke. Ilsa's the boss here, one of the most fearsome alpha females ever put on screen. At one point she's aptly compared to a black widow spider, a frightening creature that might launch into a murderous attack moments after mating. Well, aren't we all a bit scared of not being able to satisfy the lady in our life? Isn't *Ilsa* tapping into our deepest fears? Couldn't it be argued that Ilsa embodies male anxiety? Do unsatisfied women fantasize about cutting off our useless nuts and moving onto a guy with a bit more stamina?

Bear in mind *The Stepford Wives* was released the same year as *Ilsa*. In that decent, ultimately eerie movie, men attempted to stem the scary tide of female liberation (with its attendant demands for better jobs, control over their bodies and God forbid! some consideration in the bedroom) by killing their women and replacing them with obedient robots. *Ilsa* stands at the other end of such extreme behaviour, its titular character personifying female authoritarianism while subjugating and killing any man deemed a flop.

I sincerely hope *Ilsa* is not some whacked out snapshot of the future.

Would the violence make a vicar faint? Yeah, I think you'd need to whip out the smelling salts pretty quickly for this one. There's a lot of the red stuff splashed around amid some surprisingly good special effects, ranging from toenails being pulled out to less than relaxing dips in superheated baths. There's even some poor naked wench chucked into a decompression unit and left there until the haemorrhaging blood gushes out of her mouth and down between her voluptuous breasts and... Excuse me, I think I want to be alone now.

How fucked-up is this film? It starts with a written intro from the producer, Herman Traeger, in which he has the temerity to attempt a justification for its catalogue of lurid excesses, citing some guff about 'documented fact' and the like.

Come on, Herman, fess up, you're just exploiting the darkest episode in mankind's history to help fellow sickos like me get their rocks off.

'We dedicate this film with the hope that these heinous crimes will never occur again,' he concludes as an off-screen Hitler rants *Sieg Heil*. Notice how Herman doesn't say who the film's dedicated *to* coz I doubt any surviving victims would have appreciated its portrayal of their ghastly experiences within the camps.

So, how do we justify the existence of such an abhorrent flick?

Quite easily, actually.

An awful lot of movies exploit human misery; it's just they do it in a *classier* way. Yes, *Schindler's List* is a superior piece of art to *Ilsa*, but viewers are still getting some sort of vicarious jolt from its deadly goings on. Money is nevertheless being made. Reputations are being enhanced. At the end of the day Spielberg's Oscar-winning magnum opus is *entertainment* just like Edmonds' *Ilsa*.

All built on the murder of twelve million people.

Ilsa is simply more upfront and obvious about its wallow in degradation. People wanna condemn such sordid stuff yet it was successful enough to lead to three rapid-fire sequels. Whether we like it or not, there's an unhealthy fascination with the Nazis, especially what went on in the death camps, and I suggest you think about that the next time you pop on Slayer's *Angel of Death*.

Besides that, trash like *Ilsa* is nowhere near good enough to convince me even for a second it's nothing more than people with an adolescent desire to shock playing dress up in front of cheap, sparsely adorned sets while pretending to hurt one another.

Where's the harm in that?

Frankly, I get more irked by earnest, overwrought depictions of middle class angst in lauded dramas such as *Ordinary People*. Now that was one movie which needed more electrified dildos shoved up its cast.

Bloody Sam Says Hi!

Dying in his fifties seemed like a fitting final action for the maverick film-maker Sam Peckinpah. Better to burn out than fade away and all that. For whenever Sam was in town the rage-filled stories of excess flew thick and fast, tales that included wild on-set bust-ups, legendary alcohol and coke consumption, budget blowouts, and bitter clashes with studio execs, all stoked by media outrage about the graphic nature of the blood-soaked final product.

Peckinpah was a tyrannical director, capable of firing more than thirty crew on any given shoot, and yet inspired fierce loyalty as he battled to deliver unmolested artistic visions of a particular type of dysfunctional man. The result was some of the most vivid and uncompromising films of the era, films that often centred on battle-hardened adversaries hunting each other, amoral men on bloody missions of self-destruction, and tormented loners determined to do things their own way. Men who were not only lost, but had no idea if they even *had* a home.

"Sam's films were always looking for something special," regular cohort James Coburn says in the 2005 doco *Passion & Poetry: The Ballad of Sam Peckinpah*. "You got to do work that you couldn't do with other people... He not only allowed you to take it out to the edge, but sometimes he would force you out there. He might be a nasty bastard, but at least he's truthful about that... Each film he made was a sacred enterprise. He devoted not only his time and attention, but his heart and being. Some of them were worth it, some of them weren't, but they were all *interesting*."

The Wild Bunch (1969) 'I want them all back here head down over a saddle.'

I guess if *Wild Bunch* were remade today our main characters would be ethnically diverse. One of 'em might even be a woman. Back in Peckinpah's day such tedious considerations could be ignored, leaving him free to direct charismatic, convincing actors (e.g. Ernest Borgnine, Warren Oates and Ben

Johnson) while reducing the female presence to that of Mexican whores. Indeed, *Wild Bunch* is the perfect example of what's been lost in modern moviemaking, standing as a lasting testament to the clear (if blood-spattered) vision of its hard-living auteur. Now well over half a century old, it remains an epic meditation on violence, obsolescence and the fierce code that bonds certain kinds of men.

With this groundbreaking flick, Peckinpah also ran headlong into the same finger-wagging bullshit that Tarantino would face twenty-odd years later with *Reservoir Dogs* and *Pulp Fiction* i.e. the excessive use and glorification of brutality. My answer to such objectors is to politely suggest they fuck off and watch *Mary Poppins* instead. *Wild Bunch* does have a nihilistic flavour, though, best illustrated in an ominous early scene in which a bunch of kids giggle over a writhing pair of ant-covered scorpions that they're about to set on fire.

We begin in 1913 Texas. Pike Bishop (William Holden) is the leader of a gang of aging outlaws intent on robbing a railroad office. Unbeknown to him, his former comrade (now turned deputized pursuer), Deke Thornton (Robert Ryan), is lying in wait with a load of bounty hunters. The robbery is a disaster, netting the gang some bags of metal washers while leaving about a fifth of the townsfolk dead. Worse, they lose a few men in the botched raid, causing them to flee across the border with Thornton hot on their trail...

This tremendous opening shows Peckinpah's unsentimental, uncompromising nature. It's masterfully depicted with bullets thudding into chests, bodies falling off roofs, bystanders getting mown down and horses crashing through shop windows. No western had ever been so graphic and in one foul swoop a new age of bloody gun violence was ushered in.

Clearly, the money-obsessed Bishop and his men are no angels. They're committed criminals, happy to use the oblivious residents as a human shield. They will also execute a blinded gang member to avoid being slowed down. Bishop, however, is a long way from a bloodthirsty savage. "We gotta start thinking beyond our guns," he says. "Those days are closing fast." But although he's a clear-sighted, unhesitating killer, he also strongly believes in comradeship, even if that ultimately means self-destruction. "When you side with a man, you stay with him, and if you can't do that you're like some animal. You're finished."

Like Sergio Leone, Peckinpah had a real flair for bringing to life a man's world in which action set-pieces, economical dialogue, superb stunt work, a vibrant grasp of history and the ability to illustrate character predominate. Peckinpah also had an eye for populating his group scenes with memorable faces and local colour.

Still, his main interest is masculinity and *Wild Bunch* excels in this regard. His anti-heroes fight, drink, rob, frolic with hookers, party hard, play pranks, lust after gold and slay without apology ("If they move, kill 'em"). There's no balance provided by the 'good' guys, either. Thornton's posse is a motley crew of squabbling lowlifes while the gringo-hating Mexican army that Pike tangles with is filled with corrupt, untrustworthy barbarians.

Wild Bunch is so fucking manly there were times I had to put down my knitting and just sigh. It leaves us with no winners and losers, no victory of any kind. It's the cinematic equivalent of ant-covered scorpions being turned into a bug bonfire.

Straw Dogs (1971) 'What the hell is wrong with you people?'

I was always disappointed by John Carpenter's post-*Thing* output. Stuff like *Christine*, *Prince of Darkness*, *They Live* and *In the Mouth of Madness* doesn't cut it for me. It's as if the revulsion and stinging reviews that met his hard-edged 1982 sci-fi/horror masterpiece broke something in the man. His verve was never quite the same and I would've preferred it if he'd taken a whiskey-soaked leaf out of Peckinpah's battered book.

Peckinpah followed up the furore surrounding *Wild Bunch* with the unconventionally gentle *The Ballad of Cable Hogue*. However, he quickly appeared to decide that such mildness didn't represent his true artistic nature and jumped back into his rough-hewn saddle. And so we come to the troubling *Straw Dogs*, a mysteriously-titled flick that was probably even more controversial than his breakthrough hit. It's an essential watch, underlining that *Wild Bunch* was no Tobe Hooper-style flash in the pan.

David Sumner (a prime Dustin Hoffmann) is a meek mathematician, trying to cope with the simmering undercurrents of hostility in a Cornish village. He's moved there on a university grant with his sexpot wife Amy (Susan George, never better) in a bid to temporarily escape the growing social unrest of early 70s America. As the saying goes *better the devil you know* because this particular village is overflowing with misogyny, predatory men, bullies, animal cruelty, passive-aggressiveness and excessive drinking. Not to mention a child-molesting idiot, ostracism and low tricks. Even the rat catcher is a tittering fuckwit who'll ask you if you've seen 'anybody get knifed' before stealing your wife's panties.

Straw Dogs examines the latent violence in man, partly by presenting David as unmanly. A chump. Or at least that's how the locals view him. They don't like his clothes, his way of speaking, his short stature and his intellectual job. They might call him 'sir' to his face and take their hats off in his home, but their respect is the thinnest of veneers. Most of all, they resent how this 'Yank bastard' has got his hands on one of their best girls. Amy is little help here, sarcastically calling him 'tiger', complaining about his lack of DIY acumen, and obviously thinking less of him for refusing to confront the horrible, intimidating bunch of builders working on their home. Their marriage isn't quite a sham, but it's clearly fractious, full of needle and petty digs. "Don't play games with me," David warns her, but Amy doesn't heed the inherent danger in her behaviour.

This brings us to *Straw Dogs*' other concern, which is female sexuality. The first shot of Amy is her nipples doing their best to poke through a thick white sweater, immediately placing her in a sexualized context. She's aware of her effect on men, but there's some truth in David's observation when he tells her: "You act like you're fourteen." She complains about the builders' ogling and yet parades around her house naked, knowing they can see in. David suggests she wears a bra and "shouldn't go around without one and expect that type not to stare." Of course, this wanders dangerously close to the old 'asking for it' cliché, but Amy does welcome some of the attention.

Her eventual assault, in which she initially resists the first rape and then takes pleasure in the sex, only complicates matters. It's a notorious sequence that stills winds up and offends viewers, especially those who separate sexual encounters into the unambiguously consensual and plain violation. Frankly, I think life is grey and nothing captures that better than the shifting sands of physical attraction, interpersonal chemistry and sex. However, Amy's second rape by a different man makes it clear she doesn't enjoy being overpowered *per se*.

Elsewhere, the mini-skirted teenage daughter of the village's main troublemaker (a burly, menacing Peter Vaughan) is a flirtatious voyeur whose undisciplined nature has given way to precocious sexuality. *Straw Dogs* shows female sexuality can be a dangerous lure that not only leads the opposite sex into all kinds of bother, but lights the fuse of unbridled violence, a violence that men like David Sumner have little idea is already bubbling away within. Whether Peckinpah condones that aggression as a necessary way to protect territory and establish manhood ("This is where I live. This is *me*. I will not allow violence against this house") is still being debated today.

The Getaway (1972) 'Punch it, baby!'

A Walter Hill (*The Driver*, *48 Hrs*) script. Steve McQueen tearing up the screen. And Peckinpah in the director's chair.

Oh, boy. This is what you call proper filmmaking.

McQueen is Doc McCoy, a convicted bank robber struggling with a ten-year sentence in Texas. Luckily, his loyal, resourceful wife Carol (Ali MacGraw) knows a trick or two. One such manoeuvre involves wearing a low-cut blouse and sauntering into the office of the corrupt, highly influential businessman, Beynon (Ben Johnson), who happens to have the ear of the parole board. Ten minutes later Doc's back on the street, knowing there's no such thing as a free lunch. Now under Beynon's thumb, he must take part in a bank robbery, but isn't even allowed to choose his own men. "You run the job," Beynon tells him, "but I run the show. And don't forget it."

The Getaway is notable for its terse dialogue. Peckinpah establishes so much in the opening ten minutes you realize what a brilliant visual storyteller he is. Talk about *show don't tell*. There's hardly a word spoken, but Doc's pent-up frustration with the monotony of convict life, the undimmed love for his wife, his dislike of Beynon, and the tantalizing sense of freedom represented by the grazing deer on the outside of the prison's fence are all effortlessly conveyed. Even when a contemptuous prison guard tells him "You'll be back" while opening the gate, Doc doesn't reply.

It's not that kind of movie.

Doc is the personification of blue-eyed, ice-cold professionalism, but four years in the slammer has made him rusty. Plus, he's no longer working with a top crew. In particular, Rudy Butler (Al Lettieri in wonderfully slimy, vet-humiliating form) is an arrogant, duplicitous fucker who thinks the imminent job will be a 'piece of cake'.

The complications that ensue from the meticulously planned robbery feel natural and believable, leading to such memorable scenes as an encounter with a small-time con artist aboard a train, a none-too-rosy jaunt inside a garbage truck and a fucking ace hotel shootout. The shotgun-wielding, wife-slapping Doc is a tremendously amoral character, although he gets typical help from Peckinpah's thoroughly engaging cast. It's my favourite McQueen movie and proved to be the biggest hit of Peckinpah's career.

Bring Me the Head of Alfredo Garcia (1974) 'We're gonna find the golden fleece, baby.'

Peckinpah followed *Getaway's* big success with the studio-mutilated, ponderous and barely coherent *Pat Garrett and Billy the Kid*. Like *Wild Bunch* it's about changing times. Or as one character says: "Country's gotta make a choice. Time's over for drifters and outlaws." Billy's a typical Peckinpah anti-hero in that he's a piece of shit who contributes fuck all to society, but he's got his code and initially you can't help but be interested in what he's gonna do next. Unfortunately, he's portrayed by the far too old Kris

Kristoffersen, a casting decision compounded by the man's inability to play mean.

Garrett died at the box office. The director's cut was released fifteen years later, forcing a re-evaluation with many fans seeing it as one of the era's great westerns. They point to its authentic feel, the lovely cinematography and some very strong scenes e.g. a gut-shot Slim Pickens stumbling away to sit by the river as his stricken wife can do nothing but watch while *Knockin' on Heaven's Door* plays. However (and despite its regular shootouts), I still think the flick lacks momentum and becomes repetitive.

Its commercial failure meant Peckinpah was in need of a hit so he set up shop in Mexico for the low-budget *Alfredo Garcia*. It not only died on its arse as well, but probably attracted the most scathing reviews of his career. Still, at least Peckinpah could claim it was the only one of his fourteen flicks completed without studio interference.

Unlike *Garrett*, I love the gloriously off-kilter *Garcia*, especially its opening in which a heavily pregnant teenager lies beside a sun-dappled pond as ducks and geese glide by. Peckinpah's lyrical scenes are often overlooked by our moral guardians obsessed with his penchant for slow-mo, bullet-riddled deaths, but watch carefully and there's plenty of nuance, tenderness and humour in his films. *Garcia's* beginning is a classic bit of misdirection, though, because things soon turn startling.

The expectant girl is brought before her obviously powerful dad in a packed room. "Who is the father?" he asks.

A shake of the head.

Two henchmen rip her dress open to expose her breasts as the mother anxiously looks on, too intimidated to intervene. Jesus Christ, what kind of dad is this? The girl's arms are twisted behind her back as she is forced to the floor crying.

"Who is the father?" he repeats.

Another shake of the head.

A bone is heard snapping, resulting in a name finally being given up.

Then this teary-eyed Mexican crime lord says Garcia was 'like a son to me' before putting a million-dollar price tag on his head, a bounty that ensures word spreads far and wide.

Fuck, what a brilliant opening, told (as usual) with Peckinpah's marvellous directorial shorthand. Already we're knee-deep in toxic masculinity, a sleazy, dangerous world of hard drinking, grieving grave robbers and gun-toting gay hit men where women get knocked out cold or sexually assaulted. I can't recommend the blackly comic, increasingly unhinged, nihilistic nastiness of *Garcia* highly enough.

Cross of Iron (1977) 'I will show you where the Iron Crosses grow.'

Lice, diarrhoea, throat-slitting, furtive homosexual affection, a birthday celebrant taking a bayonet in the guts and children being machine-gunned... Welcome to one of my typical dreams.

No, sorry, I mean the 1943 Eastern Front.

The Germans are in disarray, suffering constant shelling as they cower in their makeshift bunkers. Corporal Steiner (James Coburn) is a grizzled, insubordinate warrior, an unpatriotic cynic who believes God is a sadist but probably doesn't even know it. He hates officers, but is fiercely loyal to his own reconnaissance platoon, a motley crew of experienced killers.

When Steiner is badly concussed he is shipped to a military hospital. His recuperation has a tinge of surreal horror and black comedy, as exemplified by a double amputee giving a visiting general a contemptuous Nazi salute with his *leg*. However, it is in this much safer and more civilized place that we start to get some understanding of Steiner's yen to be in the midst of slaughter. He romances a buxom nurse and is told he is being given home leave as a reward for his decorated service. Things are finally looking up for the old dog, but when one of his subordinates turns up he instantly makes the decision to once again take charge of his platoon. This is an intelligent, self-aware man yet he wishes to return to one of the most dangerous places on Earth. Why would anyone do this? His tear-stricken nurse can only say: "Do you love the war so much? Or are you afraid of what you'll be without it?" Steiner tells her he has 'no home', a belief that echoes David Sumner's last line in *Straw Dogs*. Steiner is a typical Peckinpah antagonist, drawn back to violence and the possibility of annihilation because of some deep-rooted manly code he must obey.

Cross of Iron was Peckinpah's sole war flick which is a bit of a shame as a straightforward focus on combat seemed like a natural fit. He gives us two hours of authentic mayhem, blowing the shit out of almost everything on screen. He also finds time for some poetic images, such as a dead soldier face down in a water-filled ditch, his newly shed blood blooming around his head. Performances are excellent throughout, especially James Mason as Steiner's sympathetic superior and the deceitful Maximilian Schell as an 'aristocratic pile of Prussian pig shit.' The indestructible Steiner endures air raids, a gripping Russian tank assault, and his men's stinky, bunker-enclosed farts while women, as usual, are sexually assaulted.

This was Peckinpah's last hurrah, following *Cross* with two inferior flicks before his relentless substance abuse ensured his self-destruction in 1984.

Fucked-Up Films #7: Death Wish II (1982)

Synopsis

Chuck loses in love, but wins at carnage. Thank God.

Director

Michael Winner

Cast

Charles Bronson, Jill Ireland, Vincent Gardenia, Robin Sherwood, Ben Frank

What are these sick bastards doing? Sending civilisation to hell in a handcart. Luckily, one man has the answer. And it isn't rehabilitation or any other namby-pamby shit.

How skuzzy are the men? Our obnoxious five-strong street gang is happy to sit around at fairgrounds scoping potential victims. Apart from having names like Stomper and Cutter, you know they're horrible because they have a ghetto blaster, a requisite piece of intimidating equipment for urban malcontents in the 1980s. Bronson later murders the anti-social machine (along with the cretinous perp carrying it) using a single shot, a classic example of killing two birds with one stone.

Fashion-wise, this lot favours futuristic pink sunglasses, a bandana, a leather waistcoat, a mesh T-shirt, a fingerless glove, a skinny tie, some earrings, a balding blonde mullet, three hats, and a pair of knee-length brown boots with a solitary spur. In other words, not good. They also lose intimidation points by dancing really badly in public, but they sure have attitude. Loads of attitude. "Look at him," one says in an unmistakably catty way as Paul Kersey (Bronson) attracts their mean-spirited attention by walking past to provocatively buy an ice-cream. Perhaps they object to his sensible wardrobe. Who knows? You get the feeling it doesn't take much to upset this bunch and have them arrive on your doorstep.

Is the villain any good? Er, who is the baddie in this right-wing flick? I think I'm supposed to name the murderous home invaders rather than Kersey, but I guess that depends on whether you're pro or anti-vigilantism. Whatever the case, Kersey's at the very least an antagonist so I'll plump for him.

By this point in his career, I don't think Bronson was putting in much effort, perhaps taking his onscreen charisma for granted. Still, he does what's required. That basically means giving a deliberately sketchy description of his assailants to the ineffective cops, being stoic when confronted with the sight of his (yet again) raped daughter on a slab, and then matter-of-factly proceeding to the business of mass murder. It really is amazing how little time he spends grieving. I don't think he even mentions his daughter's name again, the poor poppet. She must hold some sort of record for having the worst possible time in consecutive flicks.

Kersey hunts her killers by wandering the grimy streets of downtown LA aided by an apparent photographic memory. Inquisitive hookers are ignored ("What's wrong?" one sweetheart says. "Haven't you got one?") Sometimes he ends up in an abandoned, rat-filled hotel chatting about Jesus while at others he crosses patches of waste-ground skirting around half-loopy characters dancing or muttering to themselves. Most of the time he stares at young people, obviously none too impressed with their dyed hair, leather jackets and penchant for breaking into cars. One glassy-eyed automaton is even seen wearing a pair of denim dungarees without a shirt. *Christ*, you can almost hear Kersey thinking, *what's wrong with a nice jacket and tie and being a productive member of society*?

Kersey's demeanour doesn't change pre or post murder. He sports the same expression whether proposing to his dull girlfriend or pumping scumbags full of lead. However, he does manage a sort of Clark Kent transformation, utilizing a shitty hotel rather than a phone booth. He walks into it a smartly dressed architect and wanders out sans tie with a beanie and gloves as Mr. Kimble. Hey presto, he's a killing machine. With the same expression. Not bad for a reputed $1.5million payday, huh?

It has to be said *Death Wish II* lacks memorable dialogue. "Goodbye" is a pretty poor one-liner in anyone's book, but that's all Kersey can manage after wiping out one hoodlum. His best scene arrives when he takes on and somehow kills four men wielding an arsenal of high-powered weaponry, despite only having a paltry handgun and a tree trunk to hide behind. He's such a deadly shot he even gets a fleeing perp to drive off a cliff (that materializes out of nowhere) and die in a fireball.

Christ, the NRA was right. All it takes is one good man with a gun...

How do the lovely ladies fare? Not well, given the emphasis on sexual violence. The details of the gang rape, even in the heavily cut version you're likely to see, are persuasive. "Hey, man, look at that," one rapist says in a sing-song voice after breaking into Kersey's home, overpowering the convincingly terrified Mexican maid and exposing her panties. "Isn't that pretty?" Then we get licked buttocks, full frontal nudity, a belt whipping, and lots of giggling, tongue-waggling and whooping.

Later there's the eerie violation of Kersey's abducted daughter, a traumatised young woman still recovering from her first rape in New York City. "I'm gonna fuck you, lady," one of the gang tells her. Winner again captures maximum unpleasantness, particularly in the close-ups of the watching men's faces. Her attempt to flee, culminating in the most savage impalement on the railings of an iron fence, is startlingly well done.

Elsewhere, a busty woman in an underground car park is violently assaulted as Winner delights in yet more nudity. Even by his standards he's pulling out all the stops. Hang on, there's still a bit more to go as a meditating, headphones-wearing woman is briefly seen topless for no other reason than she's got great jugs while a passenger waiting in line for a bus has her skirt pulled up.

On the plus side, Kersey's journalist girlfriend Geri (Bronson's real-life wife Ireland) is a successful career woman. Unfortunately, Ireland's such a non-actress she manages to kill every scene she's in, along with whatever liberal waffle she's trying to peddle about the evils of capital punishment.

It was probably only Bronson's clout that managed to keep Winner from having her clothes ripped off, too.

Would the violence make a vicar faint? Kersey's executions are for the most part run of the mill gunplay. It's the two explicit, frontloaded rapes that are going to make any man of God hot under his dog collar.

How fucked-up is this film? We're immediately told by a newsreader on the radio of an 'alarming rise in violence' that has seen LA homicides skyrocket by seventy-nine percent in the last five years. It's not a case of statistics, statistics and damned statistics, though. Straightaway we're shown hard evidence of how things have gone to shit when Kersey can't even buy an ice-cream in broad daylight without being hassled and having his wallet stolen.

This movie is nakedly pro-vigilante, a rabble-rousing ninety minutes that clearly wants us to cheer the vengeful Kersey on. We are repeatedly banged over the head that cops are useless while treatment for hardcore criminals is a waste of time. One husband whose semi-violated wife has just been saved from a much worse fate by the gun-toting Kersey tells the police: "Where the hell were you guys? Giving out parking tickets?" Later, he labels Kersey a 'very good citizen'. A dying cop explicitly gives his approval of Kersey's blunt methods by saying: "Get the motherfucker for me." In New York the Police Commissioner admits Kersey's original crime spree (in which he killed nine people) didn't lead to a prosecution because 'street crime was down fifty percent'. Elsewhere a hospital orderly is so contemptuous of the therapy where he works that he aids Kersey's getaway after an obviously still dangerous patient has just been zapped.

I could go on, but you get the picture. And you know what? I'm fine with a movie giving both thumbs up to outlaw justice. Just like I'm fine with any flick in which rape is eroticized, serial killers are super-intelligent and glamorous, heroin is shown to be a cool drug, and war is depicted as a noble, justifiable pursuit. Why am I fine with all that? Because I form my opinions based on my experience and what actually goes on in the world rather than from the cinema. Hence, I *know* rape is bad, people like Peter Sutcliffe fell as far as any human could, skag is a soul-sucking plague on society, and war is ghastly. In other words, I don't care how cinema depicts stuff or whatever message it tries to shove down my throat. Movies are just made-up shit. All I require is they entertain, engage or at the very least distract me from the emotional wasteland that's my life. And so Kersey's an unrepentant vigilante. This is great in the movies because, you know, lots of killings, but probably not so great in real life. In fact, I strongly suspect vigilantism is a recipe for disaster, but I don't go bagging a flick just because it presents the opposite viewpoint to my own.

Nevertheless, *Death Wish II* is a long way from quality fare. It's a simplistic, button-pushing exercise that revels in the worst of human behaviour. Then again, it moves so fast that it's impossible to be bored, especially during its rancid (but action-packed) opening twenty minutes. It remains a divisive watch, loved by fans of retro-sleaze and loathed by those who prefer a slightly more nuanced and restrained take on things. Whatever the case, it was a big hit, ensuring Kersey would be unleashed to hatefully tangle with lowlife punks yet again.

My Brain...? It's My Second Favourite Organ.

Woody Allen is a prolific artist who's been making roughly a film a year since the late sixties. His timid yet talkative onscreen persona (simultaneously intellectual and stupid, riddled with self-doubt and wrapped up in his weedy, balding, bespectacled frame) surely places him among the most distinctive film stars of all time. It's a double-edged sword in that some people love his neurotic, instantly recognizable schtick while others loathe Allen on sight. I find later stuff like *Mighty Aphrodite, Small Time Crooks, Jade Scorpion* and *Vicky Cristina Barcelona* pretty poor, but I'll always stick up for his career's splendid first phase, especially whenever one of his scrawny alter egos starts boasting about having 'the coiled sexual power of a jungle cat.'

Take the Money and Run (1969)

Allen's directorial debut takes the form of a mockumentary detailing the life of inept career criminal, Virgil Starkwell. This is a lowlife who tries his hand at everything from pool hustling to bank robbery. Apart from setting it in San Francisco rather than his beloved New York, the staples of Allen's future movies are all here: the fondness for mixing up absurdity and farce with more sophisticated, intellectual humour; his Jewishness; the jibes at God, religion and psychiatry; the mocking of machismo and criminal tendencies; the jazz score; the running gags; the portrayal of a dysfunctional childhood complete with disapproving, bickering parents; and his preposterous ability to snag beautiful women, despite being a combination of runt, loser and klutz ("I don't know how to act with girls... I have a tendency to dribble.") Perhaps the only obsession missing is the reverence for art.

Money is a plotless, rapid-fire gagfest complete with voiceover, talking heads and ham-fisted cello playing. Not all of it works, but it does have a high chuckle factor as Virgil teams up with criminals who have been convicted of such appalling crimes as dancing with a mailman and marrying a horse. There's an excellent chain gang sequence in which he only gets one hot meal a day (a bowl of steam) and ends up locked in a sweatbox with an insurance salesman. This is an easygoing, undemanding watch that remains endearingly silly.

Bananas (1971)

An all right opening half-hour in New York with a couple of excellent bits of physical comedy gives way to a pretty flat forty minutes in a fictional South American country. Sure, there are some nice jabs about the cyclical nature of political violence, American foreign policy and politics in general ("Let me be vice-president, that's a real idiot's job"), but it still feels more like extended sketch comedy than a well-rounded plot. However, I did enjoy an early Sly Stallone appearance as a leather-clad mugger on a train, as well as a TV newsreader solemnly telling us: "The NRA declares death a good thing." Plus, it's hard not to wince when Woody tries to justify buying porn in a corner store to another customer: "I'm doing a sociological study on perversion. I'm up to Advanced Child Molesting."

Play It Again, Sam (1972)

Sam is my pick of Allen's early 'funny' stuff, an inspired and consistently amusing odyssey through the nightmare of post-marriage dating. Allen is Allan Felix, a ridiculously immature hypochondriac film critic who's depressed at the collapse of his two-year-old marriage. Somehow his wife's desire for greener pastures comes as a shock, even though she kept flicking through the TV channels during sex and wants out on the grounds of 'insufficient laughter.'

"Why can't I be cool?" Felix wonders aloud. "What's the secret?" Perhaps not endlessly watching movies while sucking on frozen TV dinners, mate. His married friends, Dick and Linda Christie (Tony Roberts and Diane Keaton), decide to help but fixing the chronically repressed and self-conscious Felix up with an attractive and well-adjusted female is not easy. Luckily, an apparition of Humphrey Bogart (Jerry Lacy) is along for the ride to give him those crucial, confidence-boosting tips. "Dames are simple," he tells Felix in his no-nonsense way. "I never met one that didn't understand a slap in the mouth or a slug from a 45." But Felix is the polar opposite of Bogey, immediately passing out from his first sip of bourbon and soda in a bar.

What follows is a series of disastrous dates with blowhard nymphos and suicidal nihilists. They involve our clumsy, breast-obsessed hero doing everything from drinking aftershave and knocking things over to pretentiousness and dance floor cock-ups, all while trying to practice 'tremendous poise'. *Sam* is brilliant at satirizing the absurd lengths (read: exaggerations and outright lies) that many of us employ while trying impress the opposite sex, especially when it comes to grooming, lifestyle and accomplishments. Despite its thin subject matter and liberal sprinkling of monologues, flashbacks and fantasy sequences, this *Casablanca* homage has a lovely, organic feel. There are so many fantastic one-liners ("They said they were hairdressers") that you even occasionally stop getting distracted by Keaton's hideous dress sense.

Everything You Always Wanted To Know About Sex (1972)

Not sure I've ever seen a good anthology. The approach might work for books, but film...? Believe me, I've tried with all those cheesy horror anthologies that kept popping up through the seventies and eighties like *Asylum*, *The House That Dripped Blood*, *Tales from the Crypt*, *Creepshow*, and of course, that feline fiasco *The Uncanny*. Allen's big hit *Everything*, the tenth highest grossing movie of 72, is a good example of how tantalizing but ultimately unsatisfying the format can be. Many fans put this one down as a dated, uneven collection, unable to agree on which sketches work.

At least it starts well with its opening Cole Porter song *Let's Misbehave* piped over shots of frolicking rabbits. Allen kicks things off playing a *Hamlet*-spouting medieval jester, who's desperate to get his hands on the queen's jealously guarded fleshy jewels. Regrettably, his humble status and unappreciated court act mean he hasn't got a chance in hell. What's a horny fool to do?

Cheat, of course, by slipping a prescription-free aphrodisiac into the queen's drink. What follows is a master class in ridiculousness as Allen is thwarted by her chastity belt. "I must think of something quickly," he says, "because before you know it the Renaissance will be here and we'll all be painting." Full marks, too, for Anthony Quale's irked turn as the stern king.

However, Allen fires off his best shot during the second segment about bestiality. It's an adroit exercise in economical storytelling that's both hilarious and poignant. Gene Wilder plays a respectable, but slightly bored doctor, caught off guard during a routine consultation when a patient confesses an overwhelming love for a sheep named Daisy. "It was the greatest lay I ever had," the man insists as Wilder treats us to a lengthy array of facial reactions. Unfortunately, the road to true love never runs smooth and the lovelorn patient wants Wilder to examine his 'girlfriend' as she's grown 'cold' and 'indifferent' during their lovemaking. "I'm an MD, not a veterinarian," Wilder replies. "It's not normal to experience mature love for anything with four legs." It's all played so wonderfully straight-faced, resulting in one of the greatest skits I've ever seen. Wilder's performance is comic perfection.

Everything then tails off with four duds in a row until it finds a fitting, ahem, climax. It has to be said that even *trying* to illustrate what the hell goes on during ejaculation is inspired in itself, but the fact Allen comes up with such an unforgettable sketch is testament to his potent imagination. He depicts each part of the body as being controlled by a group of scientists in the brain who pass on orders to the manual workers elsewhere. In a memorably absurd role, Allen plays an anxious paratrooper sperm. "I'm scared, I don't wanna go," he tells his much more confident fellow sperm as they prepare to launch. "Who knows what it's gonna be like out there? You hear these strange stories, like sometimes the guys will slam their heads up against a wall of hard rubber. Or what if it's a homosexual encounter?"

Sleeper (1973)

Allen's second collaboration with Keaton sees him play a cryogenically frozen patient brought back to life in 2173. Now a 237-year-old former health store owner, he's none too pleased upon being told what's happened: "I can't believe this! My doctor said I'd be up on my feet again after five days. He was off by 199 years!"

New York has become a police state and he's quickly declared a rebel, but at least the natives are just as screwed up as ever. "Sex is different today," the highly strung Keaton tells him. "We don't have any problems. Everyone's frigid."

Sleeper is an eighty-five-minute exercise in goofiness, managing to fit in everything from gags about Richard Nixon and Miss Universe to a lot of Buster Keaton-inspired slapstick and a Blanche DuBois impersonation. It has deliberately cheap effects, such as the plastic-covered cars, the robots that are merely people acting robotically, and the fact Allen's cryogenic freezing involves little more than encasing him in silver foil (while still wearing his trademark glasses).

I've always enjoyed the nose-stealing loopiness of *Sleeper*, especially Allen's clothes-shredding introductory use of the orgasmatron, its many nods to other sci-fi flicks, and its solitary NRA dig, this time describing it as 'a group that helped criminals get guns so they could shoot citizens'.

Depressingly, Allen depicts McDonald's still going strong in 2173.

Love and Death (1975)

This eighty-minute existentialist comedy is perhaps Allen's best demonstration of his cowardly, anti-machismo persona ("*You're* scared? I'm growing a beak and feathers"). He plays Boris, a 19th century Russian scholar who gets dragged into the Napoleonic Wars. Of course, he'd rather stay at home and write poetry on the basis that he 'can't shower with other men'. When forced to go by his family, he sets off clutching his framed butterfly collection. It's not long before he messes up at boot camp, experiences battlefield slaughter and fights a duel, somehow managing to not only survive but become a hero.

Boris struggles to believe in God ("You think I was made in God's image? Take a look at me. You think he wears glasses?"), sees nature as an 'enormous restaurant', occasionally talks to Death, and is in love with a promiscuous cousin. There's a lot of silly stuff here, although its comedy is underpinned by a more intellectual flavour and occasional sophisticated word play that riffs on Russian literature.

Many see *Love and Death* as the bridge between Allen's knockabout stuff and his more mature comedy. It's a decent, gently amusing watch boasting some excellent one-liners and a pastry-obsessed Napoleon. Plus, if you're being tormented by an existential crisis and/or suicidal thoughts it magically offers the solution. "I have lived many years," an elderly holy man declares. "After many trials and tribulations, I have come to the conclusion that the best thing is blonde twelve-year-old girls. Two of them wherever possible."

The Front (1976)

If you're not too keen on Allen, I suggest taking a look at this one as it might help you change your mind. There's no knockabout, neurotic, madcap stuff here, probably because he neither wrote nor directed *The Front*. This quirk in his career resulted in a dialled-down persona that immediately feels different.

The Front is a funny yet melancholy drama that captures the pain and sheer nonsense of McCarthy-era New York. It opens with a lovely, black and white Sinatra-accompanied montage of 50s America before we meet Allen. He plays the 'practically illiterate' Howard Prince and from the offset it's clear he's not a morally upright, leading citizen. In fact, he's a self-centred, arse-grabbing, vaguely dishonest small-time bookie forever telling people stories.

When a blacklisted writer friend asks him to 'front' by submitting scripts under his name to a TV studio, this bullshitting weasel jumps at the chance of earning a ten per cent commission. Suddenly Howard's got a regular income for pretty much doing nothing, his social standing is boosted, and he even starts seeing a pretty producer. She thinks he's 'genuinely modest' because he doesn't want to talk about his work whereas the truth is he hasn't read a word of the acclaimed scripts that bear his name. Soon he wants to front for extra writers on the basis it doesn't involve any more work and will triple his unearned income. At least the first writer he's feeding off has his number. "I know you, Howard," he says. "You're gonna take off and fly right up your own ass."

Meanwhile, Hecky Brown (Zero Mostel) is a talented entertainer whose unfortunate flirtation with Communism is rapidly eroding a successful career. "We're in a war against a ruthless and tricky enemy who will stop at nothing to destroy our way of life," he's told by an anti-Communist official, a quietly frightening zealot who wants Hecky to inform and spy on other suspected sympathizers. Hecky holds out, but it results in this proud family man barely being able to snag a day's work and his fee dropping from five grand to $250. With his hangdog face, Mostel paints a heartbreaking portrait of a shunned artist being pushed into quicksand. "Talent has no protection," he says. "You do as they say or else."

The Front is not a particularly well-known comedy-drama, but it features a pitch perfect supporting cast while offering a terrific insight into writing, delusion, witch hunts, show trials, ostracism, power and professional relationships.

Annie Hall (1977)

This is the one in which Allen the successful artist made a gigantic leap into the mainstream, robbing *Star Wars* of Oscar glory in the process.

Not that he did anything different. I guess it was a case of paying his dues, building his audience and letting momentum do the rest. *Annie Hall* is certainly calmer and more mature with no clowning or slapstick, but it still contains Allen's familiar collaborators, the same settings and his fondness for direct to camera stuff, inner monologues and surrealism. All right, the cartoon interlude, the Bob Dylan jibes and the withering rejection of LA are new.

Its plot is tiny, centring on the dissection of a relationship between Alvy Singer (Allen) and the titular character (Diane Keaton, up to her old sartorial missteps). We see the initial meeting, the tentative attempts to move things onto a romantic level, the satisfying sex, the camaraderie, the insecurities, the minor arguments, the big decisions like moving in together, the jealousies, the sexual problems, the semi-breakups and the good-natured dissolution. For the most part they share a simple, relaxed love built upon an intellectual, emotional and physical connection.

But it doesn't last, bemusing the already insecure Alvy: "A relationship is like a shark. It has to constantly move forward or it dies. And I think what we got on our hands is a dead shark."

Now in his over-analytical way he has to try to work out why he's failed again. This involves examining his rollercoaster-afflicted childhood, past marriages, his obsession with death and listening to a suicide-tempted Christopher Walken.

Ultimately, there's a lot to enjoy about *Annie Hall*, but it does start to stagnate during its final half an hour. I don't find it as funny as something like *Play It Again, Sam*. Perhaps that's because its long-winded attempt to illustrate the ins and outs of relationship failure is occasionally punctured by a pithy piece of wisdom, such as when a passerby tells Alvy: "Love fades."

Yep. It really can be that simple.

Manhattan (1979)

Many of Allen's movies focus on a protagonist being terrified of women and screwing up to an absurd degree whenever near them. Or as Allan Felix says in *Play It Again, Sam*: "I have a tendency to reject before I get rejected. That way I save a lot of time and money." Yet it's noticeable that Allen's immature heroes not only get plenty of girls but bloody good-looking ones, too. There must be something in this neurotic funnyman schtick that females can't resist, leaving me to wonder who gets laid the most: Allen's characters or James Bond.

In the beautifully shot, black and white *Manhattan*, Isaac Davis (Allen) is involved with a 17-year-old cracker (an excellent Mariel Hemingway), despite the fact he's forty-two. "I'm dating a girl who does homework," he tells his friends. Isaac is the usual angst-ridden disaster with two failed marriages behind him. He's also quit his TV writing job in a fit of pique.

The best thing in his life is Tracy (Hemingway), the epitome of simple, grounded sweetness. They have a great, relaxed time together. She's in love, but he won't take anything she says seriously, let alone accept such genuine emotion. "You're a kid and I never want you to forget that," he says. "You're gonna meet a lot of terrific men in your life. I want you to enjoy me, you know, my wry sense of humour and astonishing sexual technique, but never forget that you've got your whole life ahead of you... Think of me as a detour on the highway of life."

Isaac instead gets involved with the uptight Mary Wilkie (Diane Keaton in thankfully less atrocious clothing). She's representative of the pretentious, unbearably opinionated, artsy-fartsy crowd that Isaac hangs around with ("I finally had an orgasm," one such member tells him, "but my doctor told me it was the wrong kind.") Of course, it's a doomed relationship, making Isaac realise that the honest, uncomplicated, life-affirming Tracy was the one after all.

Perhaps her extreme youth is the only new ground *Manhattan* breaks because otherwise it's Allen's typical assortment of intellectualism, relationship stuff, pseudo-intellectualism, affairs and over-analytical fretting. Watching one Allen movie after another does make it clear how he likes to cover the same ground because he sure as hell shuns action and big plots. This may make it sound like I'm not a fan of the Gershwin-accompanied *Manhattan*, but it's probably just a case of mild Allen fatigue.

Like *Annie Hall*, *Manhattan* is free of knockabout comedy and just as talky. Still, it's a good standalone film and proved to be another box-office winner. Towards its end, it starts hitting its straps as Isaac lies on a sofa listing all the stuff that makes life worth living, such as Groucho Marx, the second movement of the Jupiter Symphony, Marlon Brando and Tracy's face. From here it's a lovely, eight-minute stroll to one of the most beautifully straightforward closing lines in cinema.

Zelig (1983)

Both a well-rounded oddity in Allen's early catalogue and a technically accomplished groundbreaker, this one gives us an intriguing documentary-style account of a man who can assume the physical characteristics of others. It's a long way from being laugh out loud funny, but at least it's not another wallow in relationship angst.

Allen is Leonard Zelig, a man in the 1920s whose terrible childhood has resulted in him becoming a mental cripple without self-esteem. Now he has a chameleon-like ability to copy whomever he's standing alongside, whether they're black, Chinese, overweight or a National Socialist.

Doctors are unable to agree on a diagnosis with some thinking it's glandular or a brain tumour. Others put it down to eating too much Mexican food. It's only when a kindly, dedicated female doctor takes him under her wing that the reason is revealed. "It's safe to be like the others," he confesses under hypnosis. "I wanna be liked."

Christ, have you ever heard anything so sad?

Crimes and Misdemeanors (1989)

Crimes has a dark, unsettling centre. It quietly lays bare chilling truths and can only help undermine the idiotic belief in karma, if not God himself. Don't go thinking it's a depressing immersion in futility, though. Despite a clear-sighted view of reality and human behaviour, it's so superbly written that it still manages to offer a life-affirming thread of hope.

Judah Rosenthal (the Oscar-winning Martin Landau) is an upper-class, married father of two and successful ophthalmologist. He's also ensnared in a *Fatal Attraction*-style affair with a woman who's not only a hair's breadth away from telling his oblivious wife, but threatening to expose an earlier bout of embezzlement. She can't be bought off and won't listen to reason, insisting: "I won't be tossed out."

But what's a pillar of the community like Judah to do? He hates getting his hands dirty, even though it's clear at the very least he's a rank hypocrite. As a child it was drilled into him that the 'eyes of God are on us always' yet now he's faced with the ultimate choice: self-preservation ("God is a luxury I can't afford") or the risk of losing everything ("My life's about to go up in smoke!")

Judah is also treating a Rabbi patient, whose sight is rapidly ebbing away. He's a humble, decent guy that believes in a 'moral structure' to the universe despite his steady descent into literal darkness. He urges Rosenthal to confess his long-time infidelity, suggesting there might be unforeseen benefits.

Elsewhere, Clifford Stern (Allen, now looking like a bespectacled cross between Stan Laurel and C-3PO) is a small-time, unemployed documentary-maker trapped in an unhappy marriage. His brother-in-law Lester (a funny Alan Alda) happens to be a successful, award-winning TV producer, but he's also an insufferable, pompous arse. Lester (at his wife's behest) gives Clifford a job to make a short film celebrating his achievements. Allen falls for an associate producer on the project, but his eyes are open about his chances of success both in his love life and career. "As you go through life, great depth and smouldering sensuality do not always win," he says.

Allen has long joked about the coldness of the universe, the absence of God and the meaninglessness of life. Take *Annie Hall's* Alvy Singer outlining his somewhat bleak take on things: "I feel that life is divided up into the horrible and the miserable. Those are the two categories. The horrible would be like terminal cases. Blind people. Cripples. I don't know how they get through life. It's amazing to me. And the miserable is everyone else. So when you go through life you should be thankful to be miserable."

In *Crimes*, Allen discards the flippancy and instead examines existentialist questions at length. He depicts a world in which worthwhile men commit suicide or are otherwise blighted; facile wankers prosper; genuine emotions go unrequited; the talented never find a platform; the corrupt and wicked are not brought to justice; and your own sister can go out on a date only to end up tied to a bed with a freshly laid turd on her chest.

How to navigate through such murk? *Crimes* shows us that some people believe in nothing and do whatever is necessary, giving a dark deed no more thought than pushing a button. Some think there is a moral framework to existence, regardless of religion. A persistent handful insists that the world is a cesspit without God. Others stick their head in the sand, ignoring the appalling lows of human history while admitting the idea of God is preferable to taking on board a more believable truth. Perhaps the stoic Rabbi with the failing eyesight has the answer: "Sometimes to have a little luck is the best plan."

Crimes was Allen's fourth drama and perhaps an excellent place to start if you struggle to grasp the man's divisive persona. His character Clifford essentially provides humour, but by now Allen has learned the power of restraint and there's no clowning. *Crimes* is a minor triumph, especially the way its Shakespearean quality puts such an emphasis on eyes, God, conscience, justice and, of course, the heart.

By this point Allen had been making movies for two decades, netting a boatload of Oscar nods for his relentless output. There had certainly been wobbles (the forgettable *Midsummer Night's Sex Comedy*, the unconvincing *Purple Rose of Cairo*), but *Crimes* illustrated there was still plenty of creative and insightful life left in the old dog.

Sorry, vicious jungle beast.

Macho Idiots

There's a terrific scene in *The Terminator* when Arnie strides into a nightclub looking for Sarah Connor. A bouncer tries to stop him by slapping a hand on his shoulder, but our futuristic hit man doesn't even bother looking around. Instead he grabs the offending limb and gives the fool a taste of his cybernetic strength, forcing the doorman to his whimpering knees.

I tell you this because I was once in a situation when I fantasised about doing the same thing. I'd flown to Sydney for the weekend with my mate, Trev, and we were determined to have a good time.

Except we were wandering around post-midnight and every night club either catered for a gay clientele or wouldn't let us in. It was absurd. We were in a major city on a Friday night unable to do that Wayne and Garth thing and party on. Most bouncers rejected us because we were sans girls. We tried to explain we wanted to meet a lady or two *inside*. If we'd already met the ladies, why would we be trying to get in?

No dice.

Trev 'n' me put our inebriated heads together. We could *try* a Dahmer's Deli. We'd heard plenty of girls frequented such places because they were less likely to get propositioned and pawed by horny blokes, blokes like Trev 'n' me.

No.

People might somehow hear about it back home, put two and two together, and start whispering we'd popped over to Sydney for a bout of mutual sausage admiration.

We kept going, continually flicked away by one muscle-bound meathead after another, until we came face to face with a seven-foot tall Maori bouncer. By now we were tired and determined to reason with this intimidating bastard until fair play won.

He gave us the ocular pat down, shook his head and barely found the energy to mutter the standard reason (no girls). Worse, he turned his back on us, obviously convinced we posed no threat. We thought about running past, but suspected such sneakiness would end in humiliation, pain and possible hospital time. Instead we begged and pleaded for a good ten minutes as other smirking blokes strode past arm-in-arm with those crucial females.

And, of course, I wanted to be Arnie. I wanted to march in before crushing his poncy, flower-arranging hand in a sweat-free demonstration of sheer power.

Oh, why can't I be a cyborg? Not all the time. That would be... impractical. But just... *occasionally*. You know, when faced with a bigger, stronger, infuriatingly obstinate adversary.

Well, I guess life doesn't work that way, and just as quickly my cyborg fantasy evaporated. It was time to give up on our quest to get laid, buy a greasy kebab and return to our cheap little hotel to snigger at cheesy 80s music videos on YouTube (*When you make love, do you look in the mirror?*) Trev 'n' me started trudging back, but at least I managed to have the last word. And let me tell you, ladies and gentlemen, that excruciatingly lame outburst still haunts me. For what did I shout at my terse Maori friend after spending quarter of an hour insisting Trev 'n' me were exactly the sort of cool guys every night club needs?

"Didn't wanna come in, anyway!"

Even Trev winced.

So why do I mention this pathetic encounter on a Sydney street? Because (like most guys) I hate having my physical limitations laid bare. It ignites anger, especially when I've sunk a beer or two. Such a heightened emotional state risks making me attempt something far beyond my physical capabilities. In other words, turning into a pseudo-cyborg aka macho idiot.

And there are far too many of those tools in the world already.

Bada-bing!

Macho idiots often have an abiding weakness: they're predictable. They know only one course of action, a red-misted response that involves some form of squaring up, threatening or busting chops. Nothing illustrates this better than our hot-headed gangster friend, Sonny Corleone, in *The Godfather*.

Right from the start when pushing around nosy photographers at his sister's wedding or spitting on the floor when shown FBI id, it's clear he's got a head full of testosterone rather than any real brains. He just gets angrier and angrier and is apoplectic by the time he does his energetic tollbooth dance.

As played by James Caan in his defining role, the first-born Sonny is incapable of learning that failing to check every aggressive impulse is a mistake. Perhaps that's because he's so used to getting away with stuff, whether it's banging a broad within a few yards of his wife, shoving someone up against a wall, gnawing on a brother-in-law's fingers or ordering a hit. This is a man in a man's world. He does what he wants and takes what he wants, a confidence boosted by his massive schlong and demonstrated by his permanent swagger.

But even entitled gangsters can only get away with such undisciplined behaviour for so long. Sonny never grasps that the Sollozzo-organized shooting of his father is not personal, but merely a business decision. Negotiation, concessions and patching things up are not his style. He can't see past bloody reprisals, happy to concede that 'business will have to suffer' which, of course, is the last thing his wounded father wants. Look at the open contempt he has for his much more civilized *consigliere* Tom (Robert Duvall), who proffers a subtler way forward. Sonny rules out such an unmanly response, preferring to have a hundred button men on the street 24 hours a day. "That Turk shows one hair on his ass, he's dead," he rages.

It's no surprise Sonny later laughs at Michael's (Al Pacino) unprompted proposal to kill Sollozzo and a corrupt police captain in a restaurant. This scorn is the typical reaction of a macho idiot. Sonny sees things in black and white, unable to comprehend that a 'weaker' person might be as capable of brute force. He mocks the 'nice college boy' when in actual fact the plan's so daring it's perfect. "Didn't wanna get mixed up in the family business?" he tells Michael, just about stopping short of mussing his hair. "Now you wanna gun down a police captain?"

Sonny is always spoiling for a fight, always wanting to smash through whatever obstacle that's in his or the family's way. It's a foible his enemies learn to fatally exploit by arranging to have his pregnant sister smacked around. Or as one of them earlier tells him over the phone: "Don't lose that famous temper of yours, Sonny."

Sonny, of course, does just that.

You try to be nice to some people

Macho idiots often like to hide behind a uniform. It's a lot easier to square up to someone when you're legally packing heat and know there's an entire police department backing you up. Take *First Blood's* portly Sheriff Will Teasle (the great Brian Dennehy). He picks on the longhaired drifter John Rambo for no other reason than he doesn't like his appearance and it makes him feel manly to push someone around. And what's some powerless punk gonna do it about it anyway? Hell, there's no way he'll challenge Authority with a capital 'a'.

Bad call, mate.

Even before he meets Rambo we sense there's something a bit 'off' about Teasle. Sure, he's friendly, greeting the townsfolk as he wanders out of the station and hops into his cruiser, but then there's that remark about one resident muttered under his breath: "Gonna take a bath this week?"

There it is. The rigidness. The underlying contempt for people who don't think or behave the same. He's like a super-strict schoolmaster, always looking to criticise his students' dress sense or cuff them around the ears for being cheeky.

Teasle's initial encounter with the 'smartass drifter' Rambo is a textbook example of passive-aggressiveness. There's the way he runs his eyes over the new arrival and instantly weighs him up, the faux-politeness, the justification for moving him on (such as the town being 'boring'), and the seeming courtesy in giving him a lift to the edge of town. Teasle has got the demeanour and mannerisms down pat, presenting himself as the voice of reason and order.

When Rambo inquires if there's somewhere to eat, Teasle replies there's a diner thirty miles up the highway. The message, hidden in a concrete piece of info, is clear: *you ain't welcome here, mate.*

His weary passenger can only ask a rhetorical question: "Any law against me getting something to eat here?"

"Yeah," Teasle says, finally dropping the chivalrous act and replacing it with his best steely look. "Me."

Teasle is a judgmental asshole, the sort of authority figure who always believes the other guy started the trouble. Provocation doesn't exist. The law's the law, you see, and you can't fuck with it. When Rambo fails to heed his 'friendly advice' to leave and immediately starts walking back into town, Teasle takes it personally. "You try to be nice to some people," he mutters while swinging the cruiser around.

Teasle's machismo makes him incompetent and dangerous. Worse, he knows he looks silly in front of his subordinates. Rambo whips his butt twice in succession, firstly knocking him over in the police station and then forcing him to crash his cruiser. By now, Teasle's heels are well and truly dug in, hardening an already inflexible state of mind. His macho pride has been wounded and he's incapable of backing down or reassessing the deteriorating situation.

There's a terrific few seconds when he's told over the radio that Rambo's a Green Beret, Vietnam vet and war hero. The disbelief etched onto his face as his brain emptily whirrs is fantastic. You can almost hear him thinking: *This is not what's supposed to happen when you push a sucker around.* Still, it's only the briefest impression of doubt before machismo blinds him again. A moment later he's bellowing at the posse: "What the hell's the matter with you guys? He's one man. He's wounded."

Teasle's faulty mindset shows what machismo can do to a fellah. He refuses to call in the State police or abandon the hunt, even though a chopper pilot cries off because of an impending storm. He fails to consider Rambo's specialised training will give the ex-Green Beret the edge in such inhospitable terrain. He keeps pushing on in the spirit of rightful vengeance despite a dead colleague and the fact his quarry has acquired a gun.

"I'm gonna get that sonuvabitch!" he screams at one point. "And I'm gonna pin that Congressional Medal of Honor to his liver!"

Teasle personifies pig-eared ignorance, a 'kingshit cop' who remains dismissive, contemptuous and sarcastic even when Rambo's old boss comes up with a sensible plan to defuse the escalating situation.

But Teasle can't go for it. Macho idiots never can.

Sweep the leg!

Sometimes it's easy to spot a macho idiot.

For a start they like moody pictures of themselves to be on hand, especially if in uniform and/or holding a gun. Don't be surprised to see bare biceps and facial camouflage markings. The whiff of manliness is intensified if there's a dead animal at their feet or slung across the bonnet of a car.

The Karate Kid establishes sensei John Kreese (Martin Kove) as a prime, red-blooded specimen when we're treated to an impressive array of personal pix before setting eyes on him in the flesh. As his masterful voice hammers words of steel into his young disciples ("Fear does not exist in this dojo!"), we come face to face with a life-size cardboard cut-out of him. His brow is furrowed, his fist is poised. This is a man who takes no shit. If you're not trembling yet, the camera respectfully moves left to show us a wall-mounted black and white image from his army days, revealing he was the US army's karate champion in the early seventies.

And, of course, this serial trophy winner is also shown cradling a big fuckoff weapon.

There's only one question left: Does he hunt unarmed woodland animals on the weekend? Or at least set booby traps for them? We're never told. However, he makes up for this possible lapse in manhood by shouting at and pushing around a bunch of children all week long at his deadly serious theatre of pain. He struts with a king's arrogance among his well-drilled, shorter charges, none of whom have started shaving yet, barking commands while teaching them to strike first, strike hard and have no mercy. They are studying 'the way of the fist' and this most definitely isn't something to do with gay pleasure. Oh, no. Everyone calls him *sir* and none smirk, snigger or fart in his presence. If they did, you can bet they would be killed *without hesitation*.

"You lose concentration in a fight and you're dead meat," he roars at one fourteen-year-old child he's just thrown to the floor for having the audacity to not be as tough.

It's clearly a reign of terror at Cobra Kai. Or as Kreese tells the 'pushy little bastard' Mr. Miyagi: "This is a karate dojo, not a knitting class."

I have to say Kove's ridiculous performance, in which he's unwaveringly contemptuous of whatever's in front of him, is among my favourite bits of *Karate Kid*. He's perfect as the humourless douche bag, forever spitting out words of wisdom, such as 'mercy is for the weak' before dishing out push-up punishments or ordering an indoctrinated student to 'finish' an already floored opponent. Indeed, it's easy to imagine him back in Nam torching a village before roundhousing any woman or child that managed to make it out of the flames.

And yes, I welled up at the start of the sequel when Mr. Miyagi publicly kicked Kreese's arse in the parking lot. The threat of a fatal blow from a bonsai-loving, elderly dwarf followed by a comical tweak of the great man's nose was just too much.

Some things we should never have to see.

Suck my dick!

I think I've mentioned beforehand that a Strong Female Role is not about getting a lady to act like a fellah. I've no problem with women killing men in the movies (*Repulsion*), wiping the floor with them (*Cuckoo's Nest*) or smugly sauntering away after decisively gaining the upper hand (*Body Heat*). That's all fine, but for Christ's sake, don't have them slugging it out toe to toe with a bigger, faster, physically stronger adversary.

That shit never convinces. You just end up with stuff like *Switchblade Sisters*.

Well, after enduring Ridley Scott's far-fetched box-office flop *G.I. Jane*, I doubt Demi Moore shares my opinion about Strong Female Roles. Indeed, the way the camera 'treats' us to one shaven-headed, one-armed push-up after another makes me suspect that if she ever heard me voice such sexist tripe she'd shove my head down the bog.

She plays Lt. Jordan O'Neil and has just been plucked from a desk job (on the say-so of some ambitious, publicity-seeking, double-dealing senator who wants a 'gender-blind' navy) to undergo months of hellish training in a bid to become the first menstruating Navy SEAL.

Why O'Neil? Not sure, but the senator seems to want an attractive non-lezzer.

We already know O'Neil's a macho idiot as she applied for active duty during the Gulf War, getting rejected because the submarine 'had no bathroom facilities for women'. Who in their right mind *wants* to go to war? But a knuckle-head like O'Neil believes risking life and limb is the key to 'career advancement' so she jumps at the chance to become a political hot potato. Her boyfriend, however, adopts a more cautious approach by telling her the SEALS are 'world-class warriors' that 'will eat cornflakes out of her skull'.

Not that you can talk to a macho idiot like O'Neil. And so before long she's enduring wolf whistles, nipple and tampon jokes, prejudice, gender-norming, and what can only be described as outright abuse and torture. She becomes absurdly tough, never once crying or asking for time off to go handbag shopping. Just about every expression is serious or of the don't-fuck-with-me kind. At the eighty-minute mark she's been transformed into the equivalent of a busty Patriot missile, hell-bent on proving the girls are as good as the boys, and ultimately disappointed she doesn't get to slit a hostile's throat on some foreign beach. Not once does she grasp it's a mistake to want to be like these guys or that combat is bad. Step by step she learns respect can only be earned through physical prowess, the endurance of pain, and outright violence. Look at the scene where she absorbs a criminal amount of vicious abuse from a superior, only to briefly turn the tables by head butting and booting him in the balls.

All with her hands tied behind her back.

"Seek life elsewhere," he manages to tell her, shortly before setting his broken nose.

And her snarling reply in front of her cheering fellow SEAL wannabes?

"Suck my dick!"

Scott's mistake is to present this jingoistic, testosterone-soaked, outrageous fantasy as realism ("O'Neil, I'd go to war with you any day!") Mind you, as a director I'm not sure he's ever adopted an approach involving a tongue in cheek, satire or black comedy. *G.I. Jane* feels like a mash-up of *Officer and a Gentleman*, *Deer Hunter* and *Top Gun*, failing to be as good as any of them. It's a shame as Scott's dealing with an interesting idea (female physical limitations), but his treatment is far too straight-faced and downright absurd for it to take flight. He ends up with a movie suggesting the fairer sex is also susceptible to the poisonous belief that a Real Man has to possess big biceps and be able to seriously kick arse.

Still, it was probably unfair to hand Moore a Razzie for Worst Actress. She does her best and I can see why she plumped for this ludicrous role, perhaps viewing her extreme haircut and pumped-up physique as the 90s female answer to De Niro's Jake LaMotta transformation.

G.I. Jane is good at capturing military life, such as the anal obsession with detail, appearances and posture; the doing everything at the double; the endless saluting; the love of weaponry; the bullying and routine humiliations; the fruity little tashes; and the sheer fucking silliness of it all.

To be fair to O'Neil she's also a long way from being the only macho idiot on parade. Listen to this nugget of boot camp wisdom from her instructor: "Pain is your friend, your ally. It will tell you when you are seriously injured. It will keep you awake and angry and remind you to finish the job and get the hell home. But you know the best thing about pain? It lets you know you're not dead yet."

Alternatively, you could avoid pain. I do that as much as possible and I'm pretty sure I'm not dead, either.

Oh God, I hate these people and their rigid, desperately unimaginative mindset.

So, in summary, do not join the army. Resist those cybernetic impulses. They usually only take you to a bad place. It's far better to be a wimp, bide your time, and wait for your opponent to turn his back or (better still) fall asleep.

Then stab the bastard, especially if he happens to be a seven-foot tall Maori bouncer.

Fucked-Up Films #8: 10 To Midnight (1983)

Synopsis

Nudey nutter knifes nurses

Director

J. Lee Thompson

Cast

Charles Bronson, Gene Davis, Andrew Stevens, Lisa Eilbacher, Geoffrey Lewis

What are these sick bastards doing? Celibacy makes you kill people. Sex gets you killed. Christ, what's a person s'posed to do?

Is the villain any good? I once went up to an attractive lady in a bar and said: "You are a woman and, as such, you will do my bidding." Later, after I'd wiped the stinging white wine from my eyes, I reflected that perhaps my wooing technique could do with a little polish. Mind you, I'm still infinitely smoother than our main bad guy Warren Stacey (Davis). Good grief, this guy's *hopeless*. His idea of seduction is to pull down the zipper on the back of a blonde girl's dress at work. When that fails he does the Peeping Tom and obscene phone call thing before following her into the woods and stabbing her to death. You have to say, this combination of clumsiness, grudge-holding, harassment and fatal violence is probably not the best way to secure a steady girlfriend and some nice regular num-nums.

At work, it's obvious Warren's female colleagues dislike him, despite his metrosexual good looks. Perhaps that's because he's about thirty but has the most pathetic job I think I've ever known for a serial killer or non-serial killer alike: he cleans typewriters. As well as that, Warren's apparently still a virgin. Now I'm starting to feel sorry for the guy. Thirtyish, never been laid, women despise him, and his workplace status is below that of a typist.

At one point he's hauled in by the cops and presented with a homemade masturbation device found in his apartment. It looks like a blue and white thermos flask with a flesh-coloured orifice perched on top. It needs to be plugged in, yet its rubbery tube has indentations designed for a firm grip. For the life of me (and I say this as an expert wanker) I can't quite understand how this thing works. Perhaps it vibrates and you can enjoy a steaming hot cup of oxtail soup at the same time. Disappointingly we never get to see it in action and our minds can only wonder at its efficiency, but I feel any novice user would likely end up red-faced and stammering in the ER. Whatever the case, it's a sad substitute for a loving lady's caress.

However, Warren's colourful masturbatory habits are a mere sideshow in the shit show that's his life. He's a taunting, none too bright killer who appears to be based on a mash-up of the real-life scumbags Ted Bundy (handsome, drives a VW) and Richard Speck (dedicated nurse slaughterer). I have to say Davis isn't much of an actor, but you've gotta acknowledge his bravery in taking this one on. His character is kinda unforgettable. See later.

How do the lovely ladies fare? Fine, apart from all the stabbings. This is a pic that might be free of rape, but it's still knee-deep in misogyny. We're talking obscene phone calls ("I wouldn't piss on the best part of you"), stalking, multiple murders, sobbing victims begging for their life, and shots of bloodstained corpses in their underwear or nude. They're killed outdoors or butchered en masse in their dormitory. Honestly, there's not a sniff of a Strong Female Role here, but at least we get lots of former Playboy Playmates in minor roles and a dark-haired, torpedo-breasted lass watching a retro showing of *Butch Cassidy* at a cinema that I instantly fell in love with.

How skuzzy are the men? Bronson's partner Paul McAnn (Stevens) is a decent guy, so decent in fact that no one believes he's a detective. He's educated, treats women well, knows right from wrong, and stands up to be counted. In other words, he's dull.

Lieutenant Leo Kessler (Bronson), however, is a blue-collar cop stumbling through a moral fog. "I'm not a nice person," he tells a reporter. "I'm a mean, selfish sonuvabitch." He quickly demonstrates these steely traits by putting some discarded chewing gum in his partner's jacket pocket, objecting to the use of fancy words like 'inured' and revealing he hates quiche. There's also little doubting his rightwing views in this Reagan-era pic. He's an old school, villain-hating cop who has no faith in the system with its 'shyster' lawyers, bullshit defences and legal loopholes. "The way the law protects those maggots out there you'd think they were an endangered species," he says. "Forget what's legal and do what's right."

A paunchy Bronson looks pretty bored throughout, although at least he gets to say 'penis' and 'jacking off', which might have been a first in his career. There's a particularly embarrassing scene in which he has to chase the much younger killer in the direst of circumstances but can only manage to waddle with an expression of supreme disinterest. He might be armed, but gives the impression he's making a half-assed attempt to catch the bus. Ultimately, *Midnight* is a long way from his best.

Would the violence make a vicar faint? Hmm, it's not a particularly graphic movie, but a lot of the ladies do get to feel the pointy end of our killer's hate. You don't see the knife going in: instead it's more a case of the red stuff spraying up the wall and lots of shots of the blood-stained blade. *Midnight's* ambience is unhealthy. It has an emphasis on hunting women while its amped-up final fifteen minutes are quite something.

How fucked-up is this film? Well, the title's fucked-up as it doesn't make a lick of sense, but I guess that's a minor concern. Under no circumstances would I call this a good movie, given its implausibilities, clumsy dialogue, awkward scenes, and smattering of overacting. Then again it was put together by those lovely peeps at Cannon Films, a now defunct company that delivered such quality fare as *Over the Top*, *Death Wish 5* and *Breakin' 2: Electric Boogaloo*. *Midnight* was a terribly reviewed action thriller/slasher horror hybrid, but is still worth a watch for its killer's memorable MO. Did I mention Stacey kills in his birthday suit? I reckon he spends the best part of twenty minutes prancing around in the buff with his knife out. You see his bare buttocks at such length they end up imprinted on your retinas. I'm willing to put my neck on the line and say no other movie has ever given us such nutty nudity, especially an early scene in which a naked woman is chased through the woods. We don't actually get an explanation for Stacey's unorthodox approach, but presumably it's to avoid leaving behind forensic evidence, such as fibres. Then again, I would've thought his starkers act made him far more likely to drop a pube or two. Disappointingly no serial killer since has had the courage to ape Stacey's pioneering MO.

And they say sicko movies inspire copycats.

Devilish Dwarves

There's a famous old Peter Cook and Dudley Moore sketch in which a one-legged actor auditions for Tarzan. The casting agent can't believe what he's being confronted with ("I've got nothing against your right leg. The trouble is, neither have you") while the disabled actor remains oblivious to his chances of snagging the athletic role. Pete and Dud's point is clear: some people are blind to their bleeding obvious limitations.

It's a funny skit. What's more, it's starting to look prescient. These days employers have to be bloody careful about turning applicants away. It only takes one deluded asshat to claim prejudice on Twitter and a company can find itself at the centre of a politically correct firestorm. In this kind of climate where everyone has allegedly equal aptitude, would you be surprised to hear of an upcoming one-legged Tarzan movie? Or some TV show with a handless pianist? We're supposed to be willing to accept such madness because otherwise that makes us *discriminatory*.

And so to dwarves. When it comes to the movies, they've traditionally been pigeonholed into three kinds of roles: porn, comedy and horror (and if you're lucky, you might be able to find a saucy flick that combines all three). Apparently, this is no longer enough and there now appears to be a more inclusive push. This probably has something to do with the 1.35m Peter Dinklage. He played a depressed trainspotter in 2003's *The Station Agent*, an uneventful (although surprisingly assured and satisfying) flick which did OK financially and won plaudits. *Game of Thrones* later materialised, in which he revelled as the hooker-fucking alcoholic Tyrion.

He's since had many starring roles, although you have to say he's not exactly hitting box-office home runs. I bet you've never even heard of *Rememory*, *I Care a Lot*, *I Think We're Alone Now* and *Cyrano*, let alone watched any of them. Now don't get me wrong, I'm not trying to put down this guy's extraordinary achievements. Indeed, he's been a minor revelation, partly because he's a decent actor whereas far too many dwarves... aren't. Plus, it takes an awful lot of luck to star in a good or hit movie whether someone's under four feet tall or not.

His greatest success remains *GoT*. This was an ensemble piece, leading me to suspect movie-goers are not quite ready (or plain don't want) to hand over their dosh to see a dwarf as a romantic lead, crime lord or action hero. That'd appeal about as much as a one-legged Tarzan, yes? And lest we forget, cinema is a money-driven business.

There's also a weird duality at work here. In real life we know people do the most crazy, self-defeating kind of shit while coincidences happen all the time. You know, fact is stranger than fiction. Take the German cannibal Armin Meiwes who advertised online for a victim in 2001. Are you surprised someone not only answered, but went to his home and ended up on his dinner plate? It's just another eye-rolling example of how fucked-up we are as a species, but if you saw that onscreen would you go for it? Surely half your brain would be muttering *that's ridiculous*. Well, the psychological horror movie *Grimm Love* exploring Meiwes' notorious exploits turned up in 2006. It's an over-analytical treatment so terrified of its insane subject matter that it tries to deal with it through continual voice-overs, childhood flashbacks and academic dialogue. The choppy, deadly dull story never gets going (or as one irked character says: "You will find no answers here"). *Grimm Love* fails partly because of that odd paradox: Movies have to be more believable than the real world.

Now dwarves in real life, of course, marry normal-sized people, run marathons, start fights and do other physically incredible things, but slap such stuff in a flick and credibility starts to wobble (although I'm sure our PC lefty friends love it). Frankly, I'm against movies being used to present some idealized version of life in which dwarves can do exactly the same things as the rest of us. A flick should aim to entertain first and foremost so fuck positive representations of a disadvantaged group if you merely end up with groan-inducing shite that's little more than a vehicle to peddle a worthy message.

Michael Dunn, who remains the only Oscar-nominated dwarf for his role in 1965's *Ship of Fools*, would have disagreed. "I don't want to play Charlton Heston[1] parts," the 1.19m American actor said, "but there are a lot of roles I can do." He could be right, but are investors going to stump up for projects that widen the perception of what dwarves are capable of, given that the box-office efforts of most able-bodied actors die on their arse?

I prefer dwarves in *plausible* roles (Oompa Loompas, Munchkins, Ewoks... OK, maybe not those bloody Ewoks) because that's surely the best way to play to their strengths and end up with classic movies like *Bad Santa*. And as I try to show below, little people have already been doing the movie-going public proud for a long, long time.

Hans in *Freaks* (1932)

Poor Hans. He's a nice guy but makes the classic mistake of falling in love with a heartless floozy twice his size.

Employed in a travelling circus, he's just come into an inheritance. Suddenly he's got ideas above his station, ignoring his devoted, similar-sized fiancée while throwing his newfound cash at the conniving trapeze artist, Cleopatra (an atrocious Olga Baclanova).

Biggest success: Coming into a fortune.

Biggest humiliation: A shit wedding which includes the circus strongman snogging his bride a few moments before she drunkenly taunts Hans: "What are you? A man or a baby?" And then, of course, he doesn't even get a sniff of num-nums on his wedding night.

Best one-liner: (while flatly parroting the contemptuous Cleopatra) "Dirty, slimy freaks!"

Satanic powers: None, unless he used some to conjure up his mysterious inheritance in the first place.

Number of murders: None. Sometimes keeping 'em alive works better.

1. https://www.imdb.com/name/nm0000032?ref_=nmbio_qu_1

Memorability: *Freaks* has gained serious critical respect since its reviled box-office failure back in the Depression. I'm not sure why as it's a stilted, badly acted watch with only a few memorable moments, such as the 'gobble gobble, one of us' tabletop scene, a sack-clad dude with no arms and legs amazingly lighting a cigarette, and a slightly interesting rain-lashed denouement. Hans (the 0.99m mildly slappable Harry Earles) stands at the centre of this enduring oddity, a dapper man with a case of blue balls and a barely comprehensible, high-pitched German accent. Chin up, son. You'll be a munchkin in seven years.

Evil rating: 1. A sympathetic judge would look the other way.

Hop-Toad in *The Masque of Red Death* (1964)

I have a cunning plan, my lord...

It may surprise you to know that *Blackadder's* Baldrick is not the only slightly short dude to have come up with such a plan. And unlike that medieval idiot, Hop-Toad's scheme is both well thought-through and spectacularly successful.

He's a court jester at an Italian castle, in love with a 'tiny dancer' by the name of Esmeralda. However, her latest performance also entrances a corrupt, boorish guest called Alfredo, although that doesn't stop him smashing her to the floor when she accidentally knocks over his goblet of wine. Hop-Toad goes for his knife, but knows he's unlikely to win a straight fight. Later they talk about what happened. Hop-Toad feigns indifference, but the Machiavellian wheels of his mind are already turning...

Oh, did I mention Esmeralda is a child? About seven years old, I'd say. Naughty Hop-Toad.

Biggest success: No one makes fun of Hop-Toad's short size, suggesting he's an accepted and valued member of the court. I guess I'd better also mention the way he publicly humiliates and burns Esmeralda's assailant to death, a stunt seen by his evil master as an 'entertaining jest'. Hop-Toad and his prepubescent 'pretty toy' even avoid the Red Death, a virulent disease that wipes out just about everyone else.

Biggest humiliation: None. Very few dwarves in horror flicks do as well as this one.

Best one-liner: (To Alfredo when discussing his earlier assault on Esmeralda) "She's nothing to me. I prefer a full-sized woman."

Satanic powers: None. Hop-Toad favours deceit and cunning.

Number of murders: One, but fair play, his monstrously excessive revenge is a peach.

Memorability: Skip Martin puts in a decent performance in a theatrical, but nicely shot flick that's filled with Satan wooing and anti-God talk.

Evil rating: 5. Turns immolation into a much-appreciated public spectacle and is an unabashed pedo.

Olaf in *The Sinful Dwarf* (1973)

Danish sexploitation, anyone?

This one has to be experienced once in your otherwise sheltered life, especially if you've always fancied watching a dwarf abduct ladies, get them addicted to smack in a squalid attic and proceed to sell their helpless little asses to johns.

We're introduced to Olaf (a relentlessly sleazy Torben Bille) loitering near a woman playing hopscotch on the pavement. He uses a cane and is carrying a cute, battery-powered doggie. No threat here, then. The rapt woman follows him into his house to look at his toy collection where he doesn't hesitate to bop her over the head...

Less than three minutes in and you have to ask why a grown woman is playing hopscotch alone before wandering after a dwarf to play with his toys. Honestly, it's almost as if some dunderheads *deserve* to be enslaved.

Anyway, the busy Olaf has many duties, such as administering heroin and ushering the johns in and out of the makeshift brothel. "You know what to do," he tells one. "Just ring the bell when you're finished."

Olaf also lives on the ground floor with his scarred, musically-inclined mother. She appears to be in charge of this white slavery ring despite being half-cut most of the time. When she's not bitching about the price of skag, she's dressing up in a top hat and feather boa to do a Marlene Dietrich impersonation as Olaf accompanies her on the piano. I guess there's a certain charm to watching her forlornly sing about losing at the 'game of love' as the director cuts to upstairs shots of a naked slave being whipped.

Biggest success: In between excited bouts of voyeurism, Olaf's learned to tinkle the ivories quite well.

Biggest humiliation: Always having to climb those bloody stairs to the top floor. A sex dungeon would surely have been a lot more practical.

Best one-liner: Nothing of note, although everything he says is delivered in a raspy voice that adds to the air of depravity.

Satanic powers: None. Like Ralphus (see below), he's got his real-world MO worked out just fine.

Number of murders: Possibly one with his trusty cane when the cops come to visit. However, who knows how many of his worn-out and cruelly abused harem have overdosed or otherwise been disposed of?

Memorability: High. *The Sinful Dwarf* is low-budget, badly acted dreck with a couple of deliberately surreal moments and an imaginative, even poetic, final shot. The main blonde girl also has that same innocent allure as the star of *Debbie Does Dallas*. What's more, Torben occasionally makes you believe he's a sick little fucker by managing to look genuinely demented. Surely we're due a remake with Peter Dinklage?

Evil rating: 10. Olaf's a sadistic, sex-obsessed dwarf in anyone's book, especially when getting mean with his cane. Christ, he even arranges his beloved toys in sexual positions.

The red-coated dwarf in *Don't Look Now* (1973)

Less is more is a good way to sum up the acting career of the 1.27m tall Adelina Poerio. In her only known role, she scampers around Venice tricking Donald Sutherland into believing she might be his recently deceased young daughter. Once she's caught his attention, she lures him to a deserted palazzo to reveal she hasn't got any daddy issues at all. Or a sense of fair play. "It's OK," he gently tells her. "I'm a friend. I won't hurt you."

Too right, mate.

Biggest success: Managing to sink a meat cleaver into a six-foot-three man's neck without even jumping up. Bravo!

Best one-liner: We don't get a peep. A classic case of action speaking louder than words.

Biggest humiliation: Who knows? But she's gotta be pissed at something to take such umbrage with strangers.

Satanic powers: We're given no explanation about this mysterious scurrying figure, yet *Don't Look Now* clearly taps into the paranormal.

Memorability: Very high. Once seen, the climax of Roeg's masterpiece is not forgotten whether you find it bone chillingly unexpected, headscratchingly weird or hilariously bad.

Number of murders: One confirmed kill, but you have to say it's a doozy. Unless there are two nutters running around, I guess this female fiend is also behind those other people being fished out of the drink.

Evil rating: 8. You sense she'll be up to more mischief in that foggy, waterlogged city.

Nick Nack in *The Man with the Golden Gun* (1974)

I'd love to tell you the undersized, underhanded Nick Nack (Hervé Villechaize) is the best thing about this lacklustre Bond outing, but that honour probably goes to Britt Ekland's bikini. Nick Nack gets a fair amount of screen time as the sidekick of Scaramanga (a suave Christopher Lee) yet is required to do little more than deliver champagne, give the odd sarcastic wave, officiate duels, look cute in a bowler hat and call Bond a 'big bully'. He sneaks around and has a certain yen for voyeurism, but overall it's uninspiring stuff. This manservant is not fit to shine Odd Job's shoes.

Biggest success: Not being a fucking freak like that three-nippled Scaramanga.

Biggest humiliation: Deciding to try to kill Bond while in an ideal position to perve on Britt Ekland disrobing, a mistake that ultimately culminates in him being imprisoned in a suitcase.

Best one-liner: (To Bond about Scaramanga while indicating his boss' island home) "If you kill him, all this be mine."

Satanic powers: Nada.

Number of murders: Zero. The best he can manage is showing a spontaneous desire to kill an unconscious Bond with a trident.

Memorability: Pretty low, although at least he prompts Bond to say: "I've never killed a midget before." Maybe Villechaize, who apparently insisted on being called a midget rather than a dwarf, was better in the long-running American TV show, *Fantasy Island*.

Evil rating: 1. A pretty poor effort all round. Needs to talk to Olaf.

Burns in *The Freakmaker* aka *The Mutations* (1974)

I'll be honest here: this low-budget British horror B-movie is all about the marvellous teaming of future *Halloween* luminary Donald Pleasence and imminent *Doctor Who* star Tom Baker.

Pleasence is a discreet mad geneticist who splices plants and animals so the former can move around and the latter can harness the energy of the sun, a quirk that sees him feeding lab rabbits to a giant carnivorous plant.

Inevitably, he's also experimenting on humans so that a man can grow roots (among other things) if he wants.

Baker is the disfigured, tyrannical boss of a nearby circus freak show. He abducts people for Pleasence's experiments and then employs them when the mutations go wrong. He's one fucked-up dude, stomping on a birthday cake one minute and paying a hooker to say the words he most wants to hear the next. Despite being a figure of horror, he maintains a sliver of sympathy by hoping Pleasence's medical expertise will one day cure him of his own pronounced facial deformity.

Former Oscar nominee Michael Dunn plays Burns, Baker's business partner, a man well under the thumb in a deeply antagonistic relationship. Hence, we see him following a pretty girl through an autumnal, fogbound London park, reluctantly helping to shoo her into Baker's waiting arms. At other times he's on stage talking about the 'the refuse heap of evolution' before introducing the circus' ghastly exhibits, a parade of freaks that includes a contortionist, an eyeball-popping man, a human pincushion, a living skeleton and a Lizard Woman. He's liked by the other carnies, telling them "It's just us against all the rest of the world", but desperately wants to make enough cash to get out.

Biggest success: Playing a bad guy, but still managing to project a sense of morality in a seriously out of whack flick.

Best one-liner: (While trying to calm the growing unrest among the other bullied, disabled carnies) "We're one big happy family. Let's keep it that way."

Biggest humiliation: Having to take shit from the 'ugliest man in the world' and being unable to punch him in the face.

Satanic powers: None. This movie is more about the dangers of playing God.

Memorability: *The Freakmaker* wears its influences on its sleeve, with *Freaks* being the most obvious, but there are also dashes of *Island of Lost Souls*, Burke and Hare, *Carnival of Souls*, Hammer Horror and *Eyes Without a Face*. Directed by acclaimed cinematographer Jack Cardiff, it's a fun mad scientist flick shot through with cruelty, plentiful nudity, time-lapse photography and political incorrectness. I'm going to put my neck on the line and say everyone needs to see a human Venus flytrap do its thing. Dunn is a good actor and does what he can with a fairly well developed supporting role.

Number of murders: At least two as Burns helps his boss procure and dispose of subjects, but he'll stick the knife in, if necessary.

Evil rating: 3. Clearly conflicted, Burns is a good example of an essentially decent man getting out of his depth. Still does bad stuff for money, though.

Hercules in *I Don't Want to be Born* (1975)

We all deal with rejection in different ways. Some of us consume half a ton of chocolate. Some dash off an email to an agony aunt. Some crawl inside a bottle. And some curse the womb of middle-aged strippers.

Well, that's what Hercules (George Claydon) the dancing dwarf does at a London flesh palace after his clumsy advances are not appreciated by glamorous colleague Joan Collins. Suitably hexed, her demonic spawn routinely escapes its crib to slaughter the innocent in this gloriously awful horror flick.

Biggest success: Well, he throws a curse and by Jiminy, it works beyond all reasonable expectations. He also keeps his job at the club after a clear case of sexual harassment.

Best one-liner: (To the somewhat startled Joan) "You will have a baby, a monster, an evil monster conceived in your womb, as big as I am small, and possessed by the devil himself!" In fact, it's his only line.

Biggest humiliation: Having his consummate stage act ruined by an interfering nun. There he is in his top hat and tails surrounded by lovely disrobing ladies when all of a sudden an emissary of God starts reading Bible passages and making the sign of the cross, causing him to stagger, fall over and look like a right tit.

Satanic powers: We never learn how he has the power to hex people, but presumably it's down to having an occult source and the fact that all people less than four feet tall are intrinsically evil. Well, religion taught us that for centuries with all that 'monstrous birth' shit.

Number of murders: None directly, but fuck that murderous baby goes through people like a mini T-Rex.

Memorability: Not that high for this 1.45m former Oompa Loompa as the action concentrates on Joanie and her satanic sprog.

Evil rating: 3. Prefers the proxy approach to the dirty hands on stuff.

Ralphus in *Bloodsucking Freaks* (1976)

If life hands you lemons, make lemonade. Or porn. And I tell you what, Luis De Jesus did just that during his fifteen-year movie career. He might've only been 1.3 meters tall, but given that he spent most of his acting life eschewing the Bard in favour of hardcore stuff like 1971's *The Anal Dwarf*, I bet he could've told you an eye-opening story or two in the pub (or should that be *fly*-opening story?) He did let himself down somewhat by appearing in the 1981 Chevy Chase vehicle *Under the Rainbow* and the obscure *Return of the Jedi* two years later, but this was probably to satisfy a pressing need to rehydrate. Hard to pick a crowning moment for this former circus performer, but I do like his giggly turn as the curly-haired, gold medallion-wearing assistant Ralphus in Joel M. Reed's notorious (and wonderfully tongue-in-cheek) exploitation-splatter pic.

Ralphus works for the sadomasochistic Sardu, a somewhat frustrated artist who has combined theatre, torture and death to very little public acclaim in his show, *Sardu's Theatre of the Macabre*. Audience numbers are usually below ten. Not that the lack of interest stops Ralphus from wholeheartedly committing to such a creative endeavour. He loves every aspect of the job whether it's unpacking the recently abducted 'performers' from a wooden crate, electrifying their nipples or amputating their hands onstage. Working conditions are so good he frequently jumps up and down or runs in little circles, barely able to contain his glee. Well, why not? How many jobs offer the chance to use a bare bottom as a dartboard or pull an eyeball out and devour it?

Biggest success: Ralphus is an expert with a blow dart, using his ninja-like skills to firstly hide in a prima ballerina's locker and then subdue and abduct her so she can be forcefully made to dance in Sardu's planned new show.

Best one-liner: (On explaining the tastiness of his freshly prepared chicken soup) "I used a whole chicken. The secret is cooking it alive."

Biggest humiliation: Being picked up and thrown through the air by the flick's sole good guy. Yeah, Ralphus is in the entertainment biz, but the look on his face suggests he thinks dwarf-tossing is outdated and plain mean.

Satanic powers: Ralphus is very much a product of the modern world. Who needs supernatural mumbo-jumbo when you've got a seemingly endless supply of shackled women and a collection of tools that include a hacksaw, a chainsaw and a pair of thumbscrews?

Number of murders: Four (although has an indirect hand in many more).

Memorability: Pretty high, especially whenever he's scooping out raw meat from a bucket and chucking it through the bars of a backstage cage to starving naked women.

Evil rating: 10. This is one unapologetic dwarf, a permanently grinning imp who will kiss the lips of a decapitated head in an act of pure celebration. He's so committed to turning suffering into popular entertainment that I suspect he might have been the brains behind that monstrous reality TV show, *Big Brother*.

Falcon in *Lone Wolf McQuade* (1983)

Well, this one's an embarrassing puzzle. *Lone Wolf* is a simpleminded, enjoyably silly western designed to make Chuck Norris look as manly and heroic as possible, but I couldn't figure out how the vertically challenged Falcon (Daniel Frishman) fits into the scheme of things. Initially he's seen ogling our bearded hero through binoculars, perhaps wondering why

Chuck's an action star when he's only a foot or so taller. Later Chuck bursts into his office to find him zooming around in a motorized wheelchair obsessively playing pinball. Falcon then demonstrates his yen for throwing his head back and cackling. I think this means he's a baddie. He might also be in cahoots with an evil arms dealer, but I'm unable to offer any further details. Whatever the case, Falcon's a well-dressed, confident bastard and remains unfazed when a bodyguard is slugged to the floor. Chuck tells him: "I'm gonna have your little ass." Lordy, how should we interpret such a threat? Either Chuck's up for a bit of midget porn or he's going to roundhouse a disabled dwarf during the inevitable climactic fight.

Biggest success: Evading McQuade by having one of those cool revolving walls in his office that he can smartly disappear behind like a Bond villain. And then cackle.

Best one-liner: (While pointing a long-barrelled gun at the similarly armed McQuade) "As you can see, mine's bigger."

Biggest humiliation: Called 'shorty'. When someone like Chuck (who's not exactly tall) hands out such a withering dismissal, I guess you really are short.

Satanic powers: Zero. However, even if Falcon were able to conjure up all the demons from hell, he still wouldn't be able to defeat Chuck in his prime.

Number of murders: As I couldn't follow what Falcon was up to, I'm unsure if he had an indirect hand in any of the numerous killings.

Memorability: Pretty low. He simply does not belong in this flick.

Evil rating: 1. Got the cackle down pat, but that's about it. Dwarves seemed a lot more evil in the 70s.

Lubdan the Leprechaun in *Leprechaun* (1993)

Although horror's probably my favourite genre, I've never fancied those Chucky movies. A doll isn't scary whether it's possessed by the twisted soul of a serial killer or not. It's the same with leprechauns. A six-meter shark circling your boat is scary, as is an extra-terrestrial monster with acid for blood, but a wee man with a scabby face, an Imelda Marcos-like fetish for shoes and an oft-forgotten Irish accent?

To be fair to the 1.07m Warwick Davis, the world's highest grossing supporting actor, he does play things for laughs. However, this is a good example of what can happen when you put a dwarf front and centre i.e. ninety minutes of pure shit (although *Leprechaun* made money). The joke is that Davis probably puts in the best performance because everyone else is poor and annoying, especially a pre-*Friends* Jennifer Aniston as a whiny rich girl in desperate need of being abducted by Ralphus or Olaf.

Anyway, Davis is the six-hundred-year-old, wisecracking Lubdan, a supernatural shortarse who rides a tricycle and kills whoever nicks his pot of gold. Perhaps he should try keeping it in a bank.

Biggest success: Slyly stroking Jennifer Aniston's leg while panting.

Best one-liner: (after bloodily pogoing on a man's chest) "You'll bounce back in no time!"

Biggest humiliation: Being imprisoned in a wooden crate for a decade because it's got a four-leaf clover sitting on top.

Satanic powers: Numerous. Can impersonate dead people, magically transport himself, be physically strong, shrug off the odd amputation and take a shotgun blast in the chest. Can't recognize a dud script, though.

Number of murders: Four.

Memorability: I'm doing my best to forget I ever saw the irritating little bastard and certainly won't be watching any of the five or so sequels.

Evil rating: 5. Despite numerous kills in a R-rated horror flick, Lubdan comes across like a slightly mean stage magician.

Majai in *The Island of Dr. Moreau* (1996)

An imaginative and unsettling source novel by an esteemed writer. A cast boasting the Godfather, Iceman and Jake the Muss. A $40million budget along with a director who could deliver flicks as good as *Seconds* and *The Train*.

And a dwarf by the name of Majai (Nelson de la Rosa), who happens to be one of the shortest men who ever lived.

What could go wrong?

Well, I guess when you're aiming for horror but end up with comedy, quite a lot. Poor John Frankenheimer. Seventeen years after directing the eco-horror mutant bear laugh fest *Prophecy* he once again stepped in cinematic dog shit with his version of H.G. Wells' oft-filmed novel about perverted animal experimentation.

Stranded Englishman Edward Douglas (David Thewlis) washes up on Moreau's doorstep, remaining unimpressed after an impromptu but decidedly hair-raising jaunt around his fucked-up new home that reveals one hybrid-creature after another. "Look at these people!" he bellows at Moreau (a camp, bloated Brando in a variety of ridiculous outfits) before singling out Majai's seventy-one-centimetre frame. "Look at *him*!"

Now it's true Majai doesn't have a lot to do in this travesty. He's simply a devoted mini-version of Moreau. However, I am quite fond of the scene in which he plays a grand piano duet with the identically dressed Moreau. Majai's little piano, of course, sits on top of Moreau's and the fact he has one grossly misshapen hand complete with talons does not affect his musical ability one iota. What a shame they never ended up on *Top of the Pops*.

Biggest success: Not being sat on by that weird fatso, Brando.

Biggest humiliation: Wearing a naked body suit while dancing on the back of a jeep. Thankfully, Brando doesn't reciprocate.

Best one-liner: Majai's mute throughout, although probably curious to discuss why *Island of Lost Souls*, made sixty-four years earlier, is a vastly superior version of Wells' classic novel.

Satanic powers: Zip.

Number of murders: None, although it's rumoured the director offered him a cool million to kill that prima-donna Val Kilmer during the famously troubled production.

Memorability: Well, Mike Myers obviously remembered Majai in coming up with the character of Mini-Me three years later in *The Spy Who Shagged Me*.

Evil rating: 0. Seems like a nice guy, but it must be tricky to get up to naughty stuff when you're not much bigger than a shoebox.

Marcus in *Bad Santa* (2003)

Criminal duos don't come much more foulmouthed, antagonistic and politically incorrect than Willie and Marcus in Terry Zwigoff's comedic masterpiece. Willie (Billy Bob Thornton) is a self-loathing, alcoholic, safe-cracking Father Christmas while Marcus (Tony Cox) is his organized, but none too cheery elf helper. Together they hurl insults at one another, trying to not get fired before knocking over whatever department store that has stupidly employed them.

Marcus is the team's socially competent half, constantly appalled by his partner's lack of professionalism and self-respect, such as saying 'fuck stick' to the boss, being late or smoking on the job. Or as he tells Willie during a typical pep talk: "You are an emotional cripple. Your soul is dog shit. Every single fucking thing about you is ugly."

And yes, I do like to trot that little speech out whenever I bump into an ex-girlfriend.

Biggest success: Only having to work a few weeks of the year while spending the rest of his time banging his Asian wife.

Biggest humiliation: Having to endure Willie for a few weeks of the year.

Best one-liner: (On being told by the store's security chief to singlehandedly remove the drunken Willie to his car) "In case you hadn't noticed, I'm a motherfuckin' dwarf so unless you got a forklift handy, maybe you should lend a hand, huh?"

Satanic powers: An elf in costume only. Even if he did have any magical ability, I doubt he'd be caught dead making toys in Santa's North Pole workshop.

Number of murders: One, although obviously wants to kill Willie, too.

Memorability: Very high. *Bad Santa* is a shining example of how to use a dwarf in a movie.

Evil rating: 3. He's a seasoned criminal, but the annual plundering of a department store and the occasional dispatch of a corrupt, greedy security guard is never gonna put him in the same league as the likes of Olaf or Ralphus.

Blast of Cannon

You've probably heard of MGM and United Artists, but what about the classy, restrained and very lovely Cannon Films?

It was a studio that took on the Hollywood big boys in the 1980s. For a glorious, plate-spinning few years it became the world's largest independent movie production company, cranking out up to six low-budget pictures a *month*. How the fuck was that even possible?

Well, it wasn't at the start. The company began in the late sixties, receiving a big boost in 1970 with the Oscar-nominated, bloody terrific *Joe*. It then proceeded to mess up the rest of the decade with just about no hits whatsoever. Luckily, 'salvation' was around the corner when a pair of passionate Israeli nutters called Menahem Golan and Yoram Globus took control in 79. Already hugely successful in the Tel Aviv film industry, these cousins were cinephiles, ambitious businessmen and brilliant salesmen. They were neither politically correct nor ethically upstanding with a business model built upon hoovering up shit scripts and rapidly turning them into cheapo flicks.

The pair would usually try to capitalize on whatever was hot (e.g. breakdancing), rip off a big hit (*Raiders of the Lost Ark*, *Seven Samurai*), pitch unwritten screenplays to distributors on the basis of a hastily designed movie poster, conjure up stuff ripped from the news headlines (*Sahara*, *The Delta Force*), make pictures back-to-back on the same sets to reduce costs, or try to turn successful flicks they hadn't previously made into a franchise (*Death Wish*, *Texas Chainsaw*, *The Exterminator*).

Golan, in particular, was an extraordinary, hands-on personality, forever brimming with eccentric ideas. Not that he had much patience or discipline in honing a project. Or as one observer says in the entertaining doco *Electric Boogaloo: The Wild, Untold Story of Cannon Films*: "He had this uncanny ability to just make up shit and then we'd shoot it and that's the movie you see." Hence, a flick like *Ninja III: The Domination* in which a female aerobics instructor becomes possessed by a dead male ninja, thus combining martial arts, *The Exorcist* and *Flashdance*.

Unsurprisingly, this manic, Frankenstein-like approach, in which the cousins flew by the seat of their pants while trying to hang onto the coattails of others, resulted in an avalanche of schlocky B-movies where everything was turned up to eleven. Actors did their jobs, only to be later appalled at the ton of nudity the cousins added. Writers fared even worse, often having scripts radically altered. There's no doubt those wheeler dealers Golan and Globus were capable of low tricks and perhaps worse, but at least every penny under their control ended up on the screen. They had some fans within the industry, but wider respect for their line of attack was often paper-thin or non-existent. No wonder they were called the Go-Go Boys and the Bad News Jews.

Not that anyone who worked on a Cannon pic forgot the company's distinctive ambience. In *Electric Boogaloo*, *Bill and Ted* actor Alex Winter describes Cannon as a weird bubble. "Everyone in it had this sort of wink and a nod: *We do love the movies, but we wanna make money and we don't care about your work conditions or the quality of the product*. It was kind of a weird carnival. Movies are an unreal environment at the best of times and the Cannon movies were like that times a hundred."

Now while Cannon dabbled in the odd science fiction musical and even some Shakespeare, its core output remained ninjas, superheroes, cash-ins and mash-ups, Bronson and Norris, schizophrenic outlandishness, OTT action, soft-core trash and legendary bombs. Critics were unimpressed to say the least, especially as the company's lowbrow output often had such a wildly uneven tone (e.g. the memorable *The Last American Virgin* which is part goofy sex comedy, part sobering teen heartbreak, itself a remake of the first *Lemon Popsicle* film).

Cannon's nutso style worked for the first half of the 80s with some highly profitable pics like *Death Wish II and Missing in Action*, but their sky-high ambition and too-rapid expansion proved fatal. Yes, there were a handful of Oscar nominations, but 1987 proved a disastrous year in which cinemagoers stayed away from the panned *Masters of the Universe*, the snigger-inducing *Over the Top* and the loathed *Superman IV*. The cousins had started off churning out films for a million bucks or less but $25million budgets were becoming the norm. By the late 80s the company was essentially a pyramid scheme with the (hoped for) future success of flicks financing current projects.

Despite official probes and unfavourable news reports Cannon, of course, refused to admit its monetary woes. "I can't be worried because I'm too busy making movies and I'm so excited and so into it," a defiant Golan is caught saying in *Electric Boogaloo*. "I believe that we know what we're doing and that our future is safe."

It wasn't to be, despite the odd breathless promo promising film fans 'new talent and established box office names' and another 'decade of blockbusters'. The Golan-Globus partnership finally derailed in 1989 with the company biting the dust five years later. Not too many film snobs, rivals, industry commentators and bitter, trampled-upon employees shed a tear.

However, B-movie aficionados knew they'd lost something special. This is best demonstrated by *Death Wish 3*, an excessive flick that will forever remain a bullet-riddled, explosion-scarred monument to Golan and Globus' wonderful, risk-taking, cheesy insanity.

Cannon's slashers

As far as I can tell, Cannon only made three pure slashers in the 79-89 period. This is a surprise in that the company not only loved jumping on bandwagons but liberally sprinkled a fair chunk of its output with nudity and explicit violence. On paper, Cannon and slashers seemed like a marriage made in blood-drenched heaven.

Their first stab at the sub-genre was 1980's *Schizoid*. Some women in LA are getting stabbed by a hat-wearing nutter wielding a pair of long-bladed scissors. Klaus Kinski heads the cast, this time playing a widowed shrink, and the victims happen to be members of his therapy group. Is our Germanic friend up to his old misogynistic tricks?

Schizoid features rather unimaginative kills, not much nakedness, a pathetic electronic score and some borderline negligent cops. Of interest is the suggestion Kinski's been having an incestuous relationship with his teenage daughter and... well, not much else. The writing, direction and acting are basic, but somehow I didn't mind this passable effort. Given the extremes that Golan and Globus were later capable of, the groovily-titled *Schizoid* isn't mad enough.

Next up was the festive *New Year's Evil*, released just three months later. Here the disguise-donning killer is slaughtering women at the moment midnight strikes in each of America's time zones. Why? Because it's a slasher movie and there's gotta be a gimmick. Well, that's not strictly true. The killer does give a reason. "I'm fed up," he tells the Final Girl. "You're just like every other lady in my life... Ladies are not very nice people." Such dialogue more than suggests this flick isn't top notch, but it's an entertaining piece of drivel with a couple of nice twists. It chucks in everything from angry bikers to incompetent cops (again) and the skilled manipulation of an elevator to a middle-aged mom presenting a punk music show. Indeed, the regular songs (e.g. *Dumb Blondes*) from unconvincing bands in front of a badly dressed, moshing audience only adds to *Evil's* tasteless surrealism. In its own way, shoving music and serial murder together without any real thought is distinctive and bold (or an early indication of how Cannon was establishing a slightly unhinged take on things).

Finally the subtly named *Hospital Massacre* (aka *X-Ray*) appeared in 1982. This one feels more like a typical early 80s slasher. It features a slew of red herrings, a fair old number of gorily inventive kills, and a disguised, heavy-breathing maniac who spends his time either defying the physical laws of the universe or being intensely stupid.

Former *Playboy* model Barbi Benton (I think you have to be with a name like that) pops along to her local hospital to pick up some routine test results only to be trapped inside and stalked by the lovelorn killer. Happens all the time. Not that I'm victim-blaming, but the silly cow really should have listened to her new boyfriend while being dropped off outside. "Isn't this the hospital where they had all that trouble last year?" he asks. "Some patient ran amok or something."

Her dismissive response? *"Pur-lease..."*

So there you are, this place already has a cloud hanging over it. Mind you, as not brilliantly run medical facilities go, you still have to say this one's letting the side down. A couple of its floors are being fumigated or painted. Others are strangely deserted. Elsewhere it's filled with random blokes who stare at our busty heroine with undisguised hostility; medical staff who veer between surliness, unprofessionalism and farce; privacy screens that are backlit so an apprehensive young woman can sexily undress in silhouette; and patients that run the gamut from a confused ladyboy and an amorous drunk to the obviously distressed and mentally ill. As Bill Murray opined in *Tootsie*: "That is one nutty hospital!"

Still, if you hate such places, with their antiseptic aura of distress, decay and death, you might enjoy hanging out at this hospital. Sure, it requires a massive suspension of disbelief and yes, you're much better off with a sinister classic like *Coma*, but *Hospital Massacre* still boasts a punchy score that regularly wanders into *Omen* territory, a head in a box that predates *Se7en* by thirteen years, and a creepy medical examination that's a little like the start of those doctor/patient pornos I've never seen on that YouPorn website I've never heard of.

Enter the Ninja (1981)

The whole ninja craze passed me by in the 1980s, despite being the perfect age (i.e. a teenage boy). Not sure why (perhaps I was too busy hula-hooping in my bright pink hot pants), but I preferred renting slashers and vigilante stuff to masked chopsocky high jinks. In fact, I've still seen precious few examples of the bone-snapping joys of ninjutsu. Hence, it was with some interest that I sat down to watch *Enter the Ninja*, a box office hit that kicked off a ninja craze and probably resulted in those goddamned pizza-eating turtles.

Its extended intro involves a white-clad ninja called Cole (Franco Nero) battling a load of darker coloured ninjas in Japan. It's a good example of grown men being silly, especially when his adversaries start *catching* the arrows fired at them. After five minutes of having their asses kicked, you do start to wonder why they don't pull out a gun and shoot him instead of leaping around in front of waterfalls and indulging in fancy sword play. I guess I'm not entering into the spirit of things. Wait a sec, it turns out they're *pretending* and the slightly too old Cole is merely completing his awesome ninja training. Still, that doesn't explain how arrows can be caught.

Cole then pops over to Manila to see an old army buddy, a mate who's neck-deep in aggro as some oil-seeking gangsters are trying to force him off his beloved land. Are you surprised our moustachioed beefcake hero starts righteously kicking arse left, right and centre? This is undemanding, increasingly contrived comic book stuff. There's blood, but no real nastiness, rape or torture, even if a solitary Jap ninja does his best to re-enact his country's WW2 atrocities in the Philippines. Indeed, there are so many attempts at comedy that I'm tempted to label this flick as tongue in cheek e.g. the chief bad guy has a babe-filled swimming pool in his office; a tubby, limping short-arse with a hook for a hand is one of the gangsters; a street hustler covers his bases by selling porno pics and crucifixes; and an acidic but ultra-polite henchman remains loyal even after being shot by his boss. Shame a bra-less Susan George has nothing to do except be bra-less.

Like a lot of Cannon's stuff, *Ninja* is tonally uneven and a million miles over the top. On the whole, I was mildly amused by its relentless daftness, especially the way Cole's fighting style included breakdancing moves. I wouldn't be in a hurry to sit through its two sequels, though.

Give me *Enter the Dragon* any day.

Hercules (1983)

When I was a kid there were only three TV channels. This meant we got a lot of American imports like *Starsky and Hutch*, *The Six Million Dollar Man*, *Happy Days*, *Charlie's Angels* and *The Dukes of Hazzard*. In the late seventies

The Incredible Hulk showed up. Now I'm on record as saying superhero stuff blights modern cinema, but at least I have a soft spot for this elegiac TV pilot. This is because it mixes fascinating subject matter (hidden strength, blind rage, bad luck, grief, torment, an elusive search for an answer) with Bill Bixby's subtle and believable performance ("Mr McGee, don't make me angry. You wouldn't like me when I'm angry"). David Banner's initial, rain-lashed transformation into the Hulk while changing a tire in an electrical storm is also iconic. Plus, I love its haunting, piano-driven end theme, *Lonely Man*.

And, of course, *The Incredible Hulk* introduced the world to the six-foot-five Lou Ferrigno.

This is a man whose impressive, sculpted physique resulted in me trying to split my shirt by flexing my biceps in front of the girls at school. I'd love to tell you I grew out of that none too convincing impersonation, but I was still attempting it more than a decade later whenever I got drunk at the pub. Eventually I broadened my knowledge of Ferrigno by watching his intense rivalry with Schwarzenegger as they fought for the Mr. Olympia crown in the amusing 1977 bodybuilder doco, *Pumping Iron*. This determination to win occasionally involved a sweating, grunting Ferrigno in a state of undress chanting Schwarzenegger's name.

By the late seventies both stars appeared set for bigger things. Now I think we all know how Arnie's film career turned out, but how about Lou? I guess you have to say it didn't go quite as well. His first effort was the sensibly chosen *Hercules*, a pretty similar role to Arnie's long-haired, fairly dull starring turn in *Conan the Barbarian* released a year earlier. *Conan* did well, resulting in a sequel and a 2011 reboot. Lou's virginal effort also did all right financially, but hardly ever gets a mention these days. Is this deserved?

Well, yes. *Hercules* is not a good movie. They say meeting the Star Child in *2001* is best watched tripping your tits off, but I'd suggest ingesting a tab or two is the only sensible course of action before attempting this demented sword and sorcery flick. *Hercules* is fuelled by madness, a choppy mess that blends sci-fi, fantasy, mechanical monsters, poor model work, tacky costumes, relentlessly clunky dialogue, lifeless performances, obvious budget limitations and a Tom Baker-era *Doctor Who* level of special effects.

Jason and the Argonauts, it ain't.

To get a taste of its cheap and cheerful nature you only have to watch Hercules wrestle a grizzly, a pedestrian encounter that mixes stock animal footage and a man in a bear suit. But, hang on, this is a Cannon flick so our muscle-bound hero can't just defeat the carnivorous beast. That would be understated. Or worse, unimaginative. Instead, Hercules hurls it away so hard it ends up in *outer space* to become The Great Bear constellation.

To sum up, *Hercules* is best consumed by retarded children or anyone who happens to have some LSD handy.

Missing in Action (1984)

Do you understand the appeal of Chuck Norris? This is a long-working actor. A martial artist with a cult following. A very successful man. He's doing a bit better than me, you know? And yet trying to grasp his cinematic allure is about as easy as figuring out the solar mass of a stellar black hole. I struggle to see the difference between the-not-exactly-tall-or-muscular Chuck doing his tough guy schtick and the dancing plastic bag in *American Beauty*. Both have the same level of charisma, although I guess it's easy to tell them apart as Chuck's the one with the beard. Believe me, I've tried with this guy, having sat through all that deadening, ninja-flavoured early stuff like *The Octagon*.

So as you can probably tell, it was with some trepidation that I sat down to be entertained by the exquisite subtleties of his substantial box office hit, *Missing in Action*. Colonel James Braddock (Norris), who was MIA for seven years, is sent back to Ho Chi Minh City at the request of the president to annoy the Vietnamese army brass at a top-level conference. "You're a goddamn embarrassment," one senator tells him, and I don't think he's talking about his acting. Within ten minutes of groan-inducing contrivances, Braddock has turned into some sort of half-Spiderman, half-bearded avenger, hell-bent on rescuing those noble Yankee soldiers still being held in the Southeast Asian country's secret POW camps.

Braddock is the personification of steely dignity, a man who prefers guns and male bonding to all else. At one point he threatens to slip out of character by undressing in front of the opposite sex. Gosh, is he gonna go beard to bush with a lady? No, 'fraid not, it's merely a ruse to exit his hotel in a different set of clothes so he can get into another man's bedroom and penetrate him with his penis substitute (i.e. knife). Later he's invited into bed to sample the pleasures of two naked tarts, but declines without hesitation to instead fondle some high-powered phallic weaponry.

Braddock eventually teams up with an old army buddy Tuck (the always welcome M. Emmet Walsh), who's memorably introduced in a Bangkok cathouse being chucked off a balcony onto a disintegrating table as an onstage hooker pumps out a startlingly thin version of *Da Ya Think I'm Sexy*? From here everything becomes increasingly corny, but at least we get a smattering of nudity; the odd comic interlude; hopeless, semi-blind guards being instantly knocked unconscious; and Braddock breaking an axe handle with one chop as well as out-jumping a rocket propelled grenade aimed straight down his throat.

Missing is a good example of Cannon trying to beat its rivals to the punch. Fully aware of the eagerly anticipated *Rambo: First Blood Part II*, they managed to get *Missing* out six months before that 1985 juggernaut. I have to say I liked the action-packed *Missing*, especially its uncomplicated narrative and disinterest in anything other than Braddock's point of view. The Vietnamese are just bad guys, there to hiss and get mown down by Chuck.

Simpler, more fun movie-making times.

Exterminator 2 (1984)

One of Cannon's business quirks was to latch onto successful flicks it didn't make in the first place and produce a sequel or two. *Death Wish II* was an early success, prompting Cannon to have a go with 1980's minor hit, *The Exterminator*. Its sequel isn't as nasty or good, but it's not hard to see why it has its fans. No severed heads here, but the company ups the flamethrower quotient to a typically absurd degree. I love no one noticing our fucked-up hero John Eastland (Robert Ginty) wandering the streets in a welder's mask with his dirtbag-toasting equipment encasing his body. His MO these days involves listening to a police scanner to enable him to get to an active crime scene *before* the cops. Not bad when you're weighed down by half a ton of gear.

In his first bit of street cleaning, four laughing perps, who've just terrorized and dispatched a pair of corner shop-owning old coots, run outside to find their way blocked. "Who the fuck are you?" the ringleader understandably asks. Not that Eastland answers. Well, it's hard to chat while wearing a steel, glass-fronted mask. Needless to say, the clueless cops turn up to find some smoking remains.

But a lackadaisical Eastland only gets half of them, leaving the other two to tell tales to their leader X, played by Mario Peebles. It has to be said X is a highly amusing adversary, looking like he spends more time in the gym and beauty salon than sticking it to The Man. Once told of Eastland's outrage, however, he throws away his moisturizer and goes nuts. The teased hair and light purple vest are immediately ditched for a flat top and some togs from *The Road Warrior* before giving a rousing Churchillian speech to his 'children of the streets'.

"I am declaring war," he tells them, apparently not bothered that one of his soldiers is a moustachioed roller-skater. "My destiny and yours should be to fight for what is ours. I am the Messiah and you are my warriors. Together we shall take what I want. I want everything, including this Exterminator."

Next evening they're robbing an armoured van of half-a-million bucks, downing a police helicopter and buying a shit load of heroin from the Mob. Fuck, this is a man of his word.

Despite its high body count, explosions and many shots of flame-engulfed victims, *Exterminator 2* lacks the first flick's grittiness. Not sure why, but it might have something to do with its ridiculous fashions; a fair few unintentionally funny scenes (such as a roller-skating street abduction, bouts of breakdancing and all the happy nightclub stuff); the cheap and cheerful electronic score that continually undermines any attempt at tension; and X's inability to project menace (although at least he's impeccable at spelling his name right whenever he spray-paints it on a victim). Ginty, previously so good in his blue collar ordinariness, mostly looks lost at sea in this sequel as he's saddled with a ditzy, Broadway-chasing pole-dancer girlfriend and a cheery, garbage truck-driving best mate, both of whom are begging to be offed.

Exterminator 2 is a fun romp that can't help having a camp feel. Or as one carnation-adorned Mob boss proclaims upon strolling into X's HQ and gazing upon his new spandex-clad business partners as they stand around holding flaming torches: "Jesus Christ, what is this? This is ridiculous."

Bolero (1984)

Poor Bo.

With the exception of Madonna, it's hard to think of any actress who's had a more ridiculed film career. Still, I like Bo and her amazing cheekbones, having enjoyed their leg-losing debut in the whacky whale flick *Orca*. I also thought both her relaxed, hypocrisy-free character and restrained performance in the pretty good *10* were a pleasant surprise. That 1979 flick was the artistic highpoint by some way, though, because pretty much everything else she touched went tits up.

To be fair, *Bolero* is not some serious attempt at an erotic statement. Its light touch is evident straightaway so treating it as anything other than a bit of nicely photographed fluff does seem unfair. Saying that, it is vacuous beyond belief. During its first half there's also a pronounced dearth of nudity, titillation and coupling. Neither is it smutty nor sleazy. There's only a snatch of snatch, making you wonder who the hell it's aimed at. I can't even recall any double entendres. Yes, it picks up on the home straight, but not enough to satisfy a bullish Golan. He wanted to replace the tepid attempt at romance with much more graphic fuck scenes. For once he failed to get his way, leaving *Bolero's* most memorable aspect to be the sheer boredom etched on the face of Oscar winner George Kennedy (Dragline in *Cool Hand Luke*). It's like he can't quite believe he's stumbled into an even worse movie than *Death Ship*.

It's sad to think people once had to hand over their hard-earned cash for stuff as bad as *Bolero*, *The Bitch* or Cannon's earlier effort, *Lady Chatterley's Lover* in a bid to get their jollies. The internet has since annihilated any demand for such 'sexy' cinematic shenanigans. Soft-core shite, designed around the perfect body of someone like Bo, has become almost as pointless as pixelated porn unless it's got a decent storyline, dialogue and characterization. Sadly, *Bolero*, which caused a none-too-impressed MGM to sever its distribution deal with Cannon, doesn't have any of these attributes.

Bo plays a rich college graduate in the 1920s determined to lose her virginity in the most romantic way possible. In other words, she's ruled out a boozy night out at The Dog and Duck followed by a kebab-clutching knee-trembler in a back alley. Her first attempt involves hopping over to Morocco to do it with an opium-affected sheikh. He licks honey from her naked belly, but ends up with a gooey face that looks like he's covered in snot. Then he slips into unconsciousness. Perhaps he felt that was the best way to deal with the screenplay.

Next, Bo's off to Spain to try again with a toreador. This time she gets blissfully porked but her new lover promptly goes and gets himself gored in the groin. What a load of bullocks. At least it enables Bo the chance to offer a pep talk as he nurses his wounded pride. "That thing is going to work," she says, pointing between his legs while offering her umpteenth empty-headed grin. "I guarantee you this."

Honestly, you're better off with *Confessions of a Window Cleaner*.

Lifeforce (1985)

Horror director Tobe Hooper made three flicks with Cannon in rapid succession, but the relationship only further sullied his artistic reputation. Together they coughed up the derided remake *Invaders from Mars*, a comedic sequel to his blistering *Texas Chainsaw*, and the box office bomb *Lifeforce*.

Still, at least this sci-fi flick has reached cult status and it's not hard to see why as it lobs in a 150-mile-long spaceship, a straitjacketed child killer, martial law and an exploding St. Paul's Cathedral. Not to mention zombie hordes and a drugged Patrick Stewart chatting in a woman's voice. You can't fault this one for ambition, but it sure is one overegged sci-fi pudding.

The crew of a space shuttle investigating Halley's Comet finds an alien craft hiding in its tail. Colonel Tom Carlsen (Steve Railsback) goes aboard and makes the slightly unwise decision to bring back three naked humanoids in suspended animation, despite them being surrounded by giant, desiccated bat-like creatures. Back on Earth the space girl (Mathilda May) wakes up and charmingly presents us with one of the best pairs of breasts in cinematic history. She then causes some localized havoc before walking off nude into the night...

Carlsen remains unapologetic. "She was the most overwhelmingly feminine presence I've ever encountered," he babbles which, roughly translated, means: "Oh, God! I so wanted to bang that babe!"

Amusingly, the authorities at London's European Space Research Centre decide the best way to recapture this intergalactic bit of totty is to bring in the SAS, a good indication of how in thrall the Brits were to those lionized elite soldiers in the 1980s. Hence, we get to meet the miscast Peter Firth as an SAS colonel, who spends the next ninety minutes going head to head with Railsback in trying to deliver the worst performance.

With a $25million budget, *Lifeforce* is a long way from most of Cannon's cheapo productions. The special effects range from competent to really quite good (check out a groovy autopsy) while its restrained but intriguing opening in outer space gives little indication of the grand spectacle ahead. Bit by bit this straight-faced vampiric flick becomes mad, a bizarre and unpredictable slice of fast-paced hokum that I do believe I'm recommending. Penned by *Alien* writer Dan O'Bannon, it's preferable to Ridley Scott's woefully unsatisfactory *Prometheus* and more fun than that other piece of nudey space girl trash, *Species*.

Invasion USA (1985)

In this one Chuck's an ex-CIA operative living in Florida's Everglades. He owns a pet armadillo, captures alligators and eats frogs. He loves his big truck and wears black gloves like a *giallo* killer. I think this is called characterization. On the macho front he out-jumps a rocket propelled grenade (again) and can squeeze a dude's beer bottle-holding hand so hard the glass breaks. He tells one alleged tough guy: "If you come back in here I'm gonna hit you with so many rights, you're gonna beg for a left."

We do our best to believe him.

Story wise, this is a typically ambitious Cannon effort. These guys rarely did subtlety but even so, this one *really* goes for it. A blonde Soviet terrorist Mikal Rostov (Richard Lynch) attempts his best Rutger Hauer impersonation while importing a load of trigger-happy international malcontents to attack the good ol' US of A.

Why?

You tell me.

To be fair, Rostov attempts an explanation when he tells a henchman: "America has not been invaded by a foreign enemy in nearly 200 years. Look at them. Soft. Spineless. Decadent. They don't even understand the nature of their own freedom or how we can use it against them. They are their own worst enemy."

All right, but what is the terrorists' ultimate goal? Is all this imminent mayhem just a Cold War grudge?

Anyhow, to hell with rational motivation and let's get on with the action. I liked the bad guys coming ashore in their hundreds in landing craft akin to a reverse D-Day amphibious assault. I also loved them firing RPGs into tinsel-strewn suburban homes *at Christmas time*. This is as good a depiction of wanton slaughter and destruction as I've ever seen. It's amazingly mean, kinda like that bonkers *Halloween* movie in which the baddies try to wipe out all the world's children in one night.

Invasion USA has a thoroughly enjoyable first hour. There are cool scenes like a bunch of would-be assassins streaking across the wetlands in their airboats to kill Chuck. The main villain also does a pretty good job in that he likes to hurl screaming women out of windows and shoot men in the balls. And then spit on them. However, his intense rivalry with Chuck is never explained. "As long as he's breathing, he's a threat," Rostov says before *dreaming* about his nemesis. Boy, these two really have a hard on for each other.

Invasion USA becomes increasingly daft, but my enjoyment level didn't drop off too much. With its explosions, executions, car chases, tanks, helicopters, the National Guard, and a couple of dancing topless babes, this one checks a lot of boxes. There is one major disappointment in that the terrorists attempt but fail to blow up a church full of singing Christians. Better luck next time, fellahs.

Also, I didn't care for the bolshie female news reporter who happens to be at not one, but *three* terror incidents as they kick off. I don't think so. So she meets Chuck and keeps calling him 'cowboy'. Not once does she grasp her redundancy. Listen, lady, this is a guy flick. Women are not required unless in a state of undress. You don't do this so please piss off and allow the combatants to get on with blowing loadsa shit sky high.

As for Chuck, the way he gets out of (or defuses) dicey situations can only be explained by telepathy, divine guidance, sheer bloody luck or not giving a shit about a wildly implausible script. Not that he saves every life. Take the scene where he's gazing upon the wreckage of a fairground and trying to look heavyhearted. "For every one I stop," he says, "a hundred succeed." It's tricky not to notice that as an actor he barely uses the lower half of his face. He can't communicate emotion. He appears to be feeling the same thing whether kicking someone in the face, saving a busload of children or signing up for another fitness equipment infomercial.

Perhaps one day we'll learn Chuck Norris wasn't actually human but rather some sort of bearded cyborg prototype.

Runaway Train (1985)

Three Oscar nods? For a Cannon film? And yet this action thriller managed just that, although it was a long way from being a runaway success at the box office.

Jon Voight stars as Manny, a psychopathic bank robber in an Alaskan maximum security prison who's so tough the warden has *welded* him into his cell. He's a man that 'believes in nothing and is capable of anything'. However, a court order frees him from solitary and within two shakes of a lamb's tail he's busted out with a talkative, none too bright fellow convict, Buck (Eric Roberts). Unfortunately, they jump on a departing train (naughtily without a ticket) as its engineer keels over from a heart attack. How the fuck is the speeding choo-choo gonna be stopped now?

This is a tense, well-paced and professionally constructed flick built on a mostly solid script. The dialogue might be perfunctory, but it has good stunts, plenty of outdoor filming, a decent score, faces that fit, some nifty violence and none of Cannon's usual faults. With its existentialist underpinnings, it's also open to interpretation. Or as Manny says: "Win or lose? What's the difference?"

Cobra (1986)

This major box-office hit starts with Stallone gravelly intoning there's a murder every 24 minutes in America and 250 rapes a day. Cripes, hope they don't all happen on the same street.

Cobra's tagline is one of the best in history: *Crime is a disease. Meet the cure.* Does the flick live up to such a juicy enticement? No, but nonetheless it's a violent piece of breathless nonsense that's worth a look. Its opening supermarket hostage siege holds no surprises whatsoever but, hey, this is Stallone during his action heyday. And so we get to see a shottie-wielding madman blow the shit out of the fresh fruit display before turning his weapon on warmer prey. How long before Sly turns up and wins everyone over with his sunny personality?

As it happens, about twenty-five seconds, because that's all the cops spend negotiating with the gunman before one turns to the other and says: "Call the Cobra." I don't think I really need to detail what happens next, but it's safe to say it doesn't end in hugs and kisses.

Cobra feeds into the rightwing fantasy that only a decisive good man with a gun can stop an armed dirt bag. Anyone who objects to our hero's unorthodox methods (that some might suggest wander into outright murder) is depicted as a bleeding heart half on the side of the perps. Or as Cobra later tells his boss: "As long as we have to play by these bullshit rules and the killer doesn't, we're gonna lose." Cobra, in other words, is a dead ringer for Cannon's earlier system-hating cop, *10 To Midnight's* Leo Kessler.

So what's crawled up Lieutenant Marion Cobretti's arse? Basically, the good people of LA are being terrorized by an ongoing series of murders that involves claw hammers, axes, knives and the odd supermarket shotgun blast. There's an interesting idea here in that it's not a serial killer's work but rather an 'army of killers' on the rampage. They're called The New World and want to reshape society by applying a bit of good ol' fashioned social Darwinism. Shame this half-decent idea is fumbled, but that's partly down to *Cobra's* troubled post-production in which half an hour of footage was chopped. This results in a vague and confusing depiction of The New World. What these guys are about, how they recruit, their ethnicity, age and class (some wear suits and one's a cop), the criteria for selecting victims, and their ultimate goals are all barely touched upon.

Instead we get some grimy assholes meeting in a warehouse, standing with feet apart while rhythmically clinking their double-headed axes together and... well, I'm not sure, but it seems to involve dementedly pursuing Brigitte Nielsen, our towering damsel in distress, to the ends of the Earth. Perhaps they're psychics who knew how bad *Beverly Hills Cop II* was gonna be and were determined to prevent it ever coming into existence.

Anyway, at one point the leader does his best to put across the group's perfectly reasonable philosophy by telling Cobra: "We are the hunters. We kill the weak so the strong survive. You can't stop The New World. Your filthy society will never get rid of people like us. We are the future."

And... that's it.

So, in short, *Cobra's* not a satisfying movie, despite its $25million budget. It's better to try to enjoy its moments like a bewigged Nielsen posing with some nerdy robots during a fashion shoot; the wince-inducing squashing of a security guard; the killer's knife, which is easily one of the nastiest fucking weapons you'll see in the movies; an OTT car chase; a confrontational, by the book detective played by Andrew Robinson (whom you might remember as Scorpio from the vastly superior *Dirty Harry*) in a furrow-browed role who only exists to get slugged by our matchstick-chewing, no-nonsense hero; and the sweaty killer bellowing: "I want your eyes, pig!"

Stallone appears to be channelling a *Faith*-era George Michael throughout, especially the gay icon's designer stubble, coiffed hair, dark shades, pointy boots, and pert, blue jeans-clad butt. At one point Sly even says: "You gotta have faith." Disappointingly, his flat cap-wearing partner looks nothing like Andrew Ridgeley, pre or post-nose job. Plus, I enjoyed Nielsen inquiring, "Do you ever get involved?" to which our bemused Wham! frontman, sorry, Cobra, replies: "With a woman?"

Murphy's Law (1986)

Not often women give Bronson the run around, but within the opening twenty minutes he's been kicked in the balls by a would-be car thief, had his life threatened by a budding assassin and endured the humiliation of watching his estranged wife get her tits out to appreciative hoots in a downtown strip club. One of these disgruntled ladies even calls him a 'snot-licking donkey fart' and suggests he has a two-inch pecker.

In short, the dishevelled, borderline alcoholic cop Jack Murphy (Bronson) is not having a good time. Having watched this contrived, badly written dreck, I know how he feels. There's nothing hugely wrong with its preamble, which features a good pace and regular bursts of violence, but a few dreadful scenes around the half-hour mark rapidly drain plausibility. Then you start wondering if it's turned into a comedy. After all, this is a Cannon flick. Saying that, there's nothing remotely funny about the sidekick Murphy gets landed with. Kathleen Wilhoite's performance is eye-gougingly irritating.

The Delta Force (1986)

For the first hour Chuck Norris is barely in this flag-waver. Is that why I thought *Delta Force's* first half is much better than its second?

As in *Invasion USA,* he plays a retired dude pulled back into combat by those naughty terrorists. This time they hijack an American passenger jet. For Cannon this is surprisingly well done, the well-directed scenario proving tense and compelling (although the score doesn't help). Both Muslim terrorists give convincing performances, frightening a pregnant lady and pistol-whipping American 'imperialist pigs'. They're civilized, rational and articulate, yet committed, unstable and violent. The passengers, including a bunch of Jews and a concentration camp survivor, also do a good job, portrayed by the sort of folk (Shelley Winters, George Kennedy) who regularly turned up in those 70s disaster flicks. The pic touches upon German war guilt and international politics, only occasionally embarrassing itself through clunky dialogue.

However, the tension drains away when the hostages are split and ferried to other locations. I can understand the writer's decision to do this as it broadens the action, but it mainly results in losing the relationships it built up during the first hour.

Chuck and his beard now take centre stage, demonstrating a penchant for smashing through windows or destroying things with a rocket and machine gun-equipped motorbike that belongs in a Bond flick. That grizzled old bastard Lee Marvin (*Point Blank, Dirty Dozen, Prime Cut*) is also along for the ride in his final role. Sure, he can play such army-boss-on-a-mission stuff in his sleep, but he still gets to kill a few baddies in a vaguely pleasing sign off.

Delta never reaches the nutsiness of *Invasion,* but I didn't mind it. It's weird, but Chuck doesn't seem to be an essential ingredient in a Chuck Norris flick. I 'get' the appeal of Stallone and Arnie, but Mr. Norris could be replaced by any actor, preferably hirsute, with the ability to glower, wear black gloves and never cry.

The most intriguing aspect of his role here is the way he doesn't go near a woman or even mention one in passing. Instead, he lives alone and only has eyes for a blonde, younger colleague. At the start of *Delta* Chuck runs back to a burning helicopter and (despite dire warnings) plunges in to save this guy's life. How did he even know he was unaccounted for in the first place? Later he starts calling him Butch. "Watch your ass," he tells him at one point. The only time Chuck threatens to become emotional is when Butch gets injured again, resulting in him rushing to his side, softly speaking and showing a much gentler side.

I have no further comment.

52 Pick-Up (1986)

Miracles do happen. Jesus did that walking on water stunt while Cannon managed to put out a flick or two with a consistent tone. Obviously, I'm more impressed with the latter.

Based on an Elmore Leonard novel, this one sees Roy Scheider knee-deep in porn, skag, strippers, murder and all-round aggro. He plays construction boss Harry Mitchell, a successful man enjoying an extra-marital fling with a young bit of skirt. Unfortunately, it's not love and she's setting him up. Harry is forced to watch an incriminating videotape, supplied by three memorably skuzzy blackmailers who happen to be a gay coward, a black sociopath and someone whom even Jesus couldn't save.

Fair play, I enjoyed *52 Pick-Up*. It builds smoothly, has some juicy exploitative elements, and a nice sense of unpredictability. Most of all, things play out in a natural manner.

Golan and Globus had already filmed Leonard's book as *The Ambassador* (and completely changed it) two years earlier. Perhaps that's why director John Frankenheimer was mercifully left unmolested to deliver a faithful version.

Street Smart (1987)

This is the one that got Morgan Freeman noticed. He plays a potty-mouthed, gold-toothed pimp facing a murder rap, a role that snagged his first Oscar nomination. I dunno why. Whenever he's required to act tough, he badly fails. Look at the scene where he jams a broken bottle against a tart's cheek as she pleads for him not to mark her face. "It's not your face, bitch," he snarls. "It's *my* face. My tits and my ass."

So there you go. Morgan Freeman has a whore's tits and arse.

The talky plot, which is sparked by lacklustre reporter Christopher Reeve writing a fabricated magazine story about a pimp, is hideously contrived. It just about does enough to keep you watching, but it's easy to see why barely anyone bought a cinema ticket. Mysteriously R-rated, this one is in desperate need of that extra-special Cannon touch: namely, Freeman slipping on a ninja outfit, slicing up a couple of his misbehaving girls with a Samurai sword, and hurling their bloodied remains into outer space.

Barfly (1987)

I've read some Bukowski. Stuff like *Ham on Rye*. He's a good writer, one of those brainworms who's capable of getting at the unvarnished truth. I also know a little about his life and the way he lived it. Compromise was not in his nature, a dedicated pisshead who drank so much that even his shits stank of liquor. I imagine if I had to live one day as the unapologetic fucker, I'd probably find religion the next.

Anyway, to *Barfly*, a semi-autobiographical flick in which Bukowski's portrayed by his alter ego, Henry Chinaski (Mickey Rourke). Like his writing, this movie requires an appreciation for griminess and the outlaw spirit. Chinaski is unshaven, lank-haired and lives in a God-awful hotel room. He shuffles rather than walks and spends his days drinking, fighting, thieving and writing the odd page of prose. Obviously intelligent, articulate and filled with pithy, hard-earned wisdom, he has a peculiar sense of pride, if not a code. To put it another way, he does not bow to The Man. 'Some people never go crazy,' he writes. 'What truly horrible lives they must live.'

Then he spies the damaged alcoholic Wanda (a deglamourized Faye Dunaway) sitting on a bar stool looking like 'some kind of stressed goddess.' Her first words? "I can't stand people. I hate them." It's music to Chinaski's ears, especially as he's already been told by a barman that she's crazy.

Barfly has a sprinkling of decent dialogue ("The last time you ever paid for a drink was the first time" and "Nobody in this neighbourhood can swallow paste like I can"), but barring a few fights it lacks action and feels like a filmed play. It certainly wobbles more and more the longer it goes on, especially in the blackly comic scenes involving Chinaski's neighbors, a pair of dismissive, wisecracking paramedics and an implausible book publisher. The supporting characters are undernourished. Rourke gives a mannered performance like he's channelling Brando, but Chinaski's furious honesty gives way to romantic pretentiousness. In the end, I don't think *Barfly* adds up to a lot and I certainly prefer the grimy realism of Bukowski's prose. If you want a more compelling take on alcoholism, try the nightmarish 2019 German effort, *The Golden Glove*. That one's enough to drive you to drink.

Over the Top (1987)

Nothing illustrates Cannon's insanity better than making a movie about *arm-wrestling*. You know, a 'sport' that has no variation whatsoever and might be over in half a second flat. Surely there's no way such a motion picture can be any good?

Too bloody right.

Over the Top is an unbearably sappy family drama with a bad soundtrack, a lot of product placement and the usual Cannon implausibilities. It's one long life lesson in which we mainly learn you can beat a bigger, stronger guy at arm-wrestling by using mind over matter. And if that doesn't work, then turning around your baseball cap definitely will.

Stallone is Lincoln Hawk, a mumbling, blue-collar trucker with a dying wife, an estranged kid, a hostile father-in-law, and an interest in making a bit of cash on the side through arm-wrestling. Five minutes later he's somehow at the World Arm-Wrestling Championship in Las Vegas as a 20-1 outsider with his hideous kid alongside giving motivational advice. About the only chance this movie had was for Sly to inadvertently reverse his truck over his deeply irritating offspring within the first ten minutes.

Cyborg (1989)

All insane things must end and the Golan-Globus partnership finally crashed into a flaming ditch with an appropriate depiction of chaos in a post-apocalyptic action movie by the name of *Cyborg*.

What a shame this bellow-filled nonsense rarely raises a flicker of interest. I thought Van Damme was going to be an invincible, arse-kicking cyborg in some sort of belated *Terminator* cash-in/rip-off. That's what I expect from Cannon. Instead the titular creature is a *girl* who's barely in it. I know it's unwise to expect much from the Muscles from Brussels, but here he alternates between being a long-haired doofus and a mopey avenger forever staring into space (although he does get to demonstrate how Jesus could have got off that cross if only the Son of God had some martial arts training).

What's worse, even *Cyborg's* fights are a snooze fest while the one-note bad guys look like they've just been thrown out of Twisted Sister. I'd tell you a bit more about the plot, but I can't be bothered. *Cyborg's* structure is bloody awful, resulting in a flatly directed, poorly edited film that's constantly flicking back and forth in time. It's like it's got a sheet of glass in front of it, preventing you from falling into its world. I was so bored I was left wondering how women manage to shave their pits in such an electricity-free wasteland.

But that's life, isn't it? You want worthwhile things like Cannon to finish with a big glitzy hurrah (or even something fitting like a tit-filled biopic of Icarus) but instead you get a damp, Belgian-flavoured squib.

Also by Dave Franklin

Ice Dog Movie Guide
Go Fuck an Iceberg! A Brit's Take on Guns, Tits and Other Fun Movie
Stuff
Smile, You Sonuvabitch! A Brit's Take on Catfights, Serial Killers and Other
Fun Movie Stuff

Straitjacket Blues
Straitjacket Blues: Stories of Unease
Straitjacket Blues 2
Straitjacket Blues 3
Begin The Madness: The Straitjacket Blues Trilogy

The Goodreads Killer
The Goodreads Killer
The Goodreads Killer 2
The Goodreads Killer 3
The Goodreads Killer: The Trilogy

Welcome to Wales, Girls
Welcome to Wales, Keiko
Welcome to Wales, Paola

Welcome to Wales, Kylie

Standalone
Camaraderie
English Toss on Planet Andong
Girls Like Funny Boys
Shelter: A Supernatural Short Story
Manic Streets of Perth
To Dare A Future: A Novel of Rage
Looking for Sarah Jane Smith
Evil Arse Soup: Three Ultra-Dark Comedies
Blundering Blokes
We Should Be More Like Fish: A Medieval Novella
Bawdy Blokes: Three Porno Funnies
Then Came The Last Days Of May
Nice Man Jack
Riders on the Storm and Other Killer Songs
Saving a Child from God
Near-Life Experience: A Gripping Tale of Anxiety
Eaters of Evil Spirits
The Muslim Zombies
A Promise of Pain: A Collection of Dark Psychological Writing

About the Author

Dave Franklin is a Brit who lives Down Under. He has also written ten novels ranging from dark comedy and horror to crime and hardcore porn. His naughty work includes *Looking for Sarah Jane Smith* (2001), *Begin the Madness: The Straitjacket Blues Trilogy* (2014), *The Muslim Zombies* (2018) & *Welcome to Wales, Girls: A Violent Odyssey of Pornographic Filth* (2018).